Authorspress Literary Studies

Literary Terms in Drama Theatre and Cinema

A J Sebastian • N D R Chandra

AUTHORSPRESS

Worldwide Circulation through Authorspress Global Network
First Published 2002
by Authorspress

E-35/103, Jawahar Park
Laxmi Nagar, Delhi-110 092

e-mail: authorspress@yahoo.com
quantum_soul@mantramail.com

Typeset in NewCenturySchlbk by Chitra Computers

Literary Terms in Drama: Theatre and Cinema
ISBN 81-7273-098-5

Printed in India at Tarun Offset, Delhi.

Preface

To appreciate drama, theatre and cinema it is essential that one is familiar with the tools governing them. This book is meant as a guide to students of literature who grapple with the problem of technical terms in their understanding and appreciation of these literary forms. We have consulted several authors in bringing out this handbook. We acknowledge their great contribution: J.A. Cuddon, *A Dictionary of Literary Terms,* 1977; S. Barnet, M. Berman and W. Burto, *A Dictionary of Literary, Dramatic, and Cinematic Terms*, 1971; C. Hugh Holman and William Harmon, *A Handbook of Literature*, 1986; Chris Baldick, *The Concise Oxford Dictionary of Literary Terms*, 1990; Lee T. Lemon, *A Glossary for the Study of English*, 1992; M.H. Abrams, *A Glossary of Literary Terms,* 2000; Joseph T. Shipley, *Dictionary of World Literary Terms,* 1993; John Peck and Martin Coyle, *Literary Terms and Criticism*, 1993; J. Pickering and J. Hoeper, *Literature*, 1990; Karl Beckson and Arthur Ganz, *A Reader's Guide to Literary Terms: A Dictionary*; Jonnie Patricia Mobley, *NTC's Dictionary of Theatre and Drama Terms*, 1998; Ross Murfin and S.M. Ray, *The Bedford Glossary of Critical and Literary Terms*, 1998.

We are grateful to our publishers for their keen interest in getting this work in print.

Authors

Kohima
24 May 2002

Introduction

WHAT IS DRAMA?

Drama is a form of literature, either in prose or verse, presenting a story of life and action usually intended for performance. The word *Drama* is derived from Greek 'dran' meaning 'to perform'. It implies the idea of action; hence drama cannot be purely a literary genre. It combines language, scenery, setting, costume and the actor's physical appearance. It is noted for vocal expression, tone of voice, physical gestures and facial expressions. At times music and dance are added to the performance. A written text of a play is thus only a skeletal frame which is the permanent part of a play. Often drama is thought of as a story about events in the lives of characters associated with conflict, tension, contrast and emotions.

Theatre can be found at three levels: (a) as popular entertainment by individuals or small groups in the form of farce, circus skills; (b) as a public activity through literary drama performed at public theatres such as Greek tragedy, medieval morality plays, and contemporary Broadway theatre; and (c) as an elitist art form it is meant for a particular coterie audience such as the Renaissance court performances.

The earliest period in Western theatrical history is called classical, because it encompassed the drama and theatre of the classical civilisations of ancient Greece and Rome, and plays were written in Greek or Latin. The first evidence of dramatic literature dates from Greece in the sixth century BC. Aristotle's *Poetics* (c. 330 BC) claimed that Greek tragedy developed from dithyrambs, choral hymns in honour of the god Dionysus (Bacchus), which praised the god and told a story. Greek drama, tragedy, comedy and satyr play, thus grew out of the primitive rituals at the annual festivals dedicated to Dionysus (Bacchus), the god of fertility and wine. Tragedy means 'goat song' and refers to the goat-skinned satyrs. Comedy is derived from Greek 'comos' meaning 'revelry'. Greek tragedy flourished in the fifth century BC. Noted writers are Aeschylus, Sophocles, and Euripides. Comedy developed in the mid fifth century BC, and by the fourth century BC comedy had replaced tragedy as the dominant form.

The Greek plays were performed outdoors in the basin where two hills met to allow the large audience to witness them. Later a massive open arena was used for dramatic performance with wooden benches that ascended the hillside in a semicircle. The theatre of Dionysus at Athens had at the centre, the orchestra, the chorus, the altar to Dionysus, the proskenion and the skene. The proskenion is the narrow space between the skene and the orchestra which was the main acting area. The skene is a wooden building which served as an acoustical wall which served to reflect the voices of actors to the audience and a background. The chorus remained in the orchestra. The main characters moved between the proskenion and the orchestra.

The Romans in the fourth century BC absorbed Greek dramatic form. The great period of Roman playwriting began in the second century BC and was dominated by the comedies of Plautus and Terence.

In the first century AD Seneca became known for his tragedies based on Greek myths, stressing supernatural elements, bloody violence, and obsessive passion. The content, form, and techniques of Senecan tragedy became a strong influence during the Renaissance.

LITURGICAL DRAMA

In the medieval Catholic church liturgical drama was used for instruction of the faithful. By the 10th century various church services were presented in dramatic form including the Mass (Eucharist) that re-enacted the Last Supper of Christ. Certain feasts were celebrated with theatrical activities, such as the Palm Sunday procession. The antiphons, responses and songs of the Mass and the canonical hours were like dramatic dialogue. In the ninth century antiphonal embellishments known as tropes were added to the complex musical elements of the Mass. An anonymous three-line Easter trope, a dialogue between the three Marys and the angels at the tomb of Christ from about 925, is considered the origin of liturgical drama. The dramas centred on the two important festivals of Christmas and Easter. The life of Christ from Birth to Resurrection, and the main events of the Christian year from the Annunciation (announcement of Christ's birth to Virgin Mary) to the Ascension of Christ to heaven, were observed in the church. Appropriate episodes were performed by antiphonal chanting between priest and choir or between characters themselves. By the 12th century the liturgical drama was fully developed, but the language used was Latin.

MIRACLE PLAYS

The liturgical drama slowly evolved with various stories from the *Bible* enacted by the clergy or by choirboys. In the beginning church vestments and the church served as costume and setting. Later, mansions, plateau and booths were constructed. The mansion was a small scenic structure; a booth suggested a particular place such as the Garden of Eden, Jerusalem, or heaven; and the plateau was an area in front of the mansion where scenes were enacted.

By 13th century, the liturgical drama evolved as many *Bible* stories were presented sequentially depicting scenes from creation to the Last Judgement, and the lives of Saints. These plays are also called passion, miracle, or saint plays. Mansions were erected around the nave of the church, with heaven usually at the altar end and a hell-mouth at the opposite end of the nave. As the play progressed the performers and spectators moved from one area of the church to the other. Unlike Greek tragedy, the medieval drama did not always display conflict and tension as its purpose was to dramatise the salvation history. Though the liturgical drama was enacted for its didactic qualities, in course of time entertainment and spectacle began to increase. This necessitated drama to be taken to the market squares with the same physical arrangement. Though still religious in subject-matter, the main intention was entertainment. These were called Miracle Plays and there are records of cycles of miracle plays in many parts of England from the 14th to 16th century. Miracle plays survive from Chester, York and Wakefield. The Chester cycle had 25 plays; the York cycle, 44 plays and the Wakefield cycle, 32 plays. The themes begin with the Fall of Lucifer and end with Doomsday. They include stories of Creation, Fall, Cain and Abel, Noah, Abraham and Isaac, and the various stages of Christ's life.

By the 14th century the production of plays was associated with the Feast of Corpus Christi and had evolved into cycles of as many as 40 plays. Though these cycles are similar to the liturgical dramas, they can be considered a separate development. They were produced by the community as a whole once in every four or five years. The production of each play was assigned to a trade guild, with an attempt to correlate the guild with the subject of the play—the boatwrights, for instance, might stage the play of Noah. Since the performers were often illiterate the plays tended to be written in an easily memorised doggerel type of verse. Three major forms of staging were employed. Pageant wagons were most common in England. The former mansion became an elaborate rolling stage, that would move from place to place in the city. Spectators would assemble at each location; the participants would perform on the wagons and on a plateau created on the street or with an adjoining platform.

MORALITY PLAYS

During the period when miracle plays were popular, folk plays, secular farces, and pastoral dramas emerged by anonymous authors. All these influenced the evolution of the morality play in the 15th century. It does not deal with *Biblical* stories but with personified abstractions of virtues and vices, constantly waging war for man's soul. These were usually performed by professionals such as the minstrels or jongleurs. The themes included the Seven Deadly Sins corrupting man, and Mercy and Peace pleading with God. The allegorical characters included such figures as Death, Gluttony, Good Deeds, and other vices and virtues. The earliest Morality Play was *The Castle of Perseverance* (c. 1425) in which the Good Angels and the Bad Angels with the Deadly Sins fought for the soul of man. The most famous among these plays is *Everyman* which dealt with a person's journey through life. Everyman meets characters named after qualities they represent such as Strength, Discretion, Beauty, and Five Wits. They all desert him one by one except Good Deeds.

RENAISSANCE THEATRE

Renaissance in Europe began in the 15th century ending the Middle Ages. Radical changes are brought about by the following factors: There is a revival of interest in the Greek and Roman Classical Literature; the printing of books by Caxton; the rise of the spirit of nationalism; the affirmation of faith in the possibilities of man; discovery of new lands; discoveries of Copernicus and Galileo; and Reformation leading to Protestantism.

The Protestant Reformation put an end to most religious drama by the mid-16th century, and a new dynamic secular drama developed in its place. In the dramas of Shakespeare and Molière, there is a turning to secular and temporal concerns than the late medieval themes of man's struggle and adversity. The comic and grotesque reappear in the new drama. The Renaissance began at different times in different areas of Europe and was a slow process of change rather than a sudden shift in ideas and values. In theatre, the Renaissance was an attempt to recreate classical drama. This form is generally known as neo-classicism.

ELIZABETHAN DRAMA

The reign of Queen Elizabeth (1558-1603) is a brilliant period of order and prosperity which inspired English writers to be creative. The formation of actors' companies and the building of public theatres such as the Curtain, the Theatre, the Rose, the Swan, and the Globe in London encouraged the production of popular plays reaching to a wider audience. Elizabethan drama came of age with the University Wits in the 1580s who were graduates of Oxford and Cambridge. They included John Lyly, George Peele, Robert Greene, Thomas Nashe and Thomas Lodge. Their plays were imitation of classical drama and the medieval romances. Thomas Kyd inaugurated the Revenge Tragedy tradition in imitation of the Senecan tragedy with his *Spanish Tragedy*. Christopher Marlowe with his 'mighty lines' in blank verse drama became a model for future dramatists. His *Doctor Faustus* presents the Renaissance spirit ofhumanism.

All these dramas however culminated in the diverse and complex work of William Shakespeare, the greatest English dramatist. He employed a classical act and scene structure and mixed verse with prose. He borrowed theatrical devices from Seneca, Plautus, and the *commedia dell'arte*. He combined tragedy, comedy, histories and romances. He had several plots and covered great expanses of time and space. He took his characters from royalty to low-life. In his plays there was music, dance, spectacle, violence, battles and bloodshed. The subjects of tragedy tended to be historical rather than mythical. The comedies were primarily pastoral in nature. His comedies such as *The Comedy of Errors*, *Love's Labour's Lost*, *A Midsummer Night's Dream*, *Much Ado About Nothing* primarily concern with love and marriage. His history plays like *Richard II*, *Henry IV*, *Henry V*, *Henry VI*, and *Richard III* deal with the glory of England, the Wars, and the concept of the Divine Right of Kings. Shakespeare's four great tragedies *Hamlet*, *Othello*, *Macbeth*, and *King Lear* present his intense tragic vision. *Pericles*, *Cymbeline*, *The Winter's Tale*, and *The Tempest* are plays of reconciliation.

After the death of Queen Elizabeth drama became darker and more sinister in tone. In the plays of Ben Jonson, we find a Renaissance humanist who adhered more strictly to neoclassical precepts. His sense of cynical humour is best expressed in comedies such as *Every Man in His Humour*, *Every Man Out of His Humour*, *Volpone*, *The Alchemist*, etc. During this period the masque also developed in the hands of Jonson which presented allegorical stories in dance, music, and spectacle.

JACOBEAN AND CAROLINE DRAMA

The drama during the reign of James I (1603-1625) is known as Jacobean drama. It was a time of uncertainty, pessimism and Machiavellian intrigues. Caroline drama refers to the drama written during the reign of Charles I (1625-1642). Shakespeare and Ben Jonson wrote their last plays during these periods. Other important dramatists of the period include George Chapman, Thomas Heywood, Thomas Dekker, John Webster, Francis Beaumont, John Fletcher and others.

During the civil war in 1642, theatres were closed under the influence of the Puritans.

RESTORATION DRAMA

Restoration (1660) made dramatic entertainment popular when Charles II reopened theatre. Restoration dramas were court dramas written for the aristocratic audience. When Charles II returned from France he and his courtiers brought along the influence of Moliere. Restoration drama is concerned with the life of the upper classes—their moral laxity and licentiousness. Heroic tragedy and comedy of manners became prominent.

The term Restoration comedy denotes that kind of drama which prevailed in England between the restoration of the English King Charles II and the advent of sentimental comedy early in the 18th Century. Restoration comedy is also a term that is usually used to refer to the artificial comedy or the comedy of manners that prevailed at that time. The comedy of manners is on 'surface of life'. The presence of aristocracy at the centre of action distinguishes comedy of manners from other comedies. Though Dryden is considered the father of the comedy of manners, it is Etherage who established this genre. Later 'the mannerly and witty' Wycherley had it beautifully brought out in his *Country Wife* which at times sounded very indecent and immoral. Congreve in his *Way of the World* (1700) brought the comedy of manners to perfection.

18th CENTURY DRAMA

Jeremy Collier in 1698 wrote on *The Immorality and Licentiousness of English Stage* presenting the middle class reaction against it. Soon the sentimental comedy developed in the 18th Century. It stood for domestic virtues and the triumph of Christian virtues and preaching to middle class audience. Goldsmith and Sheridan led the anti-sentimental movement. Sheridan's *The School for Scandal* (1777) is the most successful comedy of manners. In the Prologue Garrick speaks of its purpose—to expose the theme of scandal-mongering. He wrote,

'The play had less nature than wit'. It is full of wit showing absurdities. Characters have become caricatures. There is brilliant dialogue giving sophisticated wit.

19th CENTURY DRAMA

19th century is a period of poetry and fiction than drama. There are very few plays written by the Romantics such as Shelley's *The Cenci*, *Prometheus Unbound*, etc.

LATE 19th CENTURY AND 20th CENTURY DRAMA

As drama was moving toward increasing realism in its depiction of the external world, the late 19th century playwrights developed three-dimensional characters placed in realistic settings and situations. The leading playwrights of this style were the Norwegian dramatist Henrik Ibsen and the Swedish author August Strindberg who are often considered the founders of modern drama. Henrik Ibsen with his plays like *The Pillar of Society*, *A Doll's House*, *Ghosts* and *An Enemy of the People* introduced a new trend of plays dealing with social problems and human relationships. George Bernard Shaw was influenced by Ibsen in the area of social commentary. There was a Renaissance of the English drama with the coming of Shaw with his realistic theatre. Shaw popularised Ibsen in England with his essay *The Quintessence of Ibsenism*. He wrote, "Formerly, you had, in what was called a well made play, an exposition in the first act, a situation in the second, and unravelling in the third. Now you have exposition, situation, and discussion: and the discussion is the text of the playwright." For Shaw ideas were of prime importance rather than characters in his plays that were didactic. Every play dealt with some social, economic, political, or religious problem with discussion, e.g., *Mrs. Warren's Profession* on prostitution; *Arms and the Man* on war and heroism; *Candida* on marital relations;

The Doctor's Dilemma on medical profession; *Pygmalion* on aristocracy; *Man and Superman* and *Back to Methusela* on Life Force.

The theatre of realism developed by Bernard Shaw and his followers continue to be a force in the 20th century. Noted dramatists in the genre include John Galsworthy, J.M. Barrie, J.B. Priestley, Noel Coward and Terence Rattigan.

Irish Drama with its distinct Irish quality developed in the hands of W.B. Yeats, J.M. Synge and Sean O' Casey. W.B. Yeats and Lady Gregory founded the Irish Dramatic Movement in 1899 and got the Abbey Theatre to stage Irish drama. Noted Irish plays include Yeats's *The Countess Cathleen*, *Cathleen Ni Houlihan*; Synge's *Riders to the Sea*, and *The Playboy of the Western World*.

There was a revival of Poetic Drama in England with T.S. Eliot's *Murder in the Cathedral* in 1935 and his subsequent plays *The Family Reunion*, *The Cocktail Party*, *The Confidential Clerk* and *The Elder Statesman*.

Many movements, generally lumped together as the *avant-garde*, attempted to suggest alternatives to the realistic drama and production. Paralleling modern art movements, they turned to symbol, abstraction, and ritual in an attempt to revitalise theatre. Although realism continues to be dominant in contemporary theatre, its earlier functions are now better served by television and film.

Symbolist Drama called for the removal of all the technological and scenic encumbrances of the 19th century. The texts were laden with symbolic imagery not easily construed, rather they were suggestive. The general mood of the plays was slow and dreamlike. Strong symbolist elements can be found, however, in the plays of Chekhov and the late works of Ibsen and Strindberg. Symbolist influences are found in Americans Eugene O'Neill and Tennessee Williams and the Englishman Harold Pinter. It also served as the model and inspiration for future *avant-garde* dramatic movements and the absurdist drama of the 1950s.

Expressionist Drama was popular in the 1910s and 1920s, largely in Germany. It explored the more violent, grotesque aspects of the human psyche, creating a nightmare world on stage, distorting and exaggerating with light and shadow effects. Other movements of the first half of the century, such as futurism, Dada, and surrealism, sought to bring new artistic and scientific ideas into theatre.

Other significant developments in theatre include the *ensemble theatre movement* influenced by Artaud in the 1960s; the *Polish Laboratory Theatre of* Jerzy Grotowski; Peter Brook's *Theatre of Cruelty Workshop*; *the Open Theatre* of Joseph Chaikin.

Absurdism is the most popular non-realistic genre of the 20th century evolved from the plays of Jarry, the Dadaists, and the surrealists. It was influenced by the existential theories of Albert Camus and Jean-Paul Sartre. The absurd drama of Beckett, Ionesco, Adamov, Genet and others have no consistent plot or characters. The language used is irrational and broken with silence and pauses. Samuel Beckett's *Waiting for Godot* (1952) is a typical absurdist drama with archetypes. Absurdism was at its peak in the 1950s, but continued to influence drama through the 1970s.

CONTEMPORARY DRAMA

In the 1950s the New Drama began in England with John Osborne's *Look Back in Anger* (1956) presenting the post-war "angry young men". In the USA, David Rabe expressed the anger and frustration of many toward the war in Vietnam in the 1970s. Brecht influenced many post-war German playwrights to attempt documentary dramas based on historical incidents centred on the moral obligations of individuals. In the 1960s and 1970s some playwrights built plays around language such as Tom Stoppard in England, and Sam Shepard in the USA. They concentrated on language as a reflection of society.

Drama in a realist form with stress on psychological realism continued to be popular in the USA with the plays of Arthur Miller and Tennessee Williams. They use memory scenes, dream sequences, symbolic characters and projections.

Feminist Theatre began with the American dramatist Megan Terry in the 1960s, and has become popular in the hands of dramatists such as Caryl Churchill, Pam Gems and Michelene Wandor.

In the early 1960s and 1970s there were some radical experiments in dramatic forms, however, since 1980s there has been a considerable decline in this literary form.

A

Abbey Theatre opened in Dublin in 1904, became the centre of the Irish Revival. It was meant to present Irish plays about Irish subjects. The revival was inaugurated by William Butler Yeats. He exhorted Irish writers to draw their inspiration from Irish life and traditions. The Irish Literary Theatre was established in 1899 by Yeats and Lady Isabella Augusta Gregory. In 1902 it was christened the Irish National Theatre Society. From 1904 the company is known as the Abbey Theatre. Notable Irish dramatists whose works were performed at the theatre include W.B. Yeats, Lady Gregory, John Millington Synge, George William Russell, Padraic Colum, St. John Greer Ervine, and Sean O'Casey. The Company performed plays like *Cathleen ni Houlihan* (1902) by Yeats, *Riders to the Sea* (1904) and *Playboy of the Western World* (1907) by Synge, and *Juno and the Paycock* (1924) and *The Plough and the Stars* (1926) by O'Casey. In 1951 the Abbey auditorium was damaged by fire, and the company moved to the Queen's Theatre. In 1966 the Abbey Theatre was rebuilt (*see* Irish Literary Theatre).

Abstract set is an imaginary stage setting with free doors, windows and frames without actual constructions. Abstract setting was popular in the early 20th century influenced by the Swiss designer Adolphe Appia and the English designer Edward Gordon Craig. Their concept has influenced contemporary theatre to a great extent. Such setting does not represent a particular time or space but is made up of platforms, panels, drapes, etc. These settings are excellent in depicting timelessness giving emphasis to language. It arouses the imagination of the audience with costuming and lighting.

Abstraction is a device by which individual traits of a character is presented in isolation and in a stylised manner. The term was used first by Sarah Siddons (1755-1831).

Absurd is a term derived from the existentialism of Albert Camus presented in his essay "Le Mythe de Sisyphe" (1942) and is applied to 'The Theatre of the Absurd' consisting of a body of plays written primarily in France from the mid-1940s through the 1950s. Camus wrote about the human situation in a world of shattered beliefs and speaks of man "in a universe that is suddenly deprived of illusions and of light, man feels a stranger.... This divorce between man and his life, the actor and his setting, truly constitutes the feeling of Absurdity." Hence, to understand the Absurd as a serious form of literature, one has to be familiar with the preoccupations and anxieties of the post-war modern world. The basic assumptions of the previous ages have been discarded as illusions. Religious faith declined and was substituted by progress and nationalism. The absurdists regarded themselves as loaners and outsiders isolated in their private world. They were sensitive in projecting thoughts and feelings of their contemporaries. Their works were characterised by illogical situations, unconventional dialogue, and minimal plots to express the apparent absurdity of human existence and metaphysical anguish. The word 'absurd' meant for them 'out of harmony', incongruous, unreasonable and illogical. Eugene Ionesco defined it as 'devoid of purpose'. Albert Camus and Jean-Paul Sartre conveyed their inability to find any rational explanation for human life with meaningless, confusing, hostile situations in an indifferent world. The Theatre of the Absurd believes that reality is meaningless and senseless.

Man has to face it in all its senselessness and have the courage to laugh at it.

For the Absurdists, reality being meaningless, there is no God and man's life is reduced to a mere circular progress from nothing to nothing. According to them the true field of battle is inside us, in the Unconscious. Hence the theatre of the Absurd attacks us below the threshold of consciousness using mainly visual devices and language in a state of fragmentation. They mainly concern themselves with the doomed individual, the man in despair and distress, alone and bitter in the wide world. It was the British scholar Martin Esslin who first used the phrase "theatre of the absurd" in 1961 referring to several contemporary dramatists, such as Samuel Beckett and French playwrights Eugène Ionesco, Jean Genet, and Arthur Adamov. In their drama they departed from the conventional Western theatre by rejecting logical characterisation, language, and plot. For example, Beckett's *En attendant Godot* (1953) translated as *Waiting for Godot* (1954) presents two tramps waiting for a character named Godot. They are not sure who Godot is. They spend day after day waiting for him in uncertainty. Contemporary playwrights whose works show the influence of the theatre of the absurd include British dramatists Harold Pinter and Tom Stoppard, American dramatists Edward Albee and Sam Shepard.

Though absurd theatre is a modern form of literature Martin Esslin considers it having derived from the old archaic traditions with mimes, clowning, fooling, mad scenes, dream and fantasy with allegorical element. Herman Reich traces its relation to the Latin 'mimus' through the comic characters of the medieval drama to the Italian comedia dell' arte and to Shakespeare's clowns. In the old mime-play, the clown is a 'moros' or 'stupidus' who behaves in an absurd manner due to his inability to understand logically. In the middle ages, the clowns continued in the tradition of the mimes. In the mystery plays in France and England such comic characters appear as personified devils and vices. The Shakespearean clowns with illogical reasoning and feigned madness are forerunners of the Theatre of the Absurd. In France the '*commedia dell'arte*' was absorbed into drama through dramatists like Moliere. In England the 'harlequinade' kept the tradition of '*commedia dell'arte*' alive. This became the basis of the English 'pantomime' which continues in the folk-theatre. The literature of the 'verbal nonsense' has also contributed to the growth of the theatre of the absurd. In Freud's opinion, "Delight in nonsense has its root in the feeling we enjoy when we are able to abandon the straitjacket of logic." Nonsense literature and nonsense poetry go beyond the language of logic to reveal the hidden battles within the human psyche. The literature of dreams with its allegorical element has also its impact on the theatre of the absurd, e.g., *The Piers Plowman*, Dante's *Divine Comedy*, Bunyan's *The Pilgrim's Progress,* etc. Absurdists have been influenced by dream fantasy literature of the 18th century and early 19th century such as Swift's *Gulliver's Travels* and Walpole's *The Castle of Otranto*. August Strindberg was the first to depict on stage a world of human psychology through *To Damascus* (1898-1904), *A Dream Play* (1902) and *Ghost Sonata* (1907). These plays are precursors of the theatre of the absurd with presentation of the inner states of mind being presented. Writers like Dostoevsky, Joyce and Kafka also wrote in similar manner peeping into the states of human consciousness. The Dada movement in literature and art, Expressionism, and Surrealism had their influence on the absurdists. The theatre of the absurd attempts to express the senselessness of the human condition and the inadequacy of human reason.

An analysis of the plays by the absurdists reveal their basic tenets and characteristics. They abandoned the concept of character and motivation, and concentrated on the states of mind and human situations. We do not find in them development of a plot from exposition to solution. They confront the audience with harsh facts of isolated life in an alien world. The movement began in the 1940s and became very popular in the 1950s and early 1960s. Many young playwrights of this period were influenced by the absurdist tradition, such as N.F.Simpson, Harold Pinter, Edward Albee, John Osborne, John Arden and Peter Weiss. They adopted many of the techniques from the theatre of the absurd.

Academic or **school drama** is a Renaissance practice of instructing university students in Latin drama, especially of Platus and Terrence. Performance was often done in Latin or translation. e.g., Nicholas Udall's *Ralph Roister Doister* (c.1552). Academic theatre is generally non-professional and is produced by educational institutions such as colleges and universities with educational purpose.

Act is a division of a drama into units. It grew from the episodes in the Greek tragedy with chorus that broke up the action. The Elizabethan and Jacobean dramatists generally followed the Greek and Latin form of five acts corresponding to the divisions of the action. In the 18th century the practice of dropping the curtain between acts began. Modern dramatists take liberties in their breaking up of a drama into acts like Ibsen, Chekhov, Pinter, etc.

Action refers to the chain of events that occur on stage in a drama. Action can be *external or internal*. External actions are the physical events on stage. The internal actions refer to the mental thoughts and feelings of the characters like Hamlet's soliloquy: 'To be or not to be.' Action is essential to a drama according to Aristotle's *Poetics*. The unity of action does not admit plurality of action. For tragedy is an imitation of action that is complete and whole, and of a certain magnitude. It has a beginning, a middle and an end. The movement of action progresses from the initial entanglement, rising action, climax, falling action and resolution.

Act drop is a device by which a painted cloth is lowered to close the proscenium that opens between acts.

Acting area is the space for dramatic performance. It includes the stage, platform or the floor.

Actor is used for both male and female performers who represent a character on stage.

Actors' Equity is an association of actors in the USA that looks after the salaries, terms of employment and working conditions of actors. In Britain the Actors' Equity looks after the welfare of actors in various fields such as dramatics, television, film, etc.

Actors' studio is the acting workshop that began in New York in 1940s under the leadership of Lee Strasberg. Later it came to be known as a method acting due to the techniques employed (*see* Method acting).

Actress is a female performer. Nowadays both male and female performers are called by the common term *actors*.

Act tunes are musical interludes between acts of a play. Formerly such music used to be performed by musicians on stage, however due to the development of electronic media these are rendered more effectively through studio-recorded music.

Actor-audience relationship is defined by the expectation of the audience, dramatic conventions employed, and the qualities of the actor. In conventional plays the 'actor-audience relationship' is loose and it does not arouse much tension in the audience since they are familiar with the outcome. In new forms of drama like those of Ibsen, Chekhov, Beckett or Pinter, there is an element of surprise and tension aroused. The performance of the actors through soliloquies, monologues, and things said aside contribute to good actor-audience relationship.

Adaptation is the remodelling of a play to suit the taste of the audience and the theatrical conditions. This is done by certain changes made in the characters, text and action. Adaptation occurs mostly in the case of translations.

Ad-lib is improvised addition to a dialogue or stage management. It is an unrehearsed and spontaneous response at an emergency such as when actors forget their script or when props and stage setting get disrupted.

Aestheticism is derived from Greek *aistheta* meaning 'things perceptible by the senses'. Aesthetic signifies that which concerns the criticism of the beautiful. The aesthete is the one who is devoted to the beautiful in art, music and literature. Aestheticism began as a cult of beauty as an end in itself disregarding all moral, didactic, political or utilitarian considerations. The movement began in Germany in the 19th century under the influence of Kant, Schelling, Goethe and Schiller. They sought to make art independent in itself. Aestheticism took roots in France as a self-conscious movement from Theophile Gautier and was developed by Baudelaire, Flaubert and Mallarme with the maxim "l'art pour l'art" (art for art's sake) that stood for a religion of beauty.

In English literature the term is loosely applied to the literary movement which began in the 1880s under the influence of the Pre-Raphaelites Ruskin and Pater, and rooted in the reverence for beauty instilled by Keats. Keats's 'Ode on a Grecian Urn' sums up the aesthetic philosophy: "Beauty is truth, truth beauty—that is all / Ye know on earth, and all ye need to know." Oscar Wilde, perhaps the best representative of the group, furthered the movement taking his inspiration from Walter Pater who held the view that aesthetic considerations were absolutely independent of morality. The movement came as a revolt against realism and Victorian moralism. The phrase 'art for art's sake' became the credo of the aesthetes. The beautiful form is to be valued more than moral content even to the extent of considering morality irrelevant to art. Art became an end in itself having to serve no moral or intellectual considerations. Those who took the movement to the extreme levels are known as 'decadents' due to their contempt for orthodox morality and belief that an artist ought to break traditional moral principles to have an understanding of all aspects of life. The movement reached its peak in the 1890s under Walter Pater, Oscar Wilde and Aubrey Beardsley who lived more in a world of art and beauty than goodness. However, the movement was not so enthusiastically received by some Victorians like Tennyson who wrote: 'Art for Art's sake! Hail, truest lord of Hell! / Hail Genius, Master of Moral Will!'

Aesthetics is the philosophy of art which studies beauty as an end in itself in art, music and literature. There are two major approaches to aesthetics: the philosophical and the psychological. The philosophical approach is through deductive reasoning to establish the nature of art and beauty as well as their relations to truth and goodness. The psychological approach stresses the study of the process of creation in the artist and of appreciation in the beholder.

Aesthetic or **psychic distance** refers to the degree of emotional and psychological involvement of a reader in a work. The aesthetic distance is great when the reader is least involved in the action or the fate of the characters in the work. If the reader is influenced emotionally or psychologically by the action or characters in the work, the aesthetic distance is the least. The ideal aesthetic distance according to many theorists is when the reader is able to establish an involvement that is deep yet with sufficient degree of detachment that allows tranquil recollection of the aesthetic and thematic quality of the work.

Afterpiece is a brief comedy performed after a main play. It aimed at entertaining the latecomers and to give comic relief like the satyr plays in the Greek tradition. Afterpiece was common in the 18th century London Theatre.

Agitprop refers to the Russian propaganda theatre promoted by the Communist party's central committee after the 1917 revolution. German director Erwin Piscator began a kind of a political theatre in the 1920s with presentations of montage with multimedia, film, slides, placards, etc. These propaganda plays were relevant to the audience.

Agon is an argument between two characters which forms the major part of the Greek comedy of Aristophanes. In Greek drama this debate was primarily between the protagonist and the antagonist, e.g., Aristophanes in *Lysistrata* presents a debate between *Lysistrata* and the magistrate on war and sex. She goes on a sex embargo to end a war.

Aldwych farce refers to the farcical plays of Ben Travers and other dramatists staged by Aldwych theatre of London in the 1920s and 1930s. These were usually bedroom plays depicting sexual adventures and conjugal infidelities.

Alienation effect, generally known as 'A-effect', comes from the German *Verfremdungseffekt* or *V-effekt*, an epic theory propounded by Bertolt Brecht. He used the device in his epic dramas like *Mother Courage* and *The Good Woman of Setzuan*. It aimed at an alienation effect of detachment in the audience. The audience as well as the actors are encouraged to keep a distance from the dramatic action. This is maintained by sudden change of scenes, songs to interrupt dramatic action and switching roles. Its purpose is to prevent identification of the audience to characters and events portrayed. It reminds the audience and actor of the artificial nature of drama. This lack of emotional involvement makes the audience accept the political or philosophical ideal conveyed.

Allegory literally means *other reading*. It is a way of interpreting a narrative or a text to extract a more general, or a less literal meaning from it, e.g., Reading Bunyan's *The Pilgrim's Progress* as a journey of humanity to the Divine—the Pilgrim representing all men. Hence it is a literary device by which people, objects or events in prose or verse are presented symbolically giving a meaning other than the one actually described. In the Middle Ages allegory was associated with the interpretation of the Biblical Old Testament in relation to the New Testament. Allegory is often used to convey a moral lesson. The main technique used is personification by which abstract qualities are presented in human form. To this genre belongs allegorical lyric poetry, allegorical drama and allegorical narrative. The allegorical sensibility prevailed in the Christian literature of the Middle Ages in Morality Plays and Dream Visions, e.g., Dante's *Divina Commedia*, medieval morality play *Everyman*, Langland's *Piers Plowman*, Spenser's *The Faerie Queene*. Allegory is used in 20th century 'Expressionist Drama' and 'Theatre of the Absurd.' These dramatists include Samuel Beckett, Harold Pinter, and Edward Albee.

Alternative theatre refers to some fringe group performances since the 1960s with a mixture of socialism, feminism, song and satire. It was an alternative to conventional theatre.

Amateur theatre is a term applied to poor performance by inexperienced and unpaid actors.

Ambiguity means multiple meaning or different interpretation of an idea. William Empson in *Seven Types of Ambiguity* (1930) justifies ambiguity as a poetic technique with verbal nuance which allows alternative reactions to the same piece of language. Ambiguity occurs in drama with ambiguous characters and situations that instil a sense of suspense in the audience. Ambiguity can be non-verbal, expressed through actions, gestures and moods.

Amphitheatre is a spacious open-air building, generally oval in form. Originally constructed of wood and later of stone, it was used by the Romans for gladiatorial combats and other spectacles. Seats for the spectators encircled the area for exhibition. Later the shape of the amphitheatre was used for arena stage for dramatic performances. The first amphitheater in Rome was constructed in 59 BC by the Roman *pontifex maximus* Gaius Scribonius Curio. The famous Colosseum of Rome was built by the emperor Vespasian and dedicated by his son Titus in AD 80.

Anachronism is setting a person, thing, or event not in its historical perspective, for instance, the use of modern-day costumes while staging a play of Shakespeare. Some playwrights have tried to experiment with anachronism to create the 'Alienation - effect', setting the past in the present, e.g., a clock striking in Shakespeare's *Julius Caesar*. Historically there were no clocks in the Roman times, yet Shakespeare brings it as an anachronism.

Anagnorisis is a Greek word used by Aristotle in *Poetics* meaning 'discovery'. It brings about a climax in the chain of events when the protagonist discovers the truth, e.g., in *Oedipus Tyrannus*, Oedipus discovers that he himself had killed his father and married his mother. In Shakespeare's *Winter's Tale*, King Leontes gets his queen Hermione back, though he had thought her dead.

Angry young men is a journalistic term derived from a work of the Irish writer Leslie Paul entitled *Angry Young Man* (1951). The name also came from John Osborne's play *Look Back in Anger* (1956). The term came to be applied to a group of British authors in the 1950s. They were anti-establishment and revolted against the post-war society with its traditions and values. In their writings they brought out the middle class hypocrisy and self-complacency. They wrote against the establishment and the middle class 'old boys' with their Oxford and Cambridge background and posh accents. John Osborne's *Look Back in Anger* presents his protagonist Jimmy Porter, a middle class angry rebel of his time. The group includes authors such as Kingsley Amis, John Osborne, Sillitoe and C. Wilson.

Angst is a term used by the Existential philosophers meaning 'anxiety or dread'. Danish theologian Soren Kierkegaard writes about it in *Begrebet Angst* (The Concept of Dread, 1844). Man's life depends on his actions and decisions in this absurd universe. This individual self-responsibility makes him live anxiously as he is confronted by the burden of freedom and responsibility that accompanies it. This feeling of *Angst* brings him to confront death and the ultimate meaninglessness of life. This makes him experience a sense of dread. Kierkegaard interpreted it as God's way of calling each individual to make a commitment to life. The word *Angst* has a similarly crucial role in the work of the 20th century German philosopher Martin Heidegger. Anxiety leads to the individual's confrontation with nothingness and with the impossibility of finding ultimate justification for the choices he or she must make.

Antagonist is the major character that opposes the protagonist or the hero of a drama or narrative. He sets the conflict in motion. The antagonist is often the villain who represents negative values in the theme developed, e.g., Satan is the antagonist in Milton's *Paradise Lost*; King Claudius is the antagonist in Shakespeare's *Hamlet*; Iago is the antagonist that disturbs the 'Othello music' in *Othello*.

Anti-Aristotalianism in drama refers to the rejection of Aristotalian principles of Dramatic Unities, Catharsis (Purgation), and the idea of a beginning, middle and end in a drama. The Anti-Aristotalian movement began with Brecht with his 'Alienation-effect' (*see* Alienation-effect).

Anti-climax is an abrupt and deliberate descent from the sublime to the ridiculous, when the action is about to reach its climax. This brings about the reduction of tension in the play. This device is employed to provide humour and surprise. In a comedy the performer intentionally speaks of something serious and suddenly climaxes it with a joke.

Anti-hero is a protagonist who lacks traditional heroic qualities such as valour, honesty, generosity, goodness, etc. He is often found in modern drama, especially in the theatre of the absurd in which he is a failure and a victim of circumstances. Anti-hero is a misfit and a dropout, e.g., Arthur Miller's protagonist Willy Lowman in the *Death of a Salesman*; John Osborne's Jimmy Porter in *Look Back in Anger*.

Antimasque is a device introduced by Ben Jonson to present grotesque characters through a humorous dance that occurred between serious actions during a masque. Often it preceded the masque and Jonson used it as a burlesque of the action.

Antistrophe in Greek means 'turning round'. It is the returning movement after the strophe of the chorus dancers in a Greek drama. Greek choral odes have three movements: (i) 'the strophe' in which the chorus sings and dances from right to left; (ii) 'the antistrophe' in which the movement is reversed; (iii) 'the epode' in which the chorus moves to the centre of the stage and sings standing still.

Anti-theatre is generally referred to the theatre of the absurd. Since the 1950s it is also applied to plays that do not follow the conventional patterns and are considered illogical.

Antoinette Perry Awards is given every year to the best in the field of theatre in the New York Theatre. It is also known as 'Tonys'.

Apocalyptic drama is based on the sense of impending doom of the world. The belief in doomsday is found in the medieval mystery plays. In the Jacobean drama of Webster and Shakespeare, the sense of doom is present. In the 20th century, after the two world wars, the end of the world was strongly felt. During the cold war era, writers like Harold Pinter, Edward Bond and Samuel Beckett wrote in the same strain.

Apocalyptic literature is one of revelation of the future. The Book of Revelation in the *Bible* is an excellent example which is rich in allegory and continues to be the subject of different interpretations. The book is sometimes called the

Apocalypse. At times such literary works predict doom and concern with the end of the world and its destruction.

Apron is the area of the stage in front of the curtain. It is also called the forestage.

Archetypal character is a character who represents a group of people that share some common features. We have such archetypal characters such as Oedipus, Macbeth, Samson and Faust. They evoke philosophical and psychological thoughts. Archetype is associated with myth criticism where symbols such as the rose and the sun appear besides themes of love and death. The setting is mythical with a paradisal garden with stock characters in search of something. Northrop Frye presents his findings in *Anatomy of Criticism* (1957). J.G. Frazer's *The Golden Bough* (1890-1915) ushered in studies in archetypal criticism in the modern period. Psychologist C.G. Jung developed his concepts of archetypes in mythology through a dream analysis. He opined that ancestral memories are transmitted through 'collective unconscious' in man.

Architectural stage is a fixed form of stage setting with scenes, stairs, platforms, pillars, etc., e.g., Japanese No and Kabuki stages have such features.

Arena stage is a theatre-in-the-round and an open stage where the audience sits on three sides. This arrangement has been largely used in non-dramatic forms such as the circus. It has some constraints as at some times the audience has to see the performer's back. It is difficult to present illusions on arena stage as entrances and exits must be made in full view of the audience. This eliminates the surprise effect. However, arena stage can create a sense of intimacy not often possible with other stage arrangements. It is most suited to many non-dramatic forms.

Aristotle's six elements of tragedy are defined in his *Poetics*. They are character, diction, music, plot, spectacle and thought.

Arlecchino or **Harlequino** is a character in the *Commedia dell'arte* prevalent in Italy from the 16th to the 18th centuries. An Arlecchino was usually a comical, witty yet cunning servant.

Artistic failure is when a production has only some merits and does not receive a favourable theatre review. It can also refer to a play that has been reviewed favourably, but has little commercial success.

Aside is a dramatic device by which a character directly addresses the audience or another character which the others on stage do not overhear. Aside is meant to give simple information, intentions, thoughts and decisions of a character. It also links the characters and situations.

Asphaleian system is a stage that is operated with a hydraulic lift system. Different sections of the stage can be brought out for performance.

Atmosphere (*see* Mood).

Attitude is a character's relationship to other characters and situations.

Audition is the trial performance by an applicant for an acting role. It checks the physical appearance and gives an opportunity to perform with others and to show one's talents and skills.

Audience is an assembly of spectators who are interested in a common spectacle. They all share the same space to witness the spectacle. They communicate with the actors by their stillness, concentration, applause and disapproval. They sit in the stalls, circle or gallery. An audience can be divided among themselves according to the appeal made by different sections of the play on their sensibility. The audience-actor relationship is important for the success of a play.

Auditorium known also as the house is the place for the audience in a theatre building. In a wider sense, it can be applied to the entire theatre set-up. Modern auditoriums are fan-shaped in which seats are inclined upward from front to back. This gives an unobstructed view of the stage. Some auditoriums have balconies and boxes.

Augustan Age is a term applied to the era of Augustus, ruler of Rome from 27 BC to AD 14. It was called the Golden Age of Latin literature being distinguished for a number of classical writers of learning like Horace, Ovid, and Virgil. The reign of Queen Anne in early 18th century is also known as the Augustan Age in England. The major writers of the period are Jonathan Swift, Alexander Pope, Joseph Addison and Sir Richard Steele. Led by Pope and Swift, they attempted to create an urban literary environment through satires and epistles. Dryden may also be considered part of this movement. They were neoclassical as their style imitated the Roman forms. They emphasized intellect, common sense, correctness, moderation and reason over emotion. Arnold called it the "Age of Prose and Reason."

Autoclesis is a rhetorical device by which a character introduces a topic, but does not speak of it, e.g., During Mark Anthony's oration in *Julius Caesar*, he introduces the topic of Caesar's testament, but does not read it.

Auto sacramental is a term applied to Spanish religious drama of the 16th century. It consisted of a street procession, exposition of the Blessed sacrament (Eucharist) on the altar for adoration, and a religious play being performed in the church. Auto sacramentals were usually performed on the Feast of Corpus Christi.

Avant-garde is a French term designating innovative writing in form and method. From the late 19th century it is applied to writers who are dedicated to the idea of art as an experiment and revolted against tradition. They were distinctly modern and their innovations were far ahead of their contemporaries. They drew inspiration from the invention of new or unconventional techniques with new styles. Participants in the creative process can be considered members of the *avant-garde*. Hence we have classical *avant-garde* composers like Pierre Boulez, *avant-garde* pioneers in electronic music, *avant-garde* rock music, *avant-garde* approaches in jazz like the recording of Ornette Coleman. In the late 1950s, 1960s, and 1970s there were directors, producers, and screen-writers of *avant-garde* films like Michelangelo Antonioni, Ingmar Bergman, Luis Buñuel, Sergey Mikhaylovich Eisenstein, Abel Gance, etc. The Avant-Garde Precursors of Modern Theatre are Antonin Artaud, Samuel Beckett, Bertolt Brech, Jean Cocteau and Friedrich Dürrenmatt. The *avant-garde* theatre is experimental and unorthodox. Known theatre groups in this genre include La Mama Troupe in New York, Jerzy Grotowski's Polish Lab Theatre in Poland, and Antonin Artaud's Theatre of Cruelty in France.

Avista is a method of changing scenes during a performance in front of the audience without closing the curtain. Often it is done by the stage crew dressed in black uniform dress and in full stage lights or dim lights.

B

Backdrop is a canvas hanging from the flies at the back of the stage with the appropriate painting for the scene. When the sky is painted as the background it is known as the sky drop.

Backing consists of the materials such as flats, screens and drops used at the back of the stage to block the audience from seeing through the gaps of the doors and windows.

Backstage is the area behind the backdrop or the sets.

Back projection is an 'alienation device' to create realism in drama. It consists of projecting photographs or film on a back-drop. This projection can present the general theme of the drama with a flashback of a scene which helps the character to recollect a past scene.

Ballad opera is an 18th century opera form which parodied the Italian grand opera by presenting some of its popular tunes and ordinary lower class content. In it dialogue is mingled with popular songs, e.g., John Gay's *The Beggar's Opera.*

Ballet is a form of theatrical dance with stylised movements and positions. It began to evolve in Europe during the Renaissance (1300-1600). The word *ballet* can also mean an individual artistic composition using this dance technique. It is usually accompanied by music, scenery, and costumes. Toe dancing is often considered synonymous with ballet, but ballet technique can be performed without toe dancing. The steps were first named and codified in France. The earliest precursors to ballets were lavish entertainment given in the courts of Renaissance Italy. These spectacles which united painting, poetry, music, and dancing, took place in large halls that were used also for banquets and balls. The Italian court ballets were further developed in France. Most French court ballets consisted of dance scenes linked by a minimum of plot. The court ballet reached its peak during the reign (1643-1715) of Louis XIV, whose title of the Sun King was derived from a role he danced in a ballet.

Barker is the person who tries to attract audience to a performance. He stands at the entrance of the show in attractive costumes and tries to lure the customers.

Barnstormer is a 19th century ranting actor who preformed with his travelling troupe for people working in barns.

Baroque is applied to queer, extravagant and superficial styles in literature, art, music and architecture especially after the Renaissance in Europe from late 16th to 18th century. In Italy baroque began as a reaction to the classical exuberance and took to present through art and religious stories in the church with the purpose of instructing the Catholics in the faith during the counter-Reformation. The word 'baroque' may have derived from the Portuguese *barocco* or the Spanish *barueco* referring to an uneven pearl, oddly shaped rather than a spherical one. However, the word does not define exactly the style it refers to. By the end of the 18th century it entered the terminology of art criticism as a term applied to 17th century bizarre art. In England, Sir Thomas Browne and the Metaphysical poets with their conceits were considered baroque in style. To typify the spirit of the baroque the relation between the poetry of Crashaw in English and Latin, and the sculpture and architecture of Gianlorenzo Benini are compared. Baroque Drama developed in the European court theatres in the 17th century. It aimed at spectacular pompous style in presenting a court drama in very impressive theatres.

Bathos is a term used to refer to the intentional use of anti-climax to give humorous or satiric effect. By it an author comes down from the most exalted to the most trifling subject for ironic effect. The term was introduced by Alexander Pope in the 18th century (*see* Anti-climax).

Beginners are the actors who appear in the opening scene of a play.

Beginning, middle and end is the threefold movement in a drama according to Aristotle. In his *Poetics* he writes, "Now a whole is that which has a beginning, a middle and an end. A beginning is that which does not necessarily follow anything else, but which leads naturally to another event or development: an end is the opposite of that which itself follows something else and is followed by another thing."

Berliner Ensemble is the company that Brecht established in East Berlin where he directed his major plays during his exile. His new techniques of acting and directing had a great influence on the new generation of journalistic and politically conscious writers in the 1950s.

Biomechanics is a method used by the Russian director Vsevolod Meyerhold by which the actors can project certain emotions or expressions through muscular movements, e.g., to show intense joy an actor could jump around.

Black comedy is a drama with a cynical attitude to life based on the belief that man exists in a purposeless universe. It causes bitter laughter and amusement dealing with subjects such as death, disease or warfare. The purpose is to offend and shock by exaggeration through caricature and repetition, giving an effect of insanity. Death looms large in black comedies creating a nightmare world. It is prominent in the theatre of the absurd.

Blackbox is a small theatre fully painted in black inside.

Blackout is the switching off of stage lights between scenes to enable actors to enter and exit. This is a device to give time for lapse effect and change of location. Harold Pinter uses this in his plays.

Black theatre is a term used to refer to the black theatrical movement in the 1960s among the black Americans. It was a theatre meant primarily for a black audience. Prominent exponents are Leori Jones and James Baldwin.

Blocking is a device by which effective portions of the dialogue are marked at the rehearsal, giving details as to when the characters should sit, stand or move. This helps the actors to be spontaneous and natural as there is perfect synchronisation of dialogue and movements.

Body language is the unconscious postures and movements of a person that can reveal his thoughts and feelings. The audience can interpret the mind of the character from the gesticulations. The body language emerges spontaneously from the dialogue and movements. An actor can draw the attention of the audience by such exaggerations in course of the dialogue.

Book-holder (book-keeper) is the one who monitors the movements of the players on stage and their dialogue with proper cues. He is assisted by other stage-keepers.

Booth-stage is a movable stage used by travelling actors in the middle ages consisting of a booth and a stage. It was a simple wooden platform. A booth was made behind the platform from where the actors made their entrances and exits to the front portion.

Bombast is verbose and exaggerated language with bombastic words. It is derived from 'cotton stuffing' depicting the hollowness of such high-sounding expressions. Elizabethan Tragedy, especially Senecan plays, are known for bombasts.

> As are the elements, such are the heavens,
> Even from the moon unto the empyreal orb,
> Mutually folded in each other's spheres,
> And jointly move upon one axle-tree,
> Whose termine is termed the world's wide pole.
>
> (*Doctor Faustus* : Marlowe)

Border is a narrow strip suspended over a scene to represent the sky, clouds or trees.

Boulevard theatre refers to drama meant for commercial success in the theatres of Paris main roads. It is a form of farce and domestic drama in the 19th century France. It depicted the materialistic pleasure-seeking life of young men.

Bourgeois drama deals with the problems of the middle class characters in the 18th century. It reflects the psychology of the middle class audience. It keeps out aristocratic presentation as in Elizabethan and Restoration drama. It is bourgeois in content and form, and reflects the attitudes and wants of the middle class. However, these elements can be relative at times as a play may be bourgeois in content, but not in attitude and vice versa.

Bowdlerise is the practice of omitting certain sexual references in the presence of women. It is a practice introduced by Thomas Bowdler (1754-1824).

Box-set is a stage arrangement with flats and ceiling cloths, and with doors and windows which give it the illusory look of a perfect room. Three walls and ceiling are present. The fourth wall is left to be imagined.

Boy companies refer to boy players chosen from the royal choirs into the Elizabethan drama troupes in the 16th century England.

Braggadocio is a stock character in drama who is generally a coward. He is a braggart who makes empty boasting. He is called *alazon* in Greek comedy. In Shakespeare, Falstaff is such a braggadocio.

Bread and puppet theatre was a New York theatre company in the 1930s that presented mythical and folk themes through mime, masks and puppets representing mythical and supernatural beings. Since there was a practice of sharing bread by actors and audience, the company was tagged 'bread and puppet theatre'.

Broadway is a New York street known for the entertainment industry with big theatres.

Burlesque is a term derived from Italian *burla* meaning "mockery" with comic and ridiculous effect. A burlesque can be satiric and can have two forms: (i) as a mock epic in which a trivial subject is treated in an exalted manner as Alexander Pope in *The Rape of the Lock*; and (ii) and as a parody in which a serious subject is treated as a trifle, as Cervantes in *Don Quixote*. Burlesque should not be confused with farce and parody. Parody is a mocking imitation of a particular work or of the style of a writer, while farce is written to excite laughter. The earliest use of burlesque was in the Greek mock epic poem *The Battle of the Frogs and the Mice*. Aristophanes and Euripides employed it in drama. In England, burlesque began with Geoffrey Chaucer. French comic playwrights Paul Scarron and Molière excelled in its use. Samuel Butler's *Hudibras* is an excellent mock epic poem. In the modern times the *Nonsense Novels* (1911) of the Canadian author Stephen Leacock is an example. In the USA, burlesque is considered a kind of theatrical production popular between the two world wars. American burlesque began in the late 19th century with minstrel show and vaudeville. In 20th century it took the form of ribald comedy and striptease in which a female performer strips herself on stage. Of the many strippers who achieved fame, Gypsy Rose Lee was the most prominent. Interest in burlesque declined as films became popular.

Burletta is an 18th century three-act play with more than five songs performed in minor theatres.

Bus and truck company is a theatrical troupe that goes around the countryside giving performances in small towns. The bus carries the actors and the truck takes all the costumes and scenery.

Business means stage activity consisting of clever play with props which the actors or directors use to strengthen a dramatic action.

Buskin is a thick soled boot reaching up to the knees, worn by Elizabethan actors. It came to be associated with tragedy as buskin was worn by tragic actors to give them stature.

Byplay refers to the side actions in a drama as the main action continues. Such byplays are meant to distract the audience with some humour in the course of the main action.

C

Cabaret in the 17th century was a drinking shop. In course of time it came to be associated with entertainment during meals and drinks in a restaurant or night club especially during World War I. Cabaret form attracted the futurists and dadaists with its musical setting. Being a means of social and political satire, cabaret developed into a new kind of theatre combining humour and imagination.

Call-board is the notice board near the stage door on which announcements and rehearsal schedules are put out.

Cape-and-sword play is a Spanish comedy in which performance involves sword play among gallant lovers in the midst of nobility and beautiful ladies. Lope de Vega (1562-1635) is the most popular author in this genre.

Capitano is a stereotyped cowardly soldier. Such a character has his private fears, yet he puts on an outward look of courage. He is a character the audience sympathises with yet mocks at. Such characters occur in Shakespeare's *Henry IV & V*.

Caricature is the likeness of anything so exaggerated or distorted as to appear ridiculous. In it physical features as well as mental characteristics are comically exaggerated, e.g., In Shakespeare, Falstaff's large belly is caricatured as belonging to creatures who live and change.

Carnivalisation is a theory developed by the Russian formalist critic Bakhtin. According to him, in popular carnival there is a mingling of the sacred with the profane and noble with the ridiculous.

Carnival play is a one-act play performed during Shrove-tide (the carnival days preceded Ash Wednesday when people went about singing and collecting money). In the play elements of Catholic Mass and liturgy were included. The play used masks, puppets and the usual wise-fool. The custom was prevalent in the 15th and 16th centuries, especially in Germany.

Caroline theatre is the theatre during the reign of Charles I (1625-49). Caroline comes from the Latin 'Carolus' for Charles. The age is marked by the English Civil War between the Cavaliers (the King's supporters) and the Roundheads (Parliament's supporters). Caroline theatre consists of the drama written during the reign of Charles I and until 1642 when theatre was closed. There is a transition during this period from the Jacobean to restoration drama in dramatists like James Shirley.

Carriage and frame is a devise to change the scenery wings in a theatre with the help of carriages or platforms.

Cast comprises a list of actors who play different roles in a drama.

Casting is the selection of actors by audition. A director has to get suitable people for different roles and see to the best interaction. Casting is a very important process of allotting proper roles to fitting actors. Often popular actors are given important roles in a drama, leading to 'type casting.' This can deprive new faces their opportunity to play key roles.

Catastrophe is the final tragic conclusion of a tragedy or the denouement of the plot which climaxes with the struggle and usually the death of the hero. It can consist of: the resolution of the plot, the revealing the full identity of characters, the reversal of fortunes of the hero, reconciliation, etc. The term was used by the German critic, Gustav Freytag.

Catharsis is a term derived from Aristotle's *Poetics*. In Greek *katharsis* means "purification" denoting purgation through tragic drama. According to him tragedy should succeed in "arousing pity and fear in such a way as to accomplish a catharsis of such emotion." Aristotle spoke of Catharsis through Pity and Fear. He rejected Plato's theory that emotions are in themselves bad. He rejected Plato's view that by rousing the emotions, poetry produces a dangerous excess of emotions in real life. Aristotle's theory of Catharsis is his answer to Plato on these points. *Pity and Fear* are two tragic emotions and Aristotle uses them mostly in conjunction with each other as a pair. In chapter 13 of *Poetics* he says : 'Pity is occasioned by undeserved misfortune and fear by that of one like ourselves (i.e., by the misfortune of one like ourselves).' This is expanded by him in Book II of *Rhetoric*. In it he defines fear as 'a kind of pain or disturbance due to a mental picture of some destructive or painful event in the future.' He adds that this impending evil must be near at hand, not distant. He further says, 'anything causes us to feel fear that when it happens to or threatens others, causes us to feel pity.' Thus pity and fear are very closely linked. In *Rhetoric* he defines pity as 'a sort of pain at an evident evil of a destructive or painful kind in the case of somebody who does not deserve it, the evil being one which we might expect to happen to ourselves or to some of our friends and this at a time when it is said to be near at hand.' Again he says that pity turns into fear when the object is so nearly related to us that the suffering seems to be our own, and we pity others in circumstances in which we should fear for ourselves. Thus in Aristotle's treatment pity is not an altruistic and disinterested emotion. There can be no pity where there is no fear also. Both pity and fear are derived from the self regarding instinct and pity springs from the feeling that a similar suffering might happen to ourselves. The object of pity therefore should be like ourselves. This is the basis of the very possibility of sympathy of the feeling with somebody else. When the good prosper, we rejoice with them, when the good suffer or expect to suffer, we share their pains and fears, and that is pity. If we do not have a tendency to fear for ourselves we cannot share the fear of others. Rash and presumptuous people therefore tend to be incapable of pity. On the other extreme, if we ourselves are already in terrible suffering and have nothing worse to suffer or fear, we also tend to be incapable of pity because we are absorbed in our own fear and cannot share anymore with others. Ideally the two scales of goodness and badness and of pleasure and pain should be in harmony so that the good have pleasure and the bad, pain.

Causality in philosophy is the relationship of a cause to its effect. It is the sequence of events arranged in such a way that a cause-and-effect relation seems probable. However in ancient times superstitions and religion made people believe in spirits, demons or gods controlling the events in the universe. Fate and destiny controlled everything. But with scientific discoveries and better understanding of natural phenomena, man has sought rational explanations to natural and social causality. These changes are also reflected in drama if we peep into the history of Greek classical drama to the present day. In Greek drama, gods and spirits wield their supernatural influence in the form of fate and destiny; in Elizabethan drama, the fear of the spirits and witches are present in a different scale; in modern drama, there is greater thrust towards psychological and social conflicts as for example in Ibsen's social tragedies. The theatre of the absurd on the other hand, returns to the play of chance and fate in a meaningless universe. Drama is an outcome of the tension between casual belief systems and the individual's choice and responsibility. The Greek philosopher Aristotle enumerated four different kinds of causes: the material, the formal, the efficient, and the final.

Cavalier drama consisted of court plays of the 17th century such as James Shirley's *The Triumph of Peace*; Sir John Suckling's *The Goblins*; and Thomas Killigrew's *The Parson's Wedding*.

Ceiling cloth is the canvas on the ceiling of a box that represents a room.

Cellar is the space below the stage used for keeping the equipment for changing scenery and other props required for the play.

Censorship was practised in the English theatre during the time of Henry VIII when Lord Chamberlain was appointed to check heresy and sedition presented in drama. Later, Licensing Acts were promulgated under James I in 1713 and 1737. The Theatre Act came into effect in 1843 giving licences to theatres and plays for public performance. The 1968 Theatre Act abolished Lord Chamberlain's power to censor tests. The 1959 Obscene Publications Act controls writers, directors and the media.

Centre 42 is a movement began by Arnold Wesker in 1962 to manifest his political commitment to the working classes. It aimed to popularise the arts through trade union support. The movement died out due to debt and lack of trade union support.

Centring is a technical term referring to an actor's concentration and focus of attention during the play.

Centrestage is the very centre of attention at the dramatic performance taking place in the central portion of the stage.

Central action refers to the series of events or the general movement in the play.

Central staging is the same as the arena stage on which the audience surround the area where the action takes place.

Centres Dramatiques were French centres established outside Paris after World War ·II to promote French theatre.

Prominent among them is the Theatre de la cite near Lyons founded in 1957.

Chamber play is a play written to be read aloud or to be performed in a chamber for close friends. It is not meant for commercial performance on stage.

Chamberlain's Men was the most successful Elizabethan dramatic company of Shakespeare taken in 1594. Later King James I became their patron and the company was christened 'King's men.' It flourished until 1642 when theatres were closed by the puritans.

Chance, a causeless occurrence, is a concern in drama which is a mimetic art. Chance is given its due place even in philosophy and science, e.g., Darwin's 'theory of natural selection', Bergson's 'principle of creative evolution' and Heisenberg's 'uncertainty principle.' Chance becomes a device in the hands of the dramatist. e.g., in Shakespeare's *Othello* a lost handkerchief by chance brings about the death of Desdemona.

Character is the person in a play or his personality. Aristotle in his *Poetics* considered character that aspect of the plot from which the action arises. In Chapter 6 of *Poetics* he argues that plot is more important than character. It looks as though there is an antithesis between character and plot. But it is not so in reality as character is formed by plot. Speaking about characters he demands that they be 'good' (ch.15). Good means ethically good. The goodness he requires is the moral purpose which is inseparably linked to the goodness of the whole action. In Chapter 15 of *Poetics* Aristotle discusses that character should be 'good', 'appropriate', 'like reality' and 'consistent.' It looks as though there is a sharp antithesis between 'character and plot' or 'character and action.' But in reality they are not opposed but inseparable. In each individual, character is formed by action. By 'tragedies without character', Aristotle meant plays in which personages go through a change of fortune.

Probably a change from happiness to misery, rather than the opposite in which they suffer and act.

Characterisation is the process by which an actor creates a character. Through it the dramatist communicates with the audience. Once characterisation is defined, an appropriate name is given to the character. Then the dialogue and other devices of communication by the character are specified.

Chaucerian stanza (*see* Rhyme Royal)

Chester cycle is one of the four cycles of mystery plays in medieval England. These cycles were York, Chester, Wakefield (Towneley) and Ludus Coventriae (Hegge cycle). These cycles are associated with the feast of the Corpus Christi (29th June) which was declared in 1264. The pageants vary. Chester has 25 and York 50. The plays were assigned to particular trade guilds, e.g., York shipwrights enacted the story of Noah. These stories were popular from the time of Chaucer to Shakespeare. However they declined during the Reformation.

Chew the scenery means over acting by which actors indulge in too much of gesticulations or histrionics or behave in a highly emotional manner.

Chiaroscuro is the distribution and contrast of light and shade in a painting or drawing. It is also applied to similar stage lighting to create a mood or a particular emotion in a symbolic manner. The term is derived from the Italian chiaro ("light") and oscuro ("dark") and consists of contrasting lights and shadows. Such dramatic effects are found in the works of 16th century Renaissance masters such as Leonardo da Vinci and Raphael.

Children of Paul's / Children of the chapel were boy drama companies in the 16th century.

Choregus is a title given to a rich patron in ancient Greece who paid for the training and costuming of the chorus of a drama.

Choreographer is the one who plans the steps and dances in a play.

Chorus in the theatre is a group of singers and dancers who are accompanied by music. The term chorus was used first by the ancient Greeks in Attic drama consisting of a group of dancing singers. (6th - 5th centuries BC). During pauses in the play, the chorus sang lyrical passages and performed dance movements which was a comment on the play and added to its progress. In the Elizabethan times even a single character who commented on the action of the play in a prologue or epilogue was called a *chorus*. In the modern theatre the term is applied strictly to a group of singers and dancers who assist in the action of a musical play.

Chorus character is a single person who takes the place of a chorus and makes comments on the action of the play. Shakespeare uses his fools as chorus characters.

Christmas drama consists of Biblical events of Christ's birth, the Epiphany, the Journey of the Magi, the announcement to the shepherds, the massacre of the Holy Innocents by Herod and the flight of the Holy Family into Egypt. These stories existed in independent plays and were incorporated into the mystery cycles.

Chronicle is a bare record of events in order of time. It could be of national or of universal nature. If chronicled events are considered year by year they are called *Annals*. Chronicles in England began under King Alfred in the 9th century known as *The Anglo Saxon Chronicle* consisting of legends and facts. Other chronicles include Geoffrey of Monmouth's *The History of the Kings of Britain* (c. 1136) in Latin, recording the legends of King Arthur and other legendary British history; Raphael Hollinshed's *Chronicles of England, Scotland, and Ireland*, which Shakespeare and other dramatists used in their chronicle plays.

Chronicle play is based on recorded history and the earliest Chronicles. It was popular towards the end of 16th century and early 17th century depicting scenes from the lives of monarchs or famous historical personages. John Bale (1495-1563) was the first to attempt this genre with his *King John*. This brought about a departure from the *Interludes* that were popular then. Shakespeare was one of the first to write chronicle plays. His *Henry VI* in three parts present historical events in the dramatic form. Other known chronicle plays include Shakespeare's *Henry IV, Henry VIII, Richard II*; Webster's *Sir Thomas Wyat*; Marlowe's *Edward II*; George Peele's *Edward I*. Most of these plays were based on Holinshed's *Chronicles of England, Scotland and Ireland* (1587). They were neither comedy nor tragedy but contained elements of both with an effort to recreate dramatically a movement in history. In the 18th and 19th century some plays based on the Roman history appeared. Thomas Hardy's *The Dynasts* (1904) is an epic drama in blank verse and prose, tracing the heroic life of Napoleon. Chronicle plays written after the Second World War include Arthur Miller's *The Crucible* and Robert Bolt's *A Man for All Seasons*. Thus the chronicle plays have given basic foundation to the tradition of historical drama from Shakespeare to the present day.

Chronology refers to time sequence by which events follow in a particular order. Aristotle makes a clear distinction between a 'beginning, middle and end' in drama. Drama calls for a clear chronology of events to make it comprehensible. But in certain plays the chronology of events is broken by subplots. In the modern theatre, chronology is broken to present dream materials on stage, whereby the same character appears on stage presenting different points in time. In the plays of Harold Pinter he makes use of 'stream of consciousness' technique breaking chronological sequence of events.

Cinefication is a term derived from Meyerhold (1874-1940) who insisted on using film techniques in the theatre. Films were successful in presenting things realistically in contrast to the theatre's artificial presentation of spectacular melodrama. Meyerhold suggested radical changes in dramatic presentation to withstand the onslaught of film industry by frequent change of scenes, elaborate use of machinery and constructions like the cinema halls.

Church drama belongs to a genre that developed in the Christian church based on religious subjects. It was meant for apologetics. It came into vogue in the middle ages as well as during the Reformation. In the 20th century there is a revival of such plays in the works of T.S. Eliot, Charles Williams and C.S. Lewis.

Circle of attention is some space an actor needs to have for himself to concentrate on his role. He feels secure in his territory and can be isolated from the audience and other distractions. This circle can be very small depending on the object on which he concentrates, e.g., If he is handling a gun, he concentrates on it and the circle is very narrow. If the gun is to be used for killing a person the circle widens to give that impression. This circle helps the actor to give a realistic impression to the audience.

Claque consists of the friends and well-wishers of the actors brought in to respond enthusiastically during a dramatic performance by the managers at their own expense. This is to lead critics and the audience to appreciate the play.

Classical in the restricted sense is used to portray the art, literature, and aesthetics of the ancient Greeks and Romans. In a broad sense it refers to any style or period of creative work remarkable for its qualities that are mainly suggestive of classical Greek or Roman art, literature, and aesthetics. Among these qualities are a sense of conscious restraint in the handling of themes and a sense of rational order and proportion in forms.

Classicism means the imitation of the style and aesthetic principles of ancient Greek and Roman classical art and literature. It also refers to the adoption of such principles in music today. The late 17th and early 18th centuries were the most important periods when classicism prevailed in Western thought. The term *neoclassicism* is often used in referring to revivals of classicism.

Classical drama refers to ancient Greek and Latin drama as well as the neoclassical drama. It is a general term applied to drama that follows strict rules of unities, objectivity, balance, decorum, economy and seriousness. The earliest period in Western theatrical history is called classical with drama and theatre of the classical civilisations of ancient Greece and Rome. The Greek dramatic literature began in the sixth century BC. Aristotle's *Poetics* (c.330 BC) speaks of the origin of theatre. According to him the Greek tragedy developed from dithyrambs: choral hymns in honour of the god Dionysus. Greek tragedy flourished in the fifth century BC. Of the more than 1,000 tragedies written during that century, only 31 remain, all by Aeschylus, Sophocles, and Euripides. The plays are highly formal, they are written in verse and consist of scenes (episodes) alternating with choral songs (odes). The stories are mostly drawn from myth or ancient history. They focused on humanity's place in the world and the consequences of individual actions. Little action occurred onstage and most events and information were related through dialogue and choral songs. Comedy also developed in the mid-fifth century BC. The oldest existing comedies are by Aristophanes. They have a highly formal structure thought to be derived from ancient fertility rites. The humour consists of a mixture of satirical attacks on contemporary public figures, bawdy, scatological jokes, and seemingly sacrilegious parodies of the gods. By the fourth century BC comedy had displaced tragedy as the dominant form. As the Roman Republic began to spread in the fourth century BC, it absorbed Greek territories as well as Greek drama and theatre. Native Roman drama did not develop until the third century BC. Drama was originally associated with religious festivals, however, the spiritual nature of the events was soon lost and it became primarily a secular entertainment. The most popular forms were comedy and the native Atellan farce.

The great period of Roman playwriting began in the second century BC and was dominated by the comedies of Plautus and Terence. The plays generally involve domestic intrigue, although those of Terence have a moral value as well. Although Greek and Roman tragedies were performed during this period, the only extant tragedies, from the first century AD, are those of Seneca. Seneca based himself on Greek myths, but emphasised supernatural elements, bloody violence, and obsessive passion. Seneca followed a five-act structure that included soliloquies and poetic speeches. This had great influence on the Renaissance drama which was an attempt to recreate classical drama. Due to new technologies the Renaissance theatre took on a totally new form with some classical characteristics. This form is generally known as neoclassicism. Renaissance theatre was first seen in Italy in the 15th century. The earliest plays were in Latin, but eventually they were written in the vernacular. They were based primarily on Roman models, although the dramatic theory was derived from the rediscovery of Aristotle's *Poetics*. The most important concept in Renaissance art was verisimilitude—the appearance of truth. This did not mean slavishly copying the real world, but rather eliminating the improbable and irrational while emphasizing the ideal. It sought proper moral order and a sense of decorum. Good was rewarded, evil was punished, characters were depicted as ideal types rather than as idiosyncratic individuals. Most significant were the three unities: time, place, and action. Based on a passage in Aristotle, strict rules were kept: A play could have only a single plot, must take place within a 24-hour period, and could occur only in one locale.

Climax is the turning point in the course of a play when it reaches crisis and resolution. Climax is often the scene of recognition and discovery. For example in Sophocles's

Oedipus Rex, the protagonist Oedipus discovers himself to be the man who has killed his father and married his own mother.

Cloak and sword plays belong to the 17th century Spanish romantic tradition. In it the characters wear cloaks and hide their identities. As the plot thicken they engage themselves in duels.

Closed form is a device used in drama whereby solutions to the problems posed are given to the audience. Drama being a mimetic art most dramatists seek to be articulate. But in the case of tragedies some questions may not find coherent answers. Some dramatists like Chekhov prefer not to give answers to questions posed, making it 'open form.' This is typical of the theatre of the absurd as in Beckett's *Waiting for Godot*.

Closet drama is written to be read privately than preformed on stage, dramas such as *Milton's Samson Agonistes*, Hardy's *The Dynasts*, Tennyson's *Becket*, Shelley's *Prometheus Unbound*, and Arnold's *Empedocles on Etna*.

Clown is the modern circus performer who plays the fool and does tricks to make people laugh. Clown is known by other names such as buffoon, jester, fool, mirth-maker, gleeman, mime, harlequin, etc. Each clown puts on a face or a performance personality. His face becomes the clown's unique personal property. Clowns can be classified into four categories: *whiteface, auguste, character*, and *new vaudeville*. The whiteface clown originated in the 18th century. He coloured his face with white flour and later with grease-paints. The most popular known white-face characters is Harlequin in the Italian *commedia dell'arte*. English actor John Rich was a popular white-face clown in the mid-18th century. English entertainer Joseph Grimaldi is considered the most famous clown. He has appeared in many performances including *Harlequin and Mother Goose* (1806) with exaggerated eyebrows and geometrical patterns on his cheeks and a blue topknot on his bald head.

Auguste clown is a stupid bumbling fool. He is an acrobat and horseback rider dressed in a ragged coat, a tattered wig, and with a grease-painted red nose. He usually wears oversize shoes and bright coloured oversized clothing. He is pushed into the ring by the circus owner. The auguste clown is often the butt of jokes.

The character clown is a 20th century carpet clown who performed in circus. He is the most realistic of the clown types. He makes fun of different features of the human face through exaggerated beards, whiskers, warts, large noses, bald heads, and strange haircuts. The most popular character is the tramp clown, the development of which owes much to English actor Charlie Chaplin. He played the "Little Tramp" in many motion pictures. Otto Griebling and Emmett Kelly are two other famous tramp clowns.

The new vaudeville clown is a performer who have turned away from traditional clown acts. He works alone without makeup. He tries to relate with audience. The new vaudeville clown performs with circus and in the theatre. He combines juggling, mime, and magic tricks with traditional clowning techniques. The best known such clown is Bill Irwin. He does not wear clown makeup and uses his expressive face to portray the chaos of a mechanised and unfair world. Irwin produced and preformed in *The Regard of Flight* (1982), *Largely New York* (1989), and *Fool Moon* (1993).

Code is a term from semiotics referring to certain signal between a sender and a receiver. In drama it has psychological, linguistic and cultural significance. Codes can be found together with utterances in the form of off-stage voices. Accordingly when a character speaks besides his personal opinion he may be expressing the attitudes of his social milieu, family or parents. The audience responds to these whispered codes differently. Codes can be found in the tone, posture, gestures, facial expressions, type of costumes, etc.

Cold reading is an extempore reading by an actor for audition. This can show the actor's potentiality better than when prepared texts are read.

Collaborative theatre is when a playwright develops the script in consultation with the actors. As rehearsals go on the script is modified and actors are able to contribute their ideas.

Collage is a work put together from assembled fragments. In drama it consists of materials such as dialogue, quotations, scenes borrowed from different sources. Shakespeare too resorted to this technique.

Colour is an effective theatrical language to communicate emotions. Single colours signify certain feelings, e.g., white = innocence, red = danger, black = death, green = jealousy. Colours of scenery and costume may also be effectively used to communicate emotions in the characters. A particular colour can be prominent in a play to give the impression of its theme, e.g, 'Red' in Webster's *The Duchess of Malfi* being a revenge tragedy.

Columbina is a pretty and innocent girl of marriageable age in a *commedia dell' arte*. She is generally a maidservant who becomes in course of time a ward and even the wife of the Pantaloon. She falls in love with the Harlequin and elopes with him. However, she remains unfulfilled in love.

Combat music is the musical background for a fight scene in a Victorian melodrama.

Comedy originated from the Greek fertility rites in honour of Dionysus. Aristotle defined it as written about persons of minor importance whom their faults rendered ridiculous and it dealt with 'some defeat or ugliness that is not painful or destructive.' Comedy is derived from the Greek 'komos' which meant 'merry making.' There are three periods of the Greek comedy, namely, the old, the middle and the new. Aristophanes (448-380 BC) belongs to the old period. His comedies are characterised by buffoonery, satire and social commentary. His popular works translated into English are *The Acharnians*, *The Knights*, *The Clouds*, *The Peace*, *The Wasps*, *The Birds*, *The Frogs,* etc. Aristophanes, being a satirist, targeted the politicians, poets, and philosophers of his day. *The Knights* (424 BC) is a devastating satire about Athenian politician and military leader Cleon. *The Clouds* (423 BC) satirises Greek philosopher Socrates. In *The Wasps* (422 BC) he satirised the courts of justice of the day, and in *The Peace* (421 BC) he spoke of peace between Athens and Sparta. *Lysistrata* (411 BC), his most famous work, is a satire on war in which women strike for peace by practising celibacy. The plays of Aristophanes had some influence on English satire, especially that of English playwright Ben Jonson and the novelist Henry Fielding.

Antiphanes is the main writer in the middle period with his plays marked by burlesque. The new period had Menander who was the most influential of the Greek comedy writers. The new comedy mostly dealt with love intrigues of young lovers. Menander exerted his influence on Plautus and Terence.

According to Dante a comedy begins on a harsh note and ends on a happy note. His *Divine Comedy* begins with the misfortunes in Inferno and ends on a happy note in Paradise. Sir Philip Sidney defined comedy in his *Apology for Poetry* as "an imitation of the common errors of life, which he the poet representeth in the most ridiculous and scornful sort that may be; so that it is impossible that any beholder can be content to be such a one." Sidney found a didactic purpose also in comedy though it is meant to please and entertain. Dr. Jonson considered comedy as a living form and sought to find out the sources in comedies that provide pleasure and mirth.

Ben Jonson (1572-1637) contributed a great deal to the Renaissance comedy of humours. His comedies were of satirical nature with intellectual honesty. He based his theory of humours on Hippocratic pathology. Accordingly, the human body has four fluids: blood, phlegm, yellow bile and black bile. These fluids make a person sanguine, phlegmatic, choleric or melancholic. He created character types through his comedy of humours such as *Everyman in his humour*; *Everyman out of his humour*; *Volpone*; *The Alchemist,* etc.

Shakespeare has his early comedies: *The Comedy of Errors*, *The Taming of the Shrew*, *The Two Gentlemen of Verona* and *Love's Labour's Lost*. In *The Comedy of Errors* he conforms to classical discipline and bases himself on the Roman writer Plautus. He tries to be free from the romantic comedy in *The Comedy of Errors* and *The Taming of the Shrew*. His other plays are romantic comedies that end in a happy ending like *A Mid-Summer Night's Dream*, *Twelfth Night* and *The Tempest*. Being plays of love the characters are preoccupied in wooing. Some of his plays are called dark comedies as the main characters in them undergo various misfortunes yet are happily united at the end, e.g., *All's well that ends well*, *Measure for Measure*, *The Winter's Tale* and *Cymbeline*. Shakespeare seldom uses the comedy for social criticism but primarily aims to arouse laughter. Thomas Dekker wrote sympathetic realistic comedy like *The Shoe Maker's Holiday*. Beaumont and Fletcher wrote tragic-comedies such as *Philaster*.

The Restoration drama introduced the comedies of manners. William Congreve (1670-1729) presented the narrow world of fashion with gallants, ladies, fops, and rakes in his plays like *Love for Love* and *The Way of the World*. Oliver Goldsmith wrote anti-sentimental comedies, e.g., *She Stoops to Conquer*. Richard Sheridan wrote in the same vein of the comedy of manners plays like *The School for Scandal* and *The Rivals*. There is a decadence in comedy until Bernard Shaw revived it towards the end of the 19th century.

Comedy of humours is a term applied to the form of comedy developed by Ben Jonson (1572-1637). His comedies were mostly satirical and intellectually honest. The theory of humours was based on Hippocratic pathology that the human body has four fluids: blood, phlegm, yellow bile and black bile which make a man sanguine, phlegmatic, choleric and melancholic. Jonson exploited this concept in his early plays *Everyman in his Humour* and *Every man out of his Humour*. Both plays are satires and the prologue to *Every man in his Humour* has his dramatic theory. He opposes romantic comedies and chronicles as they lack 'classically precise forms.' Humours are the bodily fluids to which medieval medicine attributed various types of human temperament according to the prominence of each within the body. He wants to put on stage, "deeds and language such as men use and persons such as comedy would choose when she would show an image of the times." His characters are not individuals but types.

Comedy of intrigue is a type of comedy that arouses laughter through intrigues and disguises. The device was used by John Fletcher (1579-1625), Behn (1640-89), etc.

Comedy of manners is a kind of Restoration comedy in imitation of the Italian mime and the plays of Moliere. Restoration (1660) made dramatic entertainment popular as Charles II reopened theatre. These dramas were court dramas written for the aristocratic audience. When Charles II returned from France he and his courtiers brought along the influence of Moliere. The Restoration drama concerned with the life of the upper classes—their moral laxity and licentiousness. Comedy of manners dealt with the artificial life of the upper classes. It concerned with love, moral infidelity and foibles of society. It presented the habits, customs, manners, follies of gay elegant aristocracy and dealt with young nobles straining after wit. The plot is mostly made up of love intrigues, clandestine love affairs, senseless prattles, scandalmongering, drinking and gambling. Love is an important theme in such comedies. Usually there is a pair of lovers. They are well versed in coquetry and noted for wit, sparkling dialogue and verbal fencing matches. The lovers will try to be united with each other, but others try to obstruct them. Thus the conflict is maintained. Usually lovers are simple and easily duped. There is a series of dramatic incidents and finally the conflict is resolved. For example, in Sheridan's *The School for Scandal,* there are two pairs of lovers who are rewarded at the end. The villains are mildly punished. Comedy has a world of sunshine with bits of passing shadows. Sheridan was not a deep thinker but well exposed to life and presented society to some extent. Comedy deals eventually with appearance and reality. The comedy of manners is on 'surface of life.' The presence of aristocracy at the centre of action distinguishes comedy of manners from other comedies.

Traditionally comedy deals with middle or low section. Therefore comedy of manners is styled artificial as they present superficial habits and manners dealing with surface of human existence of a section of society. They do not depict men and women in their emotional sides. There is no study of human psychology as done by Shakespeare.

The comedy of manners has been branded licentious. Dryden is considered the father of the genre, however it is Etherage who established it. Later 'the mannerly and witty' Wycherley had it beautifully brought out in *The Country Wife* which at times sounded very indecent and immoral. Congreve in *The Way of the World* brought the comedy of manners to perfection. Jeremy Collier in 1698 wrote on 'The Immorality and Licentiousness of English Stage' presenting the middle class reaction against it. Soon the sentimental comedy developed in the 18th century. It stood for domestic virtues and the triumph of Christian virtues and preaching to middle class audience. Goldsmith and Sheridan led the anti-sentimental movement. Sheridan's *The School for Scandal* is a very successful comedy of manners. In the Prologue Garrick speaks of its purpose—to expose the theme of scandalmongering. He wrote, 'the play had less nature than wit.' It is full of wit showing absurdities.

Comic opera is an opera with a comic plot or a romantic drama with songs and comical scenes.

Comic relief is a device employed by a dramatist in a tragedy by inserting some comical situations or the role of a fool. As the tragedy progresses, it relieves tension in the audience. This has a psychological effect on the audience, e.g, The episode of the drunken porter in *Macbeth*; the scene of the grave diggers in *Hamlet*.

Command performance is a drama presentation by a troupe for a royal person on request. Often such performances are made for charity fund raising.

Commedia dell' arte means 'professional comedy' preformed by Italian drama troupes in the 16th and 18th centuries influenced by the 'Commedia erudita' (learned comedy) of Plautus and Terence as well as the mime of the Atellan fables in Latin. It originated in northern Italy in the mid-16th century. These troupes consisted of six to 12 actors. It presented stereotyped characters each performing a conventional role in masks. They brought out humorous scenes with apparently unrehearsed dialogue, acrobatic feats, physical gestures, musical interludes, and clowning. Unlike traditional theatre, skilled actresses were brought in instead of males playing the female roles. The roles of the actors varied such as a 'Pantalone' (Pantaloon), an aged and rich merchant who disguises to attract women, a fat 'dottore (doctor) who takes pride in his skills, a 'Pulcinella' (a pot-bellied Neopolitan rogue), a 'Columbina' (an innocent pretty girl), an 'Arlecchino' (called 'Harlequin', a clown), a cowardly Captain, handsome lovers, a variety of servants, etc. From this collection of stock characters, each *commedia* troupe dramatised several plots. The troupes had also comic routines called 'Iazzi' which was a comic act to arouse sudden laughter. These were presented on demand. The plots often revolved around amorous intrigues of young lovers. The *commedia dell' arte* had its influence on the Elizabethan comedy writers. There was an attempt to censure the *commedia dell' arte* in the 1600s by the governments of Spain and France. However, eventually the humour and character types of the *commedia* were incorporated into the conventional European theatre. Elements of the *commedia* is present in the comedies of the French dramatists Molière and Pierre Carlet. An attempt was made to revive and reform the *commedia* in Italy during the 18th century by playwrights Carlo Gozzi and Carlo Goldoni.

Commedia erudita means 'learned comedy' written in Italy in the early 16th century. Most representative in this genre is Aristo's *Suppositi* and Machiavelli's *La Mandragola*.

Commercial theatre refers to theatrical performances meant for a very large audience with the purpose of making a profit. Such performances are meant for entertainment, literary, artistic or didactic purposes are secondary for commercial theatre. In United Kingdom, London's West End, and in the USA, New York Broadway theatre district are known for commercial theatres. Some of these theatrical companies tour other cities and are known as 'Bus and truck tour' or 'Road companies'.

Communication in theatre is established by the interaction between actor and spectator, character and spectator, character and character, actor and actor and spectator and spectator.

Communion is the link established between character and audience, character and character, actor and actor. This link depends also on the props the actor uses as well as their expressions.

Community theatre is amateur performances by the residents of a locality. It began in 1968 in Britain. It consisted of fringe groups that presented social problems of racial minorities. They also looked for new audiences. In their effort to present situations realistically, they even lived among communities to experience their problems and tensions.

Company is a team of actors, directors and technicians who come together for the production of a play.

Complication is the intensification of suspense due to some forces that come in opposition to the protagonist, as the plot develops. In a five-act tragedy, usually it is the second act that presents the complication. It is known as the act of complication. According to Aristotle in his *Poetics,* "Every tragedy is in part Complication and in part Denouement. The complication consists of incidents that have taken place before the opening of the play and often some also of that occurring within it; the remainder form the denouement. By complication I mean everything from the beginning of the story up to the point where the hero suffers a change of fortune; by denouement, everything from the latter point to the end.

Concentration in drama calls for the character's full attention to the role played paying no attention to distracting noise or movements. It calls for a circle of attention created by the actor by which he focuses on his own self and is aware of his physical atmosphere.

Confidant/Confidante (fem) is the person in whom the protagonist confides and seeks advice from and listens to. The author uses the confidant-protagonist dialogue to expose the mind of the protagonist as well as the innermost thoughts of other characters, e.g, in *Hamlet*, Horatio is the confidant of Hamlet.

Conflict is the opposition and struggle between two opposing forces in a plot. It arouses interest in a play from the suspense generated. The conflict can be of different types such as: (i) from the opposition of two physical forces generating intense actions; (ii) from the opposition between the wills of two characters leading to the confrontation of one quality of character with another; (iii) from the internal mental struggle in a character between opposite desires; (iv) from a character in confrontation with family or society;

(v) from the opposition between a character and the audience; (vi) from the struggle between a character and gods or fate. The interest aroused in the audience depends on the strength of the conflict. Conflicts arouse empathy and identification in the audience.

Connection in dramatic performance is the interdependence between actors which presupposes an intuitive attention to each other's feelings and emotions.

Connotation is the implication of something more than the denotation of it such as ideas, feelings and images. Denotation is that which a word denotes in contradistinction to what it connotes, e.g., *snake* denotes a reptile. But it can connote a person of intriguing and cunning character as in Sheridan's *The School for Scandal*. Connotation of a word can imply many things according to contexts and references.

Constructivism is a modern concept developed by the Russian director Vsevolod Meyerhold. He presents an illusory setting for a play with scaffolds, ladders and the like to represent houses and factories.

Contamination is a dramatic device by which parts of two plays are combined to form a third. It was a practice in ancient Rome, especially by Plautus and Terence. Renaissance dramatists like Shakespeare borrowed heavily from Chaucer and Boccaccio, e.g., in writing *Troilus and Cressida*, Shakespeare was inspired by Homer's, Chaucer's, Henryson's and Caxton's treatment of the love between Troilus and Cressida and its betrayal against the setting of the siege of Troy by the Greeks.

Continuity is the flow in the stage appearance of an actor. The individual actor's role should flow into the scenes and the scenes into acts and finally the whole play having continuous flow from act to act.

Contrast is to compare characters or ideas in a play to show their difference. The contrast of characters can be in their external appearance, age, size, expressions, posture, tone of voice, etc. Visual contrasts can be shown by settings and lighting. Contrast can be a very effective device to give emphasis.

Convention in literature is a method or style that has become an accepted form of literary expression in course of time, e.g., Pastoral elegy; Ballad tradition; use of Heroic Couplet by Dryden and Pope; Stream of Consciousness novels; Shakespearean sonnet, etc. In drama, convention is a code the dramatist shares with the audience. There are codes of behaviour, speech and costumes fit for a particular character in a naturalist drama. A pauper does not behave and dress like a monarch and vice versa. Such conventions are bypassed in burlesque or travesty. These conventions are at times unnatural devices in a drama as, for instance, in presenting a drama on conquest the audience suspends its disbelief and regards the stage as a battlefield and the actors as kings and warriors. When the characters speak in soliloquy, asides, etc., the audience understands it as a convention to reveal characters or as comments on actions or persons.

Cornish round refers to the arenas in Cornwall with circular areas where medieval plays were performed. These circular areas had scaffolds on four sides with figures of God in the East and the World, the Flesh and the Devil on the other cardinal points.

Corpus Christi plays are mystery plays performed at the feast of the Corpus Christi from 1318 until 1558 when it was suppressed by Queen Elizabeth I in England. Corpus Christi in Latin means "Body of Christ". The feast was established in 1264 by Pope Urban IV and is celebrated in the Roman Catholic church honouring the presence of Christ in the sacrament of the Eucharist. It was celebrated to affirm the Eucharistic doctrine of the transubstantiation. The feast falls on the Thursday after Trinity Sunday. Until the 16th century the feast was characterised by splendid outdoor processions in which guilds, merchants, magistrates, nobility, and clergy participated. After the procession, mystery and miracle plays were performed in the public square by members of the guild (*see* Chester cycle).

Correspondence refers to various relationships between man-state-nature in accordance with the Elizabethan worldview. Man is made up of four humours in correspondence to the cosmic elements. There are seven divisions in man's head corresponding to the seven stars in the sky. Just as the head is the one that controls the whole body, so too the king rules the state as head. This mythology of correspondence was used by the Elizabethan writers like Shakespeare, e.g., The storm in *King Lear* is compared to the psychological storm the king undergoes. The principle of correspondence is a concept in Plato's psychology by which he contrasts the will and judgement in man to legislature and executive in the state.

Corsican trap is a Victorian device by which an opening used to be kept across the stage from where ghosts and spirits could make their appearance. It was first used in the French play *The Corsican Brothers* by Boucicault (1820-90).

Costume is whatever a performer wears. Costume designing concerns mainly with clothing and accessories such as wigs, masks, and makeup. Costumes are important in setting the mood of a drama giving vital information about the characters. Since acting often involves impersonation, most costuming is actual or recreated historical or contemporary dress. Sometimes costumes may also be suggestive or abstract. Prior to the 19th century little attention was paid to period and regional accuracy in costume. In the 19th and 20th centuries designers have tried to present costumes according to style of the period. Colour, fabric, cut, texture and material used can depict particular effects in a drama. Costume can represent a social class or personality traits.

Costume can signify a character signature. Comic characters or circus clowns have their typical costume. Mask is a special element of costume. It was essential in Greek and Roman drama as well as *commedia dell'arte*.

Counterweight system is a mechanical way of putting up a scenery with the help of pulleys, ropes and weights.

Coup de theatre is a sudden unexpected change in the turn of events in a dramatic situation. It gives a sensational effect due to the surprising twist in the plot. The device makes a dead person come back to life when least expected by the audience. The Greek device of *deux machina* ('god from a machine') is a *coup de theatre* effect to resolve a conflict by surprise.

Coventry cycle is one of the full cycles of mystery plays (*see* Mystery plays).

Craft cycle refers to mystery play cycles which were performed by different crafts or guilds.

Crash box is the wooden box kept outside the stage into which an actor can throw a glass to make a breaking effect.

Creative objective is a term used to refer to the central idea or motive of a play. Each actor should have the final objective of the play in mind and reach out to it as he plays his role.

Creed play is a 15th century religious play to defend the doctrines of the Catholic faith. It is connected with the medieval morality plays.

Crescendo is the building up of a tempo and bringing a play to its climax.

Crisis is a turning point in the course of a play when a decision is made. This crisis point is the climax of the play. The term can also be attributed to a decisive and important moment in a scene or act or performance of an actor. In the 'drama of crisis' a climax in the play is presented at the beginning and the protagonist is unaware of the plot, e.g., Sophocles' *Oedipus Rex*.

Cross above means to move upstage of other actors or furniture on stage.

Cross below means to move downstage of other actors or furniture on stage.

Cruelty, theatre of is a dramatic theory spoken of by Antonin Artaud and developed by his theatre company in the 1930s. It presented on stage the merciless side of humanity by not following social conventions. Artaud was of the opinion that the actors and the audience be, "victims burned at the stake, signalling through the flames." He presented plays that showed cruelty on stage to shock the audience, e.g., Peter Weiss's *The Persecution and Assassination of Jean Paul Marat*.

Cue is the signal given by the stage manager to the actor or the stage crew to perform a particular action or role. It can be a phrase, a word, a sound or an action.

Cup and saucer dramas are those performed in a domestic setting with sipping of tea in between the dialogue. This form was popularised in the mid-19th century by Tom Robertson with his *Society* and *Castle*.

Curtain is the drape that closes the stage from the view of the audience. A curtain can be operated by raising up and down or by pulling to the sides.

Curtain line is the last line of the script that brings down the curtain.

Curtain music is the music played before the curtain rises. In the Elizabethan plays curtain tunes were played at the beginning of the play and in between the acts.

Curtain raiser is a short dramatic entertainment to warm up the audience before the main play begins. This was a method prevalent in the 19th century with the purpose of setting the mood for the play.

Curtain set refers to very simple stage setting. It consists of minimal furniture such as a table or chair to suggest a room.

Cuts is a cinematic term referring to transition in a film. By cuts a strip of film is merged with another, presenting one scene to the next. The transition is made smoother by fade-in and fade-out techniques.

Cycle in drama refers to a series of episodes as in the mystery plays, e.g., the series of events of the Biblical stories. The mystery plays were performed in a sequence at a particular festival by one of the four cycles in the medieval England. These cycles were York, Chester, Wakefield (Towneley) and Ludus Coventriae (Hegge cycle) (*see* Chester cycle).

Cycle plays are the short plays based on Biblical stories popular in the medieval England. They are also known as mystery plays (*see* Cycle).

Cyclorama is a curved fabric background for a dramatic performance. It is usually used for projecting effects for stage background such as shades of trees, clouds, city structures or scenery. Cyclorama is also known as 'cyc'.

D

Dada is an artistic and literary movement depicting the nihilistic protest against Western culture especially against militarism during and after World War I (1914-1918). The term *dada* is a French word for hobbyhorse used by the Romanian-born poet Tristan Tzara. He began the Dadaist group in 1916 with German writer Hugo Ball, the Alsatian-born artist Jean Arp, and other intellectuals living in Zürich, Switzerland. A similar revolt against conventional art began in New York led by Man Ray, Marcel Duchamp, and Francis Picabia. From 1919 the Dadaist group met in Paris and inspired the *Surrealist movement*. To express the negation of all current aesthetic and social values the Dadaists used unintelligible artistic and literary methods. Their manifestos were often bewildering with the purpose of startling the public. They used innovative materials like discarded objects found in the streets in their works. The German painter Kurt Schwitters made collages of wastepaper and similar materials. French painter Marcel Duchamp exhibited as works of art ordinary commercial products like a bottle rack which he called *readymades*. Though the Dadaists were revolutionary in their methods, they believed in the romantic goodness of humanity. The movement declined in the 1920s, however it had an influence on modern-art movements. In the mid-1950s there was a revival of interest in Dada in New York City among several composers, writers, and artists who showed Dadaist features in their works. Dada is a forerunner of the theatre of cruelty and theatre of the absurd. Tom Stoppard's *Travesties* (1974) is a dada comedy. The play is set in Zurich during the First World War where Lenin, Joyce and Tristan Tzara lived. It presents witty comments on Dada, Joyce's *Ulysses*, and socialist realism.

Dead areas are sections of an auditorium from where the performers do not receive any response from the audience.

Deadly theatre is applied to theatre that keeps to conventional form that attract audience. It is characterised by stock beginning and ending with usual jokes and effects. Peter Brook in *The Empty Space* (1968) explains this concept.

Debate occurs in drama in the form of discussions on opposing viewpoints, e.g., In *The Castle of Perseverance* there is the debate between Mercy, Peace, Truth and Righteousness for the soul of man; Bernard Shaw's plays are marked by debates to convey his ideas.

De casibus tragedy is a term derived from Boccaccio's (1313-75) *De CasibusVirorum Illustrum* which was a source book for references to tragedies by Chaucer and others. *De casibus* tragedy depicts fall from prosperity to misery of heroes and heroines.

Deconstruction is the method of analysing literature that seeks to uncover multiple layers of meaning. It considers a play as a construct and studies the author's intentions, assumptions and other meanings. It analyses how the same language, images, or ideas have been used in other cases.

Décor refers to the overall get-up of a play with its sets, costumes, and props.

Decorum is a Renaissance and neoclassical principle by which the speech and behaviour of characters in drama are appropriate to their status. An Emperor speaks a formal language; a pauper speaks a commoner's language; an old man speaks a grave language; a clown speaks a rustic language.

Denotation is that which a word denotes in contradistinction to that which it connotes (*see* Connotation).

Denouement is derived from French meaning 'untying of the knot' and refers to the final resolution of the plot in a tragedy by which the mystery is solved. According to Aristotle in his *Poetics,* "Every tragedy is in part Complication and in part Denouement. The complication consists of incidents that have taken place before the opening of the play and often some also of that occurring within it; the remainder form the denouement. By complication I mean everything from the beginning of the story up to the point where the hero suffers a change of fortune; by denouement, everything from the latter point to the end." (*see* Resolution).

Deus ex machina derived from Latin meaning 'god from the machine', refers to an unexpected intervention in a plot to resolve it. It was a practice in the classical ancient Greek drama to lower on to the stage a deity ('god from the machine') through some mechanical device to bring a solution to the crisis in the plot. Euripides used the device very often. In the modern times the term could mean any sudden contrivance in the resolution of the plot such as a sudden change of heart in the rogue or unexpected inheriting of a fortune by the protagonist. In the opinion of Aristotle the device should be employed only to enlighten the protagonist about unknown events or to predict what would happen. Bertolt Brecht (1898-1956) gave a new interpretation to the device by which the gods leave the problem for man to solve.

Deuteragonist is a character in classical Greek tragedy who is a foil or confidant to the protagonist, e.g., Horatio is a deuteragonist to Hamlet in Shakespeare's *Hamlet*.

Development in drama takes place after the exposition and entanglements of the plot which begins to build to a climax.

Dialectic is a philosophical method of investigating the nature of truth by critical analysis of concepts. Formal reasoning is done through debate. Plato's *Dialogues* is the earliest examples of the dialectical method in which he sought truth through discussion in the form of questions and answers. Aristotle used the term as a synonym for the science of logic. The German philosopher, G. W. F. Hegel (1770-1831), applied the term *dialectic* to his philosophic system. According to him the evolution of ideas occurs through a dialectical process from 'thesis' to 'antithesis' to 'synthesis.' 'Synthesis' arises out of the conflict between 'thesis' and 'antithesis.' Karl Marx took the Hegelian concept to develop his economic determinism or materialist dialectic. He argued that society moved from feudalism to capitalism to a final synthesis in socialism. In drama, the principle of *thesis-antithesis-synthesis* may operate in the relationship between characters who represent different stages of personal and social development.

Dialogue is the conversation between characters in a dramatic or narrative work. A dialogue helps to advance the plot. It gives a realistic impression of the characters and depict their ideas and personalities. In the course of a dialogue, when a character does not want to listen to the other person it is called 'simultaneous monologue.' When a character converses with himself it is 'soliloquy' or 'internal dialogue.' A good dialogue is easily understood by the audience devoid of difficult phrasing. The dialogue depends on the context in which meaning is strengthened by the voice, facial expressions, silences, pauses, etc.

Didactic theatre aims to instruct and teach the audience, e.g., Morality Plays.

Digby plays is a term applied to three late mystery plays, namely, *Mary Magdalene*, *The Conversion of St. Paul* and *The Killing of the Children of Israel*.

Dilemma in theatre is caused when a character has to choose between two opposite options such as life and death; duty and love. Hamlet in his soliloquy is in a dilemma when he utters :

'To be or not to be—that is the question;
Whether 'tis nobler in the mind to suffer
The slings and arrows of outrageous fortune,
Or to take arms against a sea of troubles,...

(*Hamlet* Act III:I)

Dinner theatre is provided in a restaurant or a nightclub with an evening entertainment along with dinner. The entertainment usually consists of a shorter version of a play in the form of a musical, murder mysteries and the like.

Dionysiac in Greek mythology means relating to god Dionysos, son of Zeus by Semele. He is the god of wine and vegetation. It is he who showed man how to cultivate grapevines and make wine. As the god of vegetation he is often represented on Attic vases with a drinking horn and vine branches. He eventually became the popular Greek god of wine. He is a deity whose mysteries inspired ecstatic, orgiastic worship. Groups of female devotees left their homes and roamed the wilderness in ecstatic devotion to Dionysus. According to Greek tradition he died each winter and was reborn in the spring bringing seasonal renewal of the fruits of the earth. The rites in honour of the resurrection of Dionysus gradually evolved into the structured form of the Greek drama. Important festivals were held in honour of Dionysus during which great dramatic competitions were held. The Greater Dionysia festival was held in Athens for five days each spring. The Greek dramatists Aeschylus, Sophocles, and Euripides wrote their great tragedies for his feast. By the fifth century BC, Dionysus was also known to the Greeks as Bacchus, a name referring to the loud cries with which Dionysus was worshiped at the *orgia*, or Dionysiac mysteries. He was worshipped at the Orgia (Dionysiac mysteries) in licentiousness and intoxication. In Italy the Dionysiac mysteries were called the Bacchanalia in the second century BC.

Dionysos is the god of drama. Aristotle held that tragedy began from the hymns in his honour or dithyramba. The drama festivals were celebrated in his honour at the theatre of Dionysos on the slopes of the Acropolis in Athens.

Direct address is made by an actor on stage to the audience, e.g., in Shakespeare's *Two Gentlemen of Verona*, Launce complains about his dog to the audience.

Director is the one who is responsible for the harmonious unity of a production. The director coordinates the actors, the designers and technicians. He takes up a concept and motif and interprets the script or scenario. He selects a cast and rehearses them. He decides on the scenery, costumes, lights and sound. All the visual and aural effects are all determined by the director. It is his vision that the audience finally sees. The director usually selects the cast through auditions in which performers read sections of the script to be produced, present prepared scenes or speeches. Actors may also be hired on the basis of reputation.

Director's note is the comments and suggestions that the director makes after a performance. It is helpful to the cast to improve in the performances later.

Disappearance trap is a trapdoor with an elevator that helps the actors to make quick exits and entrances.

Disclosure is a discovery by the character which affects his plan of action and the progress of the play. Disclosure happens towards the end of the play and brings about catastrophe or reconciliation.

Discourse is used in theatre for the utterances expressed verbally or for movements and gestures.

Discovery according to Aristotle's *Poetics,* "is a change from ignorance to knowledge, and consequently either to love or to hate, in the personages destined for good or evil fortune. The finest form of Discovery is one accompanied by peripetics, such as occurs in *Oedipus*." Hence in a tragedy discovery is the exposure of something unknown to the character which brings about a turning point in the action, e.g., Oedipus discovers that he is the killer of his own father in *Oedipus the King* (*see* Hamartia).

Discovery scene is one in which the characters are already on stage when the curtain rises and are in the midst of a continuing action.

Discussion play is a kind of problem play in which social issues are debated among characters, e.g., in Bernard Shaw's *Man and Superman* Act III, a dream sequence is set in hell in which Don Juan, Mendoza, Ramsden and Ana discuss the nature of progress, evolution and the Life Force in a Shavio-Socratic debate (*see* Problem Play).

Disguise is a device to hide the identity of a character by change of costume, gait or expressions. The audience considers it only as a stage convention though not very realistically presented.

Disguising is a medieval masque performance.

Disney cartoons began with Walt Disney's animated cartoon character Mickey Mouse. He produced cartoon series such as *Oswald the Rabbit*, *Steamboat Willie*, *Plane Crazy*, etc., with Mickey Mouse as the central character. Disney began the feature-length cartoon with *Snow White and the Seven Dwarfs* (1937), *Pinocchio* (1940), *Fantasia* (1941), and *Bambi* (1942). By the 1950s and 1960s, Walt Disney Productions became a major film, television and theatre producers. The company produces books and comic strips for children featuring characters like Donald Duck and Pluto the dog. In 1955, Walt Disney opened the amusement park called Disneyland in California. Disney World, opened in 1971 near Orlando, Florida, is a major tourist attraction today.

Disorder is a dramatic technique used especially by Elizabethan and Jacobean dramatists. Drama aims to project some disorder in life and attempts to resolve it. The plays begin on a note of crisis and failure, e.g., Shakespeare begins his *Hamlet* with the ghost; *Macbeth* in the background of war with witches uttering 'Fair is foul, and foul is fair.' The disorder can be present in nature, in society, family or in the mind of a character.

Dissociation of sensibility is a phrase introduced by T.S.Eliot in his essay "The Metaphysical Poets" (1921) to point out a fault of the poetry of the later 17th century where thought and feeling do not coalesce. He found in the Metaphysical poetry of Donne "a direct sensuous apprehension of thought, or a recreation of thought into feeling". He opined that a dissociation of sensibility began in literature from the period of Milton and Dryden. He called for a unification of sensibility by which thought and feelings are put together. Perhaps, Eliot found an absence of the theatrical with ironic jokes and the like in a play to energise it with opposite attitudes. As a result the dynamism of the 17th century drama is replaced by the dogmatic tone until late 19th century. The modernist movement claimed to have some affinity with the Metaphysicals and Jacobeans.

Distance is the physical space between the actors and the audience. If the distance is minimal it establishes an intimacy between the audience and the actors.

Dithyramb is the passionate choric hymn and dance used in ancient Greece to honour the god of wine, Dionysus. Aristotle's *Poetics* (c.330 BC) claims that the Greek tragedy developed from dithyrambs, which not only praised the god but often told a story. Thespis, a legendary choral leader of the sixth century BC, created drama when he assumed the part of the leading character in a dithyrambic story. He spoke and the chorus responded. It is believed that drama evolved from this.

Documentary drama presents contemporary social problems in a naturalistic manner and suggests how to tackle them. The movement began after the First World War. After the Second Word War, the growth in documentary films and television brought social and political problems to the forefront. Drama was found to be inadequate in presenting contemporary situations realistically due to brevity of time. TV serials began to be more effective than the documentary drama.

Domestic drama concerns with family problems. It was an early 18th century development due to the rising middle class and working class audience. The naturalistic drama of the 19th century reached its peak in this genre. The modern day TV serials have become a new form of domestic drama presenting middle class life, e.g., plays of Chekhov and Ibsen.

Domestic melodrama is a 19th century form of urban or rural family drama concerning the sufferings of a family.

Domestic tragedy concerns more with the middle class family affairs and the lives of ordinary people than the nobility. The protagonist is often a woman who faces great trials and obstacles. The plot would often revolve around a husband discovering his wife's infidelity and the subsequent murder of the woman, her lover, and even the by standers. The protagonist often takes his own life at the end. Such a tragedy presents the struggle of a middle class protagonist. Arthur Miller's *Death of a Salesman* is a domestic tragedy though the protagonist Willy Lowman does not murder anyone but takes his own life.

Double casting is usually done in academic theatre to teach students. By this practice two actors or sets of actors perform the roles alternatively.

Double plot is a combination of two stories of equal importance running side by side in a drama of which neither takes prominence. It is unlike a sub-plot or under-plot which runs in contrast to the main story, e.g., Middleton's *Women Beware Women*.

Doubling is done when an actor plays the role of more than one character.

Downstage is the part of the stage close to the audience which is usually lower than the rest of the stage.

Drama (*see* Introduction : What is drama?)

Dramatic criticism examines the various aspects of a drama such as its origin and background, dramatist's intention, its content, the performance of actors, the production, etc.

Dramatic illusion calls for a willing suspension of disbelief in the opinion of Coleridge in *Biographia Literaria* ch. 12. By dramatic illusion the reader or spectator spontaneously enters into the world of literature.

Dramatic irony occurs when a character is unaware of something of which the audience knows, e.g., in *Oedipus Rex*, Oedipus has decreed to banish the slayer of the king from his kingdom. But ironically he is the slayer who killed his father and married his mother (*see* Irony).

Dramatic monologue is a poetic soliloquy which has the following characteristics: (i) A single person who is not the poet himself utters the entire poem in a specific situation at a critical moment. (ii) The person addresses and interacts with one or more people. But we know of the presence of the hearers and what they say or do only from the clues through the discourse of the speaker. (iii) The monologue focuses on and the temperament and character of the speaker who reveals himself. Robert Browning frequently used it in his poems and his aim was the revelation of character, of thoughts and passions. He wrote to a friend, "My stress lay on incidents in the development of the soul." The dramatic monologue is built around a critical situation in the speaker's life with a silent listener. The character of the speaker is unfolded so too the character of others with subjective interpretation of the past and the present. Even the stammering and incoherent utterances are part of his mental makeup. It is like a soliloquy with a difference. A soliloquy is more interpretative and meditative; a private debate. The monologue is addressed to someone. The speaker speaks about himself at a critical moment. The listeners hardly say a word. But the speaker answers his unspoken thoughts. Eg: in

'My Last Duchess' : the envoy is the listener; in 'Andrea Del Sarto' : it is the wife; in 'Fra Lippo Lippi' : the officer and the police; in 'The Last Ride Together': it is the beloved. Cazamian calls Dramatic Monologue "studies in practical psychology" as it provides a peep into the inner working of the minds. Chesterton opined that Dramatic monologues are "defences", e.g., 'The Last Ride Together' is a defence of the lover who failed in love. Browning's main idea is to throw light upon the realm of consciousness. He investigates the whole province of the soul. Therefore, they are "soul studies". It is a self-disclosure in which we have an analyst at work; a psychologist who is dissecting and a moralist who is moralising. It is a kind of drama specially suited to those whose main interest is in the character. There is also a tendency in Browning to choose abnormal characters. The dramatic monologues are "half-confessional studies" probably influenced by Shelley. The earlier glimpses of dramatic monologue are found in 'Pauline.' Under Shelley's influence he began to be a poet of confessional excess. Tennyson used it in 'Ulysses.' But Browning developed dramatic monologue to project a certain personality and temperament. The real beginning was made in *Dramatic Lyrics* (1842). The first experiment is in 'My Last Duchess.' The later dramatic monologues were published in *Men and Women* (1855) Important poems in the genre include: 'Andrea Del Sarto', 'Fra Lippo Lippi', and 'The Last Ride Together.' In these poems he portrays a wide variety of characters: crooks, cowards, scholars, musicians, painters and dukes.

Dramatic poetry as the term implies is a poetry that is dramatic in form like the dramatic monologue. The dramatic techniques employed in the form of dialogue, monologue, strong diction and conflicting situations can render it dramatic in form. The term in its wider connotation includes even poetic dramas like T.S. Eliot's *Murder in the Cathedral* (*see* Poetic drama).

Dramatic prose (*see* Prose drama).

Dramatic time is the time period that is presented in course of the action of a play which could be several years or months. Dramatic time should not be mistaken for the actual time taken for the performance on stage.

Dramatic verse is expressing heightened emotion in metrical language. Ancient European drama was written in metrical verse. Prose began to be commonly used from the 17th century in drama. In the 19th century Romantic drama, dramatic verse was employed. In the 20th century W.B.Yeats, T.S.Eliot and W.H.Auden attempted to use dramatic verse. In a play there can be a mixture of dramatic verse, dramatic prose and dramatic poetry.

Dramatis personae in Latin means characters in a play. It could refer to a list of characters in the play usually printed at the beginning of it. A brief description of the characters may also be added to the list.

Dramatisation is the process of making a play out of materials found in other literary genre such as chronicle, novel, short story, etc. Shakespeare took stories from Holinshed's *Chronicles of England, Scotland and Ireland* (1587).

Dramaturg is a scholar who studies a play's text, language, background and historical circumstances. He is able to give an interpretation to the dramatic company and its technicians for an exact rendering of it while performing with appropriate costumes and other stage effects.

Dramaturgy is the study and interpretation of plays for performance on stage. This is important when plays belonging to earlier periods are staged (*see* Dramaturg).

Drame is the French domestic middle class drama of the 18th century which was a forerunner of the sentimental comedy. It is a play of serious nature between tragedy and comedy. A drame has melodramatic plot with superficial characterisation. English romantics like Shelley, Byron and Keats attempted it.

Drawing room comedy is a kind of farcical middle class domestic drama which takes place in a drawing room, e.g., Coward's *Hay Fever* (1925).

Dream vision is a genre in which an author puts into writing what he receives in his dream. It was a popular form of literature in the middle ages, e.g., Bunyan's *Pilgrim's Progress*.

Dream play presents itself in the form of a fantasy with unconnected series of scenes. It was developed by August Strindberg in his *The Dream Play*.

Dresser is the person who assists an actor with costumes, makeup and hair-dressing.

Dressing the house is scattering a small audience in a theatre to give the impression of being filled to capacity.

Dressing the stage is a theatrical term to refer to stage direction by which the characters on stage are properly spread out during performance. In general, the term could mean setting and decorating the stage.

Dress parade is meant to check the costumes of the various actors by the director. The actors in their costumes parade themselves and the director makes an assessment of the suitable colours and shade.

Dress rehearsal is the final rehearsal before the public performance of a play as it should be with costumes and stage props and techniques.

Drolls or **Droll-humours** were short comic performances in taverns and fairs during the Commonwealth period in England (1649-1660) when plays were banned by the puritans. These were adapted from existing plays and were often performed with dance. Francis Kirkman published most of the drolls after the restoration in *The Wits*, or *Sport upon Sport* in two parts 1662, 1673.

Dry is a term to refer to an actor who misses his lines during performance. This happens due to anxiety and loss of the trend of thought due to distractions caused by the audience.

Dubbing is a cinematic term by which words, music and sound effects are added to a film.

Dumb show is a performance in which dialogue is replaced by gestures and body movements. It is used as a part of a play especially during interludes during the Elizabethan drama. Shakespeare, Webster and Middleton employed the device.

Duodrama is a late 18th century German theatrical entertainment consisting of silent actors of whom only two spoke.

Duologue is a conversation between two characters. In Greek tragedy, duologues were common among the protagonist and another character. Shakespeare used it to give further information about the plot.

Dynamic characters change in course of the play. Such characters stand in contrast to static characters who do not change essentially in course of the play as they are evil or good throughout the play.

E

Ecclesiastical drama was performed throughout Europe in the middle ages during the liturgical worship in the church. Stories from the Gospel were dramatised to instruct the illiterate public. In course of time these were moved out from inside of the churches to their premises and then to the town squares. Most prominent among them is the Easter story of the empty tomb and the angels questioning the three Marys 'Quem Quaeritis' (Whom do you seek?).

Economy of roles means making a limited number of actors perform a drama. It was a practice in the ancient Greek classical drama like those of Sophocles.

Educational theatre is usually attached to schools of theatre with the purpose of education and instruction.

Egyptian drama has its origin from the ritual re-enacted by the priests for dead Pharaoh's (c.2800-2400 BC). A certain 'Memphite Drama' used to be performed as ritual at the beginning of spring. It used to be narrating the story of the death and resurrection of Osiris and the crowning of Horus. Later, up to 550 BC, these dramas were performed on the life and death of Orisis.

Ekkyklema is a movable platform on which some off stage event is performed, e.g., in Aeschylus's *Agamemnon*, Clytemnestra standing beside the dead body of Agamemnon is presented on an ekkyklema.

Elizabethan stage society was founded by William Poel in 1894 protesting against performing Shakespearean plays on Victorian stage disregarding Elizabethan stage direction.

Elizabethan theatre flourished in the Elizabethan age from 1558 to 1603 when Queen Elizabeth reigned. It was a time marked for its economic and commercial growth establishing England as a maritime power. The English nationalism was at its height. Often it is referred to as the Golden Age of English literature because of the luminaries in the literary scene like Sidney, Spenser, Marlowe, Shakespeare, Bacon and Ben Jonson. Broadly, the period is from c.1550 to 1660 preceding the Restoration period. Elizabethan theatre had a circular auditorium with the audience in three tiers on three sides of the thrust stage. The audience was very close to the central down stage position. The most popular playhouse was the Globe.

Emotion refers to strong feeling. In psychology it brings about certain physiological changes such as variations in pulse rate and change in body temperature. It generates anger, love, and fear. Emotions cause attraction or repulsion and are expressed in action. These are investigated by writers and actors and are reproduced through dramatic art. The dramatic presentation of emotions arouse sympathy or repugnance of the audience. The dramatic situation makes the audience experience dramatic irony as what has happened in the past might happen in the future.

Emotion memory is the capacity that an actor develops by which he is able to recall emotions and experiences in creating a role. By this device the actor goes back into his past to recreate details of it into his role to strengthen his role. For example, he may recall a past experience in a city by recollecting the room where he stayed, its details, the tables and chairs, the bed, other things which he can recall as minutely as possible. This strengthens his emotional memory to recreate a role as an actor.

Empathy is the power of entering into another's personality and experienceing in an imaginative way. It can be also the power of entering into the spirit of something like a work of art and appreciate it fully. If an author is able to arouse empathy through his writings in the readers to enter into the personality of the characters portrayed, it will give better appreciation of the work. In drama, empathy means a kind of physical sympathy with the dramatic activity. It calls for both sympathy and detachment. The audience's response to a dramatic situation is more than mere identification with the characters. The audience sees a whole situation and compares the characters and their responses. It judges who deserves sympathy. It can happen that the audience may be more aware of the tragic situation of a character than he himself.

Empiricism is a philosophical doctrine that affirms all knowledge based on experience. It denies the possibility of spontaneous ideas or *a priori* thought. Often the term is applied to the view held by the English philosophers of the 17th, 18th, and 19th centuries. John Locke was the first to give it systematic expression, though Francis Bacon had implied it in his writings. The philosophy opposed to empiricism is rationalism, represented by such thinkers as the French philosopher René Descartes; the Dutch philosopher Baruch Spinoza; and the German philosopher Leibniz. Rationalists held that the mind is capable of recognising reality by means of reason. Immanuel Kant, the German philosopher, tried to compromise empiricism and rationalism. He restricted knowledge to the domain of experience and attributed to the mind a function in incorporating sensations into the structure of experience. Nowadays the term Empiricism has a more flexible meaning. William James called his own philosophy *radical empiricism*, and John Dewey used the term *immediate empiricism* for his view of experience. The term *empirical laws* is applied to those laws that express relationships observed to exist among phenomena, without implying the explanation or cause of the phenomena.

Ending is the conclusion to a story. According to Aristotle's *Poetics* the ending should be satisfying to the audience. The ending in a tragedy is the catastrophe resulting in the fate of the protagonist. The ending of a play can result in : the solution to the problem posed; the relationship between the characters turns opposite; the premonitions and fears of the audience are realised; and the rectification of misunderstandings. In drama, the ending can be through a musical piece or a choral song, a dance, or a funeral march. A dramatist may use an epilogue as an ending.

Ends and means are central to a play. A question arises whether good ends can be sought by evil means and vice versa. The conflict between good and evil is brought out through the presentation of the opposite characters, e.g., a jealous Othello killing an innocent Desdemona in Shakespeare's *Othello*.

End stage is a raised platform facing the audience. It is usually placed at one end of a rectangular space. A simple end stage is the booth stage or a raised stage with a curtained backdrop. Such end stages were used for the Greek and Roman mimes, the wandering entertainers of the Middle Ages, *commedia dell'arte*, and popular entertainers in modern times. Probably Greek tragic theatre as well as the Elizabethan theatre used it.

Enlightenment is the intellectual movement in philosophy and science that preceded Romanticism in the 17th and 18th centuries in Europe. It is also known as the Age of Reason. It gave stress to classical models and sought formal control, decorum, refinement of language. The movement is marked by the writings of Jean Jacques Rousseau and the Encyclopedistes (*see* Encyclopedistes). It ushered in the French and American revolutions. Scientists and philosophers like Kant, Bacon, Descartes, Newton, Locke,

David Hume and Adam Smith called for human reason to pervade man's search for knowledge. It threw out superstitions and dogmas, and called for rational and scientific enquiry. In religion it led to Deism.

Ensemble is an acting company with its own techniques and styles like the Elizabethan dramatic troupes. The term is applied to modern companies that are formed into a community of members which encourages mutual understanding.

Entr'acte is a musical interlude between the acts of a play.

Entrance is the appearance of an actor on stage. It has to be precise so as to maintain the continuity of the play.

Entremes is a form of Spanish entertainment in the 16th and 17th century, performed between courses of a banquet. This developed into the interludes between the acts of a play.

Entry refers to pompous display on the occasion of a royal visit, coronation, war victory, or a wedding. It was prevalent in the ancient Greek and Roman times. Such displays were very popular during Renaissance when spectacular parade and tableaus accompanied the celebrations around the rulers who made their public appearance. Such entries were also meant to strengthen the allegiance of the people for the royal personage.

Environmental theatre is a device by which actors and audience are intermingled in a theatre space. Richard Schechner founded the Performance Group in New York in 1967 with this purpose.

Episodia are scenes in Greek drama. The scenes are separated by choral song and movement.

Epic is a long narrative poem that is magnificent in theme and style. Epics deal with legendary or historical events of national or universal significance. Most epics deal with the exploits of an individual. It has several features such as : the presentation of supernatural forces that shape the action; battles and conflicts; invocation to the Muse; statement of the theme; long lists of the protagonists involved and lofty speeches. The Greeks made clear distinction between epic and lyric poetry. Lyric poetry expressed more personal emotion than epic poetry. Lyrics were sung while the epic was recited. Examples of epic include the ancient Greek epics by Homer, *The Iliad* and *The Odyssey*. Epics may synthesize the ideals of a great religious or cultural movement. The *Divine Comedy* (1307-1321) by Dante Alighieri expresses the faith of medieval Christianity. *The Faerie Queene* (1590-1609) by Edmund Spenser represents the spirit of the Renaissance in England. *Paradise Lost* (1667) by John Milton represents the ideals of Christian humanism. Epic verses are of two types, folk or literary epic. Folk epics are popular epics that developed from the orally transmitted folk poetry of tribal bards or other authors and written in course of time by anonymous poets, e.g., *The Anglo-Saxon Beowulf* (8th century), the Indian epics *Mahabharata* (Great Story, 300 BC-AD 300) and the *Ramayana* (Story of Rama, 3rd century BC). Such folk epic stories are based on legends or events that occurred a long time ago. Literary (art) epics are the creations of known poets. They deal with the mythical or historical traditions of a nation, e.g., *The Iliad*, *The Odyssey*, *The Aeneid*, *The Faerie Queene* and *Paradise Lost*. In the 19th century the epic assumed various forms like Wordsworth's autobiographical poem *The Prelude* (1850) presenting the events of his life to explore the power of the human imagination. Walt Whitman's *Song of Myself* is a brief epic in which the first-person narrator identifies himself with all of nature and humanity.

Epic theatre evolved under the influence of Erwin Piscator who rejected the Aristotelian unities. Bertolt Brecht began a revolutionary type of drama in Germany in the late 1920s presenting detached narratives in epic manner with episodes with choral presentations with songs and commentaries. He rejected the Aristotelian principles and considered a play as a series of loosely connected scenes. He tried to minimise the identification of the audience with the characters to increase objectivity. To detach the audience from the plot of the play, they use episodic structure, exaggerated social comments, caricatures, movie clips and slides, tableaus, etc. In the opinion of Brecht, epic theatre stresses narrative than plot and makes the audience go out active into the world without involving them in the play's action by identification with characters. He divides a play into episodes allowing time for the audience to think through montage presentations. He avoids the audience reach the stage of catharsis by alienation devices such as gaps between scenes. This prevents the audience from having emotional disturbances seeing the play. They are conscious that they see it merely acted on stage. He also contrived and set his plays in remote time and places mingling the epic and the dramatic, e.g., *Mother Courage* (1941), and *The Good Woman of Setzuan* (1943).

Epilogue is a statement at the end of a play. Usually it is a speech addressed to the audience by one of the actors to establish relationship between the play and the audience. In the Elizabethan plays the character begged the audience to pardon omissions and sought appreciation. Sheridan's *The School for Scandal* has an epilogue by Colman, spoken by lady Teazle:

> I who was late so volatile and gay
> Like a trade wind must now blow all one way,
> Bend all my cares, my studies and my vows,
> To one dull rusty weathercock - my spouse!
> ... Blest were the fair like you, her faults who stopt,
> And closed her follies when the curtain dropt!
> No more in vice or error to engage,
> Or play the fool at large on life's great stage.

Episode is an incident in a narrative action. It may consist of a dialogue between two characters, a particular scene or a longer action. These episodes should have a continuous flow so as to produce a single story with a beginning, middle and end. If the episodes are not woven together, the story turns out to be episodic and not a unified whole. In Greek tragedy episodes were parts between choral odes. A tragedy is divided into to the following parts: (1) the prologue, (2) the episode, and (3) the exode. For the chorus there are the parode (choral song) as the chorus moves. An episode is "all that comes in between two whole choral songs". An episode is similar to an 'act' in our terminology. It is also used by Aristotle for a division of a poem. Exode is the last action in Greek classical tragedy after the final choral ode.

Epitasis is the section in a play where the action turns intense so as to lead to its catastrophe.

Epode is a song sung by the chorus standing still after the strophe and antistrophe.

Equiestrian drama is a Roman performance with horses in an arena. The circus of modern times is a development of this dramatic form. In the 19th century performances with horses were popular, e.g., Byron's *Mazeppa* in which Mazeppa tells the story of his early life when he was bound naked on to a wild horse.

Equity is a trade union of theatre workers founded in Britain in 1929 known as the British Actor's Association. In America it began in 1913.

Erudite theatre refers to theatre that caters to a particular class of people.

Establishing character is a technique by which a writer gives existence to a character in the mind of the audience and readers by his/her name, role given in the plot and relationship he/she has with other characters.

Estrangement is a device by which Brecht made his audience see the characters in a new light presenting them in a strange manner.

Everyman is the main character in the English morality play written anonymously in the late 15th century (c.1509-1519) consisting of 921 lines. It may have been based on an earlier Dutch morality play, *Elckerlijk*. The play presents an allegory of death and the fate of the soul. Everyman is summoned by Death at the end of his life. He seeks the assistance of his friends Fellowship, Kindred, Cousin, Goods, and Strength. But they desert him one by one. Only Good Deeds and Knowledge whom he had neglected earlier remain faithful and lead him toward salvation. All these abstractions are personified giving the play its vital dramatic quality.

Existential drama is the fruit of the philosophy of existentialism that stresses the uniqueness of each individual in the world. However, the individual is faced with the painful problem of choice. Existentialists such as Kierkegaard (1813-55), Dostoevsky (1821-81), Nietzsche (1844-1900), Sartre (1905-80), and Camus (1913-60) were very interested in drama to present their viewpoints. The Existential drama is very similar to the theatre of the absurd (*see* Absurd).

Exit/exeunt occurs when an actor or actors leave the stage. If the exit occurs in the middle of a scene it makes a dramatic impression on the audience that is kept in suspense.

Exodos is the last action in Greek classical tragedy after the final choral ode. In *Medea* of Euripides, the exodus begins with the messenger coming to inform Medea to flee in the charrior sent by the sun god : "O thou who hast wrought an awful deed and lawless, /Flee, O Medea, flee, nor once leave thou / The sea-wain, or the car that scours the plain."

Exploration is a device by which actors while rehearsing the play, work out various interpretations of the text beyond the presentation intended by the dramatist.

Exposition is the opening section of a play which presents background information that is vital in creating interest and suspense.

Expressionism is a movement in the visual, literary, and performing arts to express subjective feelings and emotions rather than to depict reality objectively. It is a movement in the late 19th and early 20th centuries which came as a reaction against the academic standard since the Renaissance (1300-1600) especially in France and Germany. Expressionism depicts an emotional experience in its most compelling form. The expressionist artist deals with reality in its inner nature and the emotions aroused than with its outward appearance. In order to stress the emotional experience, expressionists exaggerate with distortions and caricatures. Chinese and Japanese art emphasizes the essential qualities of the subject rather than its physical appearance. Artists of medieval Europe exaggerated their work for the Romanesque and early Gothic cathedrals to intensify the spiritual expressiveness of the subjects. Expressionism in literature is found in Alfred Kubin's novels *Die Andere Seite* (The Other Side). He influenced Franz Kafka and other writers. Playwrights August Strindberg and Frank Wedekind had great influence on the writers such as Georg Kaiser, Ernst Toller, Eugene O'Neill, Arthur Miller, Elmer Rice and others.

Expressionist drama aimed to create a totally unified stage picture that would increase the emotional impact on the audience. It began between 1910 and 1925, closely related to expressionist painting which was intended to express inner experiences in strong colours and powerful movements. Expressionism in theatre draws attention to the subjective and the characters are presented as revealing themselves from what they do or express. The attention of the audience is drawn to the inner working of the character's mind and the subconscious with subjective psychological analysis. Expressionist drama began a new approach to staging, scene design, and directing. It aimed to create a unified stage picture that would increase the emotional impact of the production on the audience. In the Western theatre, expressionism has been an accepted convention for the past several decades partly because of the influence of cinema. Expressionism depicts inner meaning rather than outward appearance. This may imply the use of poetic and stylised language and symbolic characterisation.

In expressionist plays the following effects may be used: (i) The supposed time may be past, present or future and the action may flow without interruption from one time period to another. More than one time period may coexist, that is to say, the audience may see present and past action at the same time. (ii) The action may be presented as a dream or a vision by one of the characters. (iii) The action may take place in more than one location simultaneously. (iv) Music and light may be used to indicate a character's state of mind. (v) The setting may be non-realistic or partly realistic. One part of the stage may be set with realistic scenery, but this may have an empty open stage area in front of it into which a single piece of furniture may be brought to suggest a location, or the area may be left empty and used for a variety of purposes. (vi) Some characters may be totally non-realistic, abstract or even non-human. Arthur Miller's *Death of a Salesman* is an excellent example for an expressionist play. In it, there are *public action* and *private action* sequences occurring side by side. It might be expected that the public action sequences would be written realistically and the private action sequences would be expressionistic. Yet we discover that there is no fixed rule followed. The writer uses the *time-switch* differently at every change of sequence. Miller did not use either the time-switch or the mixture of realist and expressionist narration techniques simply for their own sakes but because he found that this was the best way to tell the story with the minimum of delay and repetition. We see that the main plot of the play is very simple, but it contains a number of subplots. Besides telling the story, the playwright must keep the audience interested by changing the mood fairly frequently. For instance, Act II begins in a mood of expectancy and optimism, but the phone call from Biff to Lynda slightly dampens her pleasure when she is reminded of the rubber tube that Willy might have used to commit suicide.

Extravaganza is a spectacle with music presenting mythical stories. Shaw applies the technique to some extent in his fantasia *Heartbreak House*.

Extrinsic idea is the idea expressed in a play in its literal level. It is often expressed through the chorus or a character.

F

Fable is a short prose or verse narrative conveying a universal moral truth. The moral is usually summed up at the end of the story. Fables are often presented with animals, birds or insects given attributes of human beings. A fable is to be distinguished from a parable. A fable is concerned with the impossible and improbable while a parable deals with possible events. However, both are allegorical in form. The most popular collections of animal fables is that of Aesop, a freed Greek slave of the sixth century BC. Aesop's fables were orally passed from generation to generation. In course of time, Greek and Roman writers wrote down versions of Aesop's fables. A Latin edition of these fables by the Byzantine monk Maximus Planudes was a very popular collection. The Sanskrit collection *Panchatantra* (c. 3rd century) is attributed to sage Bidpai.

The writing of fables was revived in France during the 12th century. Marie de France was the most important French fabulist of the period. *Roman de Renart* was the most popular collection of animal fables from the 12th to 14th centuries. It has the central character, a cunning fox Reynard. French fabulists Jean de la Fontaine was a popular writer of fables who published his works between 1668 and 1694. Among the most popular English fables is Chaucer's *Nun's Priest Tale*. John Gay wrote his *Fables* (first series, 1727; second series, 1738).

Fabula is the general term applied to Latin plays which include rustic farce, urban comedy, historical drama and mythological drama.

Facial expression is an essential component of dramatic communication, especially in modern psychological drama. A character can convey his/ her inner thoughts powerfully through movements of the facial muscles and eyes. Dramatic forms such as mime depend primarily on facial expressions.

Facsimile stage is one in which the sets for drama is made as realistically as possible with fittings and furniture of a particular time and place.

Fade is a slow dimming of the lights at the end of a scene.

Falling action refers to a play's sliding down from its turning point to a tragic catastrophe.

Falling flap is a painted scenery on both sides of the stage which fold and open to reveal faces or hide them from the audience.

Fan effect is the falling of wings at a scene change.

Farce is a form of drama meant to arouse laughter through exaggeration than by realistic imitation of life. It differs from comedy mainly in the emphasis on plot. In a farce, characters act out the intricacies of the plot. In a comedy, the plot is subordinated to characterisation. The term farce was first used in France referring to the pieces produced by certain lay companies, or *clercs de bazoche* (organisations of notaries and law clerks) in contrast to the morality plays produced by the religious orders. Many of the early farces were a mixture of several dialects the main characters spoke. The French writer Molière later refined the farce form into the comedy of manners. In England, by the 18th century farce came to be regarded distinct from comedy. In modern times, the term farce refers to any light piece with comic effect.

Fate drama is one in which a character is led by chance to a fatal action.

Fear is a *sine qua non* emotion in tragedy. Aristotle refers to 'pity and fear' which effect catharsis or purgation.

Feast of fools was a mock religious celebration in the medieval Europe especially in France since 12th to 15th centuries. It used to be a New Year celebration or held on the Feast of the Epiphany (January 6). The origin of the feast is associated with the Roman Saturnalia, a festival during which roles are exchanged temporarily between slaves and their masters. The Feast of Fools used to be celebrated within cathedrals by sub-deacons (members of the lower clergy) who took over charge. They elected a mock bishop or pope and had burlesque parodies of church ritual. A mock king who is the lord of misrule used to be central to the celebrations. Later the celebration moved out to the town with colourful processions and music. By 16th century the feast was suppressed.

Federal theatre project was set up by President Roosevelt in 1935 as a part of his new deal to improve the effects of Depression and the economic problems faced by theatre. The object was to employ writers, actors and designers in socially useful work. In its aim to produce high quality theatre, the project had five units : a Negro theatre, a living newspaper, an experimental theatre, a unit to collaborate with commercial theatre, and production of new plays at low cost. It was meant to take the arts to the people.

Feed line is a line uttered by a character that leads the comedian to give his funny comical remarks.

Female impersonation has been done on stage by men and boys due to social exclusion of women from drama in Greek and Elizabethan times.

Feminist theatre began in the 1960s and 1970s in Britain and America, calling for equal opportunities for women in theatre. It began with the American dramatist, Megan Terry, in the 1960s. Other dramatists in the genre include Caryl Churchill, Pam Gems and Michelene Wandor. Acting and production companies like the Women's Theatre Group have encouraged the movement. Effort has been made to show how the achievements of women have been ignored by society due to the subordination of women by men. As most writers of drama were men, most characters were given male roles. Women fringe groups and women writers have demanded equal rights for women on stage. They have come up with new dramatic techniques such as 'role reversal'. Caryl Churchill's *Top Girls* (1982) depicts the powerful role of a woman named Marlene who runs an employment agency named 'Top Girls'. The drama presents several women from history such as a Japanese courtesan, Chaucer's patient Griselda, etc. Going beyond historical times, these female characters show how they have struggled against male domination.

Flashback is a device used in drama by which a character returns to a previous event. Sometimes a character can flash-forward to a future event. In cinema, flashback and flash-forward are very effective techniques. Arthur Miller employs flashback in his *Death of a Salesman* very effectively, when Willy Loman, the protagonist, talks to his long lost brother Ben who went to Alaska and made a fortune.

Flat is a piece of scenery on a frame used as wings in the Restoration stage.

Flat character is a character in a play that is known only by certain characteristics and do not grow like a 'Round character' that is life-like and grows. E.M. Forster in his *Aspects of the Novel* defines round and flat characters. The flat character remains the same in nature like 'types' or 'caricatures'.

Flies is the space above the stage which is used for suspended scenery, etc., which can be lowered to effect a scene change.

Flipper is an addition made on to a flat with hinges.

Floor plan is the ground plan of the setting with all the props and furniture and places for entrances and exits.

Fluff is a verbal slip made due to nervousness during dramatic performance.

Fly-floor is the platform over the wings.

Flying effects consist of lifting actors into the air as done in pantomimes, court masque and Greek drama.

Flymen are those who work on the flies.

Focus is the centre of attention. In cinema and television, this is done effectively through camera techniques. However, in drama, focus is given to a character through conversation, peculiarity of dress, commanding stage position, movements of limbs and some action that draws attention from the audience.

Foil is a character in a play who stands in contrast to another. A protagonist who is physically well built and handsome may have a foil in a friend who is comical, weak and not so handsome, e.g., Laurel and Hardy.

Folio is an edition of a play printed on bound sheets. It consists of one fold with four pages. Shakespeare's plays were in folio edition.

Folk drama used to be performed at folk festivals especially on May-day, Christmas, etc. Many of these folk dramas originated from fertility rites and magical ceremonies. In course of time, due to the influence of Christianity, saints began to feature in such dramas.

Fool is a stage figure derived from the medieval feast of fools and court jests. Fools are found in Jacobean and Elizabethan drama. The fool has become an amateur jester who, by his nonsensical statements, is able to reveal certain truths. In Shakespeare's plays the fool acts as a mirror and presents subtle and symbolic things, e.g., Falstaff in *Henry IV* Part I.

Foreshadowing is a dramatic irony by which the spectator is not fully aware of future events. However, some subtle hints are given by which the spectators can look back at past events and make some judgement. Ibsen employs this device in his plays like *Ghosts*.

Forestage is the downstage area in front from where an actor can directly speak to the audience.

Form refers to the structure and shape of a work and is often understood as genre or type. Form has been redefined by New Critics based on the saying 'form equals content'. The form of a play has its various elements such as its inner form with its story and dialogue, the character relationships, motifs and tensions. e.g., the *form* of Webster's *The Duchess of Malfi* is that it is a revenge tragedy in five acts. The *inner form* of the play consists of its tensions, love intrigues, contrast of the goodness of the Duchess and her wicked brothers, etc. The *surface forms* of the play includes its diction, imagery, grammatical form, semantic relationships, intonation, the language, etc.

Formalism in general refers to the movement in literature which gives importance to the artistic techniques, style and form of a work of art at the expense of subject-matter. Formalism was developed by Victor Shklovsky, Vladimir Propp, and other Russian critics early in the 20th century. They emphasized plot structure, narrative perspective, symbolic imagery, and other literary techniques. But after mid-1930s, Soviet leadership demanded that literature and criticism directly serve their political objectives. They suppressed formalist criticism considering it reactionary.

By 1926, the Prague Linguistic Circle adopted some of the methods of formal analysis developed by their Russian colleagues. In the late 1940s anthropologist Claude Lévi-Strauss, critic Roland Barthes, and others initiated French structuralism by applying linguistically inspired formal methods to literature. Structuralism tried to investigate the 'structure' of a culture by 'decoding', or 'interpreting' its interactive systems of signs. The text-centred methods of the formalist critics were also welcomed in the United States as they mingled well with the concerns of the New Critics, who focused on the overall structure and verbal texture of literary works. Many New Critics looked at metaphor, imagery, and other qualities of literary language besides its historical setting and biographical information about the author.

Fortune is personified in drama as a goddess turning a wheel. In the Elizabethan theatre fortune is associated with various characters who have their rise and fall in life. In Shakespeare's *King Lear* Kent refers to the wheel of fortune : "Fortune, good night; smile once more; turn thy wheel." (2:2-168). King Lear speaks of himself as "the fool of fortune."

Four-hander is a play with only four characters who are usually contrasting couples. Edward Albee's *Who is afraid of Virginia Woolf?* (1962) presents Prof. George and his wife, while entertaining a young couple, unfold their story.

Fourth wall is the imaginative wall that exists across the proscenium arch in the naturalistic plays in which arch and curtain separate the auditorium from the acting area.

Free theatre is a movement in drama by the end of the 19th century in France, Germany and England. In Paris, Theatre Libre began in 1887 with its noted personality Andre Antoine. J.T. Grein began the Independent Theatre Club in 1891 in London. This dramatic movement sought to present naturalistic social drama.

Freeze is a device by which there is sudden break in the flow of the drama with a tableau. This makes the audience face a dilemma in their understanding of the action of the play, e.g., In Chekhov's *Three Sisters* the freeze occurs when a soldier takes a photograph of the sisters who have been talking of moving out to Moscow.

Fringe theatre began as a protest against the established theatre in the 1960s. Effort was made to depict on stage the working classes in the plays of Arnold Wesker and Edward Bond. Thus Community theatre began since 1968 in Britain consisting of fringe groups that presented social problems of racial minorities. They also looked for new audiences. In their effort to present situations realistically, they even lived among communities to experience their problems and tensions.

Front of the house is the portion of the theatre used by the audience.

Functional setting refers to whatever is required for a particular theatrical form. It is essential for performances such as circus in which scenes depend on the needs of the performers.

Functions and nature of theatre: Aristotle discusses the origin and function of theatre in his *Poetics* (c. 330 BC). The history of the theatre tells us that the theatre has been made use of for entertainment, rituals, moral instruction, social and political influence besides purely as an art form. It presents realistic stories as well as most abstract concepts through sound and movement. Theatre production includes the use of a stage or space, an auditorium or space for the audience, sets, props, lighting, costumes, and makeup. Theatre incorporates art, architecture, literature, music, dance and technology.

Futurism is an early 20th-century *avant-garde* movement in art and literature that dropped all traditions and attempted instead to glorify contemporary life. It stressed the themes of machine and motion. The manifesto of futurism was declared by the Italian poet Filippo Tommaso Marinetti in 1909. Later the *Technical Manifesto of Futurist Painting* was signed by Italian artists Giacomo Balla, Umberto Boccioni, Carlo Carrà, Luigi Russolo, and Gino Severini. Futurism presented several successive actions of a subject at the same time which looked like a series of high-speed photographs printed on a single plate, e.g., Severini's *Dynamic Hieroglyphic of the Bal Tabarin* (1912) and *Armored Train* (1915). Though the movement lasted only upto 1914, it influenced the works of painters like Marcel Duchamp, Fernand Léger, and Robert De-launey. The futurist worship of the machine survived as a fundamental part of Fascist doctrine of Mussolini in Italy. In poetry, the influence of futurism is seen in the use of putting together senseless words mechanically. In France, the poetry of Guillaime Apollinaire, Dada movement and Vorticism are the outcome of Futurism. The interest in the beauty of machine influenced theatre after the First World War, especially in designing the sets and costumes.

G

Gaelic drama developed in the 1890s, especially in Dublin, with the desire to give expression to Irish nationalism with the founding of the Gaelic Drama League and the Abbey Theatre.

Gaff is a term by which a certain low class 19th century melodrama is known.

Gag is what an actor adds into his script in the form of a joke or remark.

Galanty show is a 19th century street show of puppet shadows.

Gallery is the cheapest seats available in the auditorium usually occupied by the riff-raff.

Gamos is a Greek word for 'marriage.' The term is applied to romantic ending of a classical Greek comedy in merrymaking and marriage.

Genre is a French word meaning 'kind' or 'class' into which works of literature can be commonly grouped into poetry, prose and drama. Sub-genres can be found in these like in poetry: epic, ballad, elegy, lyric, sonnet, etc., in drama: tragedy and comedy; in comedy : comedy of humours; comedy of manners, etc. Genre takes into account the style, manner, form and technique employed in the literary work. Often genres overlap each other. A dramatist like Bernard Shaw mingles melodrama, sentimental comedy and fantasia in his *Heart-break House*.

Georgian theatre refers to drama of London theatres, Drury Lane and Covent Garden from 1714 to 1820, when Kings George I, George II and George III reigned.

Gestalt psychology deals mainly with the processes of perception in which images are perceived as a pattern or a whole rather than merely as a sum of distinct component parts. Images play very vital roles in their context. For example, in a picture, a spire can symbolise a church steeple. Gestalt psychology concerns itself with the perceptual processes. It came as a reaction to associationism that dominated psychology in the 20th century. Associationism considered stimuli as parts and then built into images. It allowed little room for such human concepts as meaning and value. In 1910, Max Wertheimer, Wolfgang Köhler, and Kurt Koffka sought a more appropriate scientific approach in psychology. They looked at perception beyond the mechanistic atomism of the associationists. For the Gestalt psychologists, perception is heavily influenced by the context of the perceived elements. The parts cannot be understood except in the context of the whole. Perceptual process has to be seen in the context of the whole. Activities within the total field of the whole govern the perceptual processes. Gestalt psychology has been applied in various areas of research in thinking, memory, and the nature of aesthetics. Some of the contemporary psychotherapies are called Gestalt as they follow Gestalt psychological approach to perception. These therapists hold that separation of mind and body is artificial and human experiences should be approached holistically. By heightening awareness, an individual's natural balance can be re-established according to Gestalt therapists. They give due emphasis to the present experiences rather than the past.

Gestalt is a term taken from Gestalt psychology. It gives emphasis to a holistic approach to human experiences. Gestalt in drama would seek a wholesome approach by which a play is not to be judged by its parts consisting of exceptional scenes or speeches. Instead, the play should be looked at from its overall form.

Gestures are the body movements and gestures which can be normal and smooth or excited or rapid indicating the mental and physical condition of the character. Theatrical gestures are mimetic and draws attention of the audience to what it copies. In naturalist drama, gestures are used to reinforce the speech of the characters. Gestures are used to convey emotions through speech and silence.

Ghost glide is also known as Corsican trap which is an opening on stage from where the ghosts could move mysteriously arousing fear in a melodrama. The device was used first in *The Corsican Brothers* (1852).

Gimmick is a stage device, action or a phrase that draws the attention of the audience.

Globe theatre on Bankside in Southwark was erected in 1599 for Shakespeare's company, Lord Chamberlain's Men. It was a large circular building with thatches with an open centre. It was destroyed by fire in 1613 after staging *Henry VIII* and was rebuilt and used till the closure of theatres in 1642. The name 'Globe' is significant as it reflects Jaques's passage in *As You Like It*: "All the world's a stage, / And all the men and women merely players."

God from the machine is the translation of the Greek phrase 'Deus ex machina' which implies a device to resolve the problem in a play (*see* Deus ex machina).

Goliard is a wandering entertainer in the 12th and 13th centuries who was a buffoon.

Gothic melodrama is a crude offspring of revenge tragedy found in the late 18th and early 19th centuries. In a Gothic melodrama, the hero and the heroine are lost in the forest and are imprisoned in ancient castles. Suspense, fear and pathos are aroused until they make miraculous escape.

Graces are the three daughters of the god Zeus and the nymph Eurynome who are the goddesses of joy, charm, and beauty in Greek mythology. They are Aglaia (Splendor), Euphrosyne (Mirth), and Thalia (Good Cheer). They are the presiding deities of banquets, dances, and pleasure inducing events to give joy to gods and men. They were part of the entourage of Aphrodite and Eros. Together with their companion Muses they sang on Mount Olympus to entertain the gods. According to legends the Graces bestowed on artists and poets inspiration to be creative. They are usually treated as a group of young maidens dancing in a circle.

Grand guignol consists of sensational plays with gruesome murder or violence. Such plays were popular in France in the late 18th century similar to the English *Punch and Judy*.

Great chain of being presents the ancient concept of the hierarchy of beings. According to this concept, minerals exist at the lowest rung. The plants grow over the minerals. Above the plants is the animal kingdom. Man comes at the apex with the faculty of intelligence. Angels exist between God and man. There are further subdivisions in the chain of being such as a nobleman above a commoner, an eagle above a hawk, gold above silver. In the Elizabethan and Jacobean tragedy the concept of the chain of being is found. Shakespeare wrote with this concept in mind in *Troilus and Cressida* Act One. Alexander Pope writes in his *Essay on Man*:

> Vast chain of being! Which from God began,
> Natures aethereal, human, angel, man,
> Beast, bird, fish, insect, what no eye can see,
> No glass can reach; from Infinite to thee,
> From thee to nothing. On superior pow'rs
> Were we to press, inferior might on ours;
> Or in the full creation leave a void,
> Where, one step broken, the great scale's destroy'd;
> From Nature's chain whatever link you strike,
> Tenth, or ten thousandth, breaks the chain alike.

Greek theatre: The earliest period in Western theatrical history is called classical, because it encompasses the drama and theatre of the classical civilisations of ancient Greece and Rome, and plays were written in Greek or Latin. The first evidence of dramatic literature dates from Greece in the sixth century BC. Aristotle's *Poetics* (c. 330 BC) claimed that Greek tragedy developed from dithyrambs, choral hymns in honour of the god Dionysus, which praised the god and told a story. Greek tragedy flourished in the fifth century BC. Noted writers are Aeschylus (525-456 BC), Sophocles (496-406 BC), and Euripides (484-407 BC). The plays were presented at festivals in honour of Dionysus, etc. Comedy developed in the mid fifth century BC, and by the fourth century BC comedy had replaced tragedy as the dominant form. Greek theatres were large amphitheatres with spectators watching the drama taking place on the circular dancing place and the long stage. The chorus sang and danced to appeal to the audience.

Green room is the dressing room for actors. It is also a place for actors who are not on stage. It is also a place where the actors can meet people after or before performance.

Groove is a sliding device for setting scenes for the wings from the Restoration to the Victorian periods.

Grotesque is the bizarre and exaggerated depiction of human features in drama, music and the plastic arts. In drama, it is a genre found in 'puppet theatre', 'commedia dell'arte' and the modern satirical and caricatural drama. V. Meyerhold (1874-1940) is a popular promoter of grotesque drama. He aimed to take the audience away from the usual to the unusual and bizarre in drama. Brecht employed the genre to depict alienation effect. Others who used the genre are Aleksandr Blok (1880-1921), Sologub (1863-1927) and Frank Wedekind (1864-1918).

Groundlings refers to the spectators who stand right in front of the stage to witness a performance in the Elizabethan times. They were the unruly riff-raff of society.

Ground plan (*see* Floor plan).

Grouping is the placing of actors on stage according to their relation to each other. It is done to give focus on the most important scene in naturalistic drama. Characters are presented in triangular positions than in flat lines or rectangular groups. The dominant character faces outward and the other characters are positioned to look at him.

Group theatre followed the methods of Stanislavski's improvisation in theatre. It is like the Community Theatre and the Fringe Groups that stress social and political problems. The drama is a group event as it is produced in collaboration with writers, researchers, improvisers, etc. It aims to project their common purpose through performance.

Guerrilla theatre is also known as protest theatre which aims at presenting on stage skits on controversial issues.

Guild productions began in the medieval times after the church banned the clergy from participating in Easter plays as entertainment and spectacle began to increase in the liturgical drama. This necessitated drama to be taken to the market squares with the same physical arrangement. Though still religious in subject-matter, the main intention was entertainment. These were called Miracle Plays and there are records of cycles of miracle plays in many parts of England from the 14th to 16th century. Miracle plays survived from Chester, York and Wakefield. The Chester cycle had 25 plays; the York cycle: 44 plays, and the Wakefield cycle : 32 plays. The themes begin with the Fall of Lucifer and end with Doomsday. They include stories of Creation, Fall, Cain and Abel, Noah, Abraham and Isaac, and the various stages of Christ's life. By the 14th century the production of plays was associated with the Feast of Corpus Christi and had evolved into cycles of as many as 40 plays. Though these cycles are similar to the liturgical dramas, they can be considered a separate development. They were produced by the community as a whole once every four or five years. The production of each play was assigned to a trade guild, with an attempt to correlate the guild with the subject of the play—the boat-wrights, for instance, might stage the play of Noah. Since the performers were often illiterate the plays tended to be written in an easy doggerel type of verse. Three major forms of staging were employed. Pageant wagons were most common in England. The former mansion became an elaborate rolling stage, that would move from place to place in the city. Spectators would assemble at each location. The participants would perform on the wagons and on a plateau created on the street or with an adjoining platform.

Gypsy is a member of the chorus. Since such a member has to move from place to place and from show to show, has a nomadic lifestyle.

H

Ham acting is referred to exaggerated and unconvincing acting. Naturalistic drama drew attention to the artificiality of the 19th century melodrama with caricatures. Ham acting presents the artificial in life and mocks at the roles played, e.g., in Samuel Beckett's *Waiting for Godot*, the dramatist presents characters giving ham performances.

Hamartia is the Greek term for error of judgement. Aristotle discusses it in his *Poetics* (4th century BC) as that which brings about the downfall of the protagonist in a tragedy. In his opinion a tragic hero should not be perfect for two reasons: (i) His misfortunes would be odious to us and it would offend our sense of justice, and (ii) He is less than perfect in order to allow scope for action. He should be neither extremely virtuous nor intentionally wicked but should suffer from hamartia which is some kind of error of judgement, frailty or ignorance which brings about his downfall. It is a single defect of character in a good and reasonable man. Aristotle does not say what kind of moral imperfection. He states in chapter 13: "Misfortune... is brought upon him not by vice and depravity, but by some error of judgement." Again in a second passage he gives clear emphasis: "The cause of it must lie not in any depravity, but in some great error on his part." Hamartia is not a moral state, but a specific error which a man makes. The phrase "tragic flaw" should be treated with suspicion. It cannot be identified with hamartia. Hamartia is a characteristic moral failing in a predominantly good man. Thus the tragic flaw of Oedipus in *Oedipus the King* was that he was hasty in temper; Samson was sensual in Milton's *Samson Agonistes*; Macbeth was ambitious and Othello jealous in Shakespeare. According to Aristotle, Hamartia is accompanied by moral imperfection; but it is not itself a moral imperfection. Hence, the hero is not morally to blame. In ancient forms of tragedy the error is imposed from above by the gods. For example, King Oedipus voluntarily aims to discover the polluted person to release Thebes from plague. But he is ignorant of the circumstances in which he has killed his own father. Things become clearer when Hamartia is seen in relation to *Peripety (reversal) & Discovery*. "The hamartia of the hero is closely connected with the peripety (reversal) and the discovery which are characteristic features of what Aristotle calls a 'complex plot.' This is distinct from a 'simple plot.' The action... I call simple when the change in the hero's fortunes take place without peripety or discovery; and complex when it involves one or the other or both." This makes it quite plain that peripety is not just the general change in the hero's fortunes which is essential for all tragedy. Even the simplest plot involves a radical change from good to bad fortune. *Peripeteia* must not be translated as 'reversal of intention.' From the point of view of the spectator or reader it is a reversal of the direction of the action in the plot of the play as a whole. "A peripety is the change from one state of things within the play to its opposite... in the probable or necessary sequence of events." (ch.11) Aristotle nowhere says that a peripety can happen only in relation to the hero. It is worth noting that even in *King Oedipus* one character was not involved in the reversal: *Tiresias* all along knew that Oedipus was the guilty man. Within any tragic plot a minor peripety may occur within the main course of the action involving primarily some other character than the hero. For instance, there is such a subordinate peripety in the *Oedipus at Colonus* when Polynices comes to his father in hope of a blessing and gets a curse instead. The very means that he chooses produces the unexpected result. In the word peripety is contained the idea of *boomerang or recoil effect* of ones own action, or falling into the pit that one has dug for someone else. The action is complex because it moves on two levels: as it appears to the doer and as it really is; and because the cause of the disaster is woven—in with the good intentions and right means to achieve them. *Discovery* is closely linked to Hamartia. It is a change from 'ignorance to knowledge' (*Poetics* ch.11). The recognition of a person by another is a 'change from ignorance to knowledge.' According to Humphry House, Hamartia, peripety and discovery all hang together in the ideal scheme of a tragic plot. The common phrase 'getting hold of the wrong end of the stick' may illustrate best. The hamartia is not to know that you have got to hold the wrong end or not to know which is the right or wrong end; and to hit yourself very hard with it as a result. The peripety is a real reversal, a turning of the stick round the opposite way brought about by force of circumstance or by the action of other characters. The discovery is the realisation of which really is the right end and of the fact that you had got hold of the wrong one.

Hand-props are the properties actors bring on stage in the course of their performance besides those already set on stage.

Harlequin is a name derived from the quick witted Arlecchino in *commedia dell'arte*. In traditional Italian and early English comedy and pantomime, he is the lover of Columbine. He is a buffoon who is simple and open.

Harleqinade is a play in which a Harlequin is the central character. It was found in the 17th century English pantomime in imitation of the *commedia del'arte*. In such plays the Harlequin is a lover who faces a lot of troubles, but is helped by good fairies.

Heavy father is a term applied to a type role played in Victorian melodrama by a serious father.

Hellenistic Age is the period between 4th to first century BC, extending between the conquest of Alexander the Great and the establishment of Roman supremacy. It was a time when Greek culture and learning were unsurpassed in the Mediterranean and the Middle East. Hellenistic is derived from 'Hellas' meaning Greece; hence it is used to differentiate from the classical Greek culture. This period was dominated by three great monarchies after Alexander: Ptolemies in Egypt; the Seleucids in Syria, and the Antigonid dynasty in Macedonia. The elite in these kingdoms spoke common Greek, which became the new international language. Their religion, art, and literature were a cosmopolitan blend of Greek and native elements. The city of Alexandria was founded in Egypt under the Ptolemies. They used their wealth to attract poets, scholars, artists, and scientists. The Alexandrian Library became very prominent in encouraging scholarly studies in philology, grammar, prosody, lexicography, and literary criticism. Advances were made in medicine, astronomy, and mathematics. The age was known for Euclid, Apollonius of Perga, Eratosthenes, Aristarchus of Sámos, Hipparchus, Hero of Alexandria, and Archimedes. Two prominent philosophical schools of the age were Stoicism and Epicureanism. In religion, they followed syncretism as they combined the Greek gods with Eastern deities. The Hebrew *Bible* was translated into Greek at Alexandria. Hellenistic monarchies declined by first century BC as the Romans began to control Greece and the Middle East. The Roman civilisation became a continuation of Hellenistic culture.

Hellenistic theatre refers to the period of Greek theatre between the death of Alexander the Great (323 BC) and that of Cleopatra (31 BC). There is very little information regarding theatre. Drama was acted on a raised stage with a circular orchestra. Some fragments of Menander's (c 342-292

BC) plays are found. There is a shift from the comedies of Aristophanes.

Hero or Heroine is the chief character or protagonist in a narrative or dramatic work. The protagonist can fall into different types. The Aristotelian tragic hero is aristocratic in origin. He is an important person in society and is a good man who falls due to a tragic flaw or error of judgement, e.g., Shakespeare's King Lear, Othello, Prince Hamlet, etc. The protagonist can be a cultural hero in legends and myths who idealises values, e.g., Achilles is the embodiment of Greek courage. The protagonist can be anti-hero who is a common man lacking heroic qualities. In modern times hero and heroine are referred to the main male and female characters.

Heroic comedy is a form of drama with happy ending imported from Spain. This Spanish form is found among the plays written by Vega Carpio (1562-1635) who is known to be the father of Spanish drama.

Heroic drama / tragedy is a form of tragedy that developed after the Restoration of English monarchy in 1660. Traces of it is found in Beaumont (1584-1616), Fletcher (1579-1625), Richard Brome (1590-1652) and James Shirley (1596-1666). It is characterised by the qualities of a heroic poem or epic with the theme of love, beauty and honour. The hero is of gigantic proportions possessing supernatural powers. Heroic drama presents emotions very artificially and had no elements of comedy in it. It dealt purely with nobility. Such dramas are usually written in rhymed heroic couplet. In the Preface to *The Conquest of Granada* Dryden defines this genre as "an heroic play to be an imitation in little of an heroic poem... love and valour ought to be the subject of it." He defended the character of his hero Almanzor in *The Conquest of Granada*: "The first image I had of him was from the Achilles of Homer: the next from Tasso's Rinaldo (who was a copy of the former), and the third the Artaban of Monsieur Calprenede, who has imitated both." Their ideals of medieval Christian romance are superimposed on

Homeric pattern stressing the ideals of "Love and Valour". These heroes are supermen who have great energy, imagination and magnanimity. The purpose of such a drama is to evoke the admiration of the audience and to arouse pity and fear besides a sense of exaltation. Elements of the French classical tragedy such as dramatic unities and epic grandeur are found in them. These plays imitated the epics in presenting great warrior heroes fighting for empires. Most of them were written in heroic couplets. Dryden's *The Conquest of Granada* is considered the best example of this genre. It has an epic grandeur with rhetorical flourish in the rhymed verse couplets employed. Dryden adapted Shakespeare's *Antony and Cleopatra* in his *All for Love* where he contrasts Roman law and Egyptian love. Thomas Otway (1652-1685) wrote in this genre his three great tragedies *Don Carlos, The Orphan, and Venice Preserv'd.* Nathaniel Lee (1649-1692) wrote his extravagant and passionate tragedies *Nero*, *Sophonisba*, *Gloriana*, and *The Rival Queens*.

High comedy is a term coined by George Meredith (1828-1909) to refer to comedy consisting of verbal wit that generates intellectual amusement. High comedy is contrasted with low comedy consisting of farce and slapstick. The high comedy deals with follies of social manners. The writers of such comedies includes William Wycherley, William Congreve, Oscar Wilde, G.B. Shaw, Noel Coward and Simon Gray.

Himation is the long mantle worn by actors in Greek classical tragedy depicting gods or heroes.

Hints are the clues given in a drama that help the audience to discover the hidden secrets in it. Hints foreshadow the action with suspense and dramatic irony, e.g, Sophocles in *Oedipus Rex*, gives hints about the king's origins. Such hints arouse empathy in the audience.

Historical drama depicts historical events either wholly or partly, e.g., Marlowe's *Edward II*, Shakespeare's *Richard II*,

Dryden's *All for Love*, Ibsen's *The Pretenders*, Shaw's *St. Joan*. In writing a historical drama the dramatist has to be selective in presenting a limited number of characters and appropriate events. He may take liberties in selecting and eliminating historical details. The dramatist often selects critical moments and individual conflicts as focus of attention. Though the term historical drama usually refers to Chronicle plays, in a wider sense it is also applied to plays with subjects associated with the impact of historical changes on some fictional characters, e.g., *Licking Hitler* (1978) by David Hare (*see* Chronicle plays).

Histrionics is the affected and highly emotional dramatic performance.

Holy theatre is a term defined by Peter Brook in his book *The Empty Space* (1968). He discusses the sacred origin of drama and claims that this genre 'makes visible invisible' as it breaks out of the ordinary world. Through dramatic art can take an action beyond the ordinary and the spectator can be carried beyond reality.

Hot spot is a spot on stage that is the focal point of the audience's attention during a performance.

House is the seating area of a theatre. It is also a term applied to the audience as a whole.

House curtain is the main curtain that closes the stage from the view of the audience.

House manager is the one who runs the box office and sees to the seat reservations and the sale of tickets for a performance.

Hubris is a Greek concept prevalent in ancient Greek culture and in classical tragedy. It refers to an over-weening pride, confidence or self-complacency that results arrogance in thoughts, words, and deeds. This attitude arouses the jealousy of the gods who punish the victim of hubris, e.g., in Aeschylus's *Oresteia*, Agamemnon walks on the sacred carpet and is guilty of hubris. Shakespeare in *King Lear* presents King Lear a victim of hubris by his imagining himself god-like in power.

Humours are the various bodily fluids according to the physiological concepts of Hippocrates (c.460-357 BC) of ancient Greece. The human body has the four chief liquids (humours) : blood, phlegm, yellow bile (choler) and black bile (melancholy). These fluids were related to the four elements: air, fire water and earth. Blood is like air, hot and moist. Yellow bile is hot and dry like fire. Phlegm is cold and moist like water. Black bile is like earth cold and dry. A person's temperament depended on the predominance of these humours. These were classified as: Sanguine (when blood predominated); Phlegmatic (when phlegm dominated); Choleric (when yellow bile dominated); Melancholic (when black bile dominated). Elizabethan used these human characteristics in their drama, e.g., *Hamlet* in Shakespeare's Hamlet is melancholic; Cardinal in *The Duchess of Malfi* is a melancholic clergyman (*see* Comedy of humours).

I

Icon or **iconic sign** was defined by the American logician, C.S. Pierce, as a sign which refers to the object it denotes merely by virtue of characters of its own. Hence, a photograph or a portrait is an icon since it has the characteristics of the person it represents. The word is occasionally used in drama criticism, especially in naturalism which presents similar characteristics of a time and place. The sign may become a symbol or icon, e.g., in Chekhov's *The Seagull* (1895) the stage prop represents a real seagull which in turn is an icon. Even characters refer to 'sea-gull' symbolically. Nina calls herself, "I'm a seagull." In a naturalistic play, a sign can be seen differently by different characters. For example, in Ibsen's *The Wild Duck* (1884), the duck is seen as a commonplace bird by ordinary people in the street; but it is seen symbolically by neurotic characters. The tension between the icon and the symbol becomes the central psychological concern of Ibsen.

Iconography is the study of subject matter in art. It is the pictorial representation and writing of signs. The purpose of iconography is to identify, classify, and explain specific objects the artist chooses to portray. Iconography is important in the study of religious and allegorical painting, where many of the objects such as crosses, skulls, books, or candles have special symbolic significance. In drama, certain visual codes are shared by the writer and the audience.

Shakespeare makes iconographic refers to 'Fortune's wheel' which the audience is able to perceive.

Ideal spectator is the average person for whom the dramatist writes or a representative of the audience who is present among the characters of the drama, e.g., In Shakespeare's *Hamlet* the character of Horatio is an ideal spectator. He is the university friend and confidant of Hamlet who is left alive to tell his story at the end of the play. Horatio has an identity of his own and he tells us where we are and reveals the identity of the characters.

Identification is the manner in which a writer, an actor, a spectator or a reader gets a new identity while writing, acting, watching or reading about dramatic characters. The degree of identification can vary with reference to different genre like tragedy, naturalistic drama, comedy, etc. There are different psychoanalytic types of identification such as primary, secondary projective and introjective. In primary identification no separate identity is recognised. In secondary identification separate identity is recognised as for instance the identification with parents. In projective identification both actors and spectators imagine something inside which has control over some external object. This is the central concern of drama. Introjective identification is opposite of the projective identification. In it the subject imagines some external object to be himself.

Ideology is the beliefs clearly or ambiguously contained in a play. In some plays such ideologies are easy to ascertain as in the morality plays. However, conflict of opposing ideologies among characters is central to most plays. In some cases the playwright may not resolve the crisis and the conflict. Though primarily it is the ideology of the author that is presented, the ideological views of actors, designers and directors can be projected in a play to some extent. Sometimes, the author's attitudes or intentions get expressed in the play. For example, Shakespeare's presentation of the Ghost in *Hamlet*. Primarily it presents the Pagan

Christian conflict; however it presents the Catholic-Protestant ideologies as well. A Ghost coming from Purgatory is a Catholic interpretation as the Protestants do not accept Purgatory.

Illegitimate drama is a term by which popular drama grew up in minor theatres of England in the 18th and 19th centuries. These theatrical performances consisted of much music and popular spectacle unlike the classical performances in the legitimate theatres. The legitimate theatres were the patent theatres such as Covent Garden, Drury Lane and Haymarket that held the monopoly in staging classical plays.

Image in literary study is a verbal imitation of a sensory reality held in the mind. Many images are conveyed through figurative language such as metaphor, simile, metonymy, synecdoche, onomatopoeia, etc. Images can be visual, auditory, tactile, olfactory and gustatory. These images may mix with each other to become a composite memory. Memory images focus on the past experiences. Freud would refer to dream images that are drawn from memories expressing fear, hope, anxiety, desire, etc. In drama it is the present that is often depicted. Yet images of the past and future strengthen dramatic process. For example, a mystery play is aimed at the theme of salvation; a political play may aim at a future utopian society.

Imagery is a collective term for images used in poetry or prose in the form of figurative language suggesting mental or visual pictures. Imagery is a term to refer to sensory or extrasensory experiences. Hence it differs from image which need not mean a mental picture. Imagery arouses an imaginative response from the reader which can be vivid. George Herbert in his poem 'Love' uses the image of love to refer to the love of God.

> Love bade me welcome; yet my soul drew back,
> Guilty of dust and sin.
> But quick-eyed Love, observing me grow slack
> From my first entrance in,
> Drew nearer to me...

Imitation/mimesis is the capability that art has in imitating natural objects or actions, etc. Aristotle in his *Poetics* defined poetry as the imitation of human actions. It is not counterfeiting of sensible reality, but presentation of universals. Imitation is not mere copying of ordinary reality, but an idealised rendering of character in action. By imitation an artist presents imaginative reconstruction of life. By imitation the artist imitates not the created nature but creative nature. An imaginative picture can be more real than the original. Drama has been considered an imitation of human behaviour. It imitates historical events, particular literary model, etc.

Impersonality is a device by which writers hide their presence in the play and create instead a wide variety of characters. For example, Shakespeare is the greatest impersonal dramatist. T.S. Eliot considers impersonality an essential feature of good poetry when he writes in his *Tradition and Individual Talent*: "...it is not expression of personality, but escape from personality."

Impersonation is dramatic method whereby someone pretends to be someone else. In Shakespeare's comedies women impersonate men. In a tragedy like *Othello*, the evil Iago disguises himself.

Impressionism is a movement in painting and music that developed in late 19th century France in reaction to the formalism and sentimentality that characterized academic art and the 18th and early 19th century music. The impressionist movement is often considered to mark the beginning of the modern period in art and music. Impressionism in painting arose out of dissatisfaction with the classical and sentimental subjects and dry, precise techniques of paintings that were approved by the Académie des Beaux-Arts in Paris. Rejecting these standards, the impressionists preferred to paint outdoors, choosing landscapes, street scenes and figures from everyday life.

Their primary object was to achieve a spontaneous, undetailed rendering of the world through careful representation of the effect of natural light on objects. The foremost impressionists included Edgar Degas, Claude Monet, Berthe Morisot, Camille Pissarro, Pierre Auguste Renoir, and Alfred Sisley. In literature, impressionism refers to very personal manner of writing depicting scenes and characters as they are seen and felt by the readers (*see* Expressionism).

Improvisation is the natural response of an actor during a play or rehearsal to a particular situation. It becomes a technique to assist actors enter deeply into the characters they portray. Stanislavski (1863-1938) employed the technique to a great extent even in improvising scenes and story. It is a creative process that leads to a sub-text which eventually helps in the origin of new plays. Tom Stoppard's *Rosencrantz and Guildenstern are dead* (1967) is a play resulting from improvisation. In the play he brings out the 'attendant lords' from *Hamlet* and gives them central place. They are presented as the bewildered witnesses and predestined victims. Improvisation technique is used in the 'Theatre in Education' (*see* Theatre in Education).

Incidental music is the music written for songs and dances in a dramatic performance. In a melodrama incidental music was played at the entrance and exits of characters besides at dramatic moments of suspense. Dramatists like Shakespeare and Dryden used it. Purcell (1659-1695) was a popular musician of the 17th century who composed music for many plays.

Incorporated stage society was founded in 1899 with the aim of staging quality plays with no commercial end in mind. The society produced some of Bernard Shaw's plays as well as several European plays of distinction.

Independent theatre club was founded in 1891 in London by a Dutchman J.T.Grein. Ibsen's *Ghosts* was the first drama staged by him.

Indian theatre can refer several things such as: (i) the Sanskrit drama from the third to the eighth century AD. The best known writer is Kalidasa in the fourth century noted for his Shakuntala. (ii) The Classical dances found in India in the 11th to the 18th century. (iii) The Modern Western style drama in India that began to be staged by the British after they opened the Playhouse in Calcutta in 1776.

Induction in a play is the exposition that takes place through the opening scene or the prologue. It can be through presenting a character speak out in the opening scene to watch the action of the play. For example, Shakespeare's *The Taming of the Shrew* begins with an induction of Christopher Sly, a drunken Warwickshire tinker, picked up by a lord from the heath. He is brought to the castle and treated like a lord who has gone out of his mind. The rest of the play is presented as seen by this drunken tinker.

Information is all that a dramatist attempts to provide such as the names of characters and details concerning each of them. He may hold back some information which can arouse curiosity and suspense in the audience as well as in the readers. Information can be passed on through prologue, messengers, chorus, soliloquy and asides.

Initiating action consists of initial proceedings or events in the play that arouse the interest and suspense of the audience. Such actions bring about the state of conflict and tension throughout the performance.

Inner creative state is a concept popularised by Stanislavscki (1863-1938) which calls for the proper frame of mind to render well a dramatic performance. The actors need to know fully the texts and render them properly according to their talents (*see* Circle of attention).

Inner proscenium is a proscenium arch which is the part of the main proscenium. This area can be used like a separate stage area for staging a different style of acting.

Inner reality refers to the working of a character's mind as well as to the inner form of the play. Dramatic tension in the play depends on what a character keeps hidden from the others. It is revealed through soliloquies of the character, through a chorus or a narrator.

Inner stage of the Elizabethan stage is the area between the two upstage doors and below the gallery.

Institute for Advanced Studies in the Theatre Arts is a New York based American association for theatre study. It brings eminent theatre personalities and directors to New York and gives opportunity to American actors and those involved in theatrical performances to interact with them and learn about their various approaches to theatre.

Intention in drama refers to the original conscious wish of the author. It is modified by other factors such as the language, the director's interpretation, the economic position of the theatre company, the size of the stage and its facilities, the expectations of the audience, etc.

Interludes were the dramatic and non-dramatic forms of entertainment prevalent in the 15th and 16th century. It used to be short entertainment between the courses of a banquet or the acts of a play. In Italy, it was known as *intermezzi*. In France and Spain interludes were known as *entremets* and *entremeses*. In England, interludes were popular especially between 1550 and 1580. Harbage in the *Annals of English Drama 975-1700* records around 90 plays belonging to this genre which is a link between the mystery plays, miracle plays and the morality plays. It was difficult to differentiate interludes from them as the characters are often allegorical. However the farcical element is prominent in interludes with the purpose of entertainment. Interlude comes as a break from the earlier moralising and religiosity with the elements of secular and the profane. They are also shorter than the morality plays. They were allegorical, didactic and farcical. Written in rough verse or doggerel, the interludes used to be about a thousand lines meant for entertainment at court banquets, in the houses of nobility, at the University Colleges or at the Inns of Court. The following are interludes some of which are also classified under morality plays: Henry Medwall's *Fulgence and Lucrece* (1490-1500); John Rastell's *Four Elements* (c.1520); Heywood's *The Play of the Weather* (1533) *A Play of Love* (c.1534), *The Four P's* (1545),; *Wit and Science* (1531-47) by Redford; *Appius and Virginia* (c.1567); *Like Will to Like* (c.1567), etc.

Intermezzo is a light comical entertainment like the interlude between the acts of a serious play or opera in Italy in the 15th and 16th century.

Interpretation is the attempt to state the theme and meaning of a text depending on the intention of the author, inner meaning of the play, understanding of the actors, impressions of the director and the response of the audience.

Intertextuality refers to the relationship between the codes of a text and the codes of the audience or reader. The interpretation by actors or the audience is often coloured by their milieu and social experiences (*see* Code).

Intonation is the various levels of pitch in pronunciation which gives a rhythmic pattern to speech. This is an important element in drama giving it proper tone and stress. For example, when an actor is angry he speaks in a higher pitch.

Introit trope is a medieval liturgical music drama which celebrates in the Church. Most prominent among them is the Easter Introit *Quem Quaeritis* (Whom do you seek?) on the resurrection of Christ.

Irish Literary Theatre was founded by W.B. Yeats and Lady Gregory along with George Moore and Edward Martyn. They aimed at staging new Irish plays to revive the Irish national and cultural movement. It led to the establishment of the Abbey Theatre in Dublin in 1904. They wished to dispel the influence of English literature and turned to the Irish heritage of myth and legend (*see* Abbey Theatre).

Irony is a literary device of humorous or lightly sarcastic mode of speech in which words are used to convey a meaning contrary to their literal sense. For instance, words of praise is used as a criticism or condemnation, e.g., Jonathan Swift in his *Modest Proposal* wrote: "...that the poor people of Ireland should rid themselves of poverty by selling their children to the rich to eat." Irony can be classified into : verbal irony, structural irony, dramatic irony, tragic irony, cosmic irony, romantic irony, etc. Shakespeare uses it in *Julius Caeser*: "For Brutus is an honourable man; So are they all, all honourable men". In drama, hidden ironies can arouse interest and suspense in the audience. Ironies can make actors and audience aware of certain possibilities they do not wish to think of. The best example of irony is in *Oedipus Rex* where the audience is aware of the tragedy while Oedipus is ignorant.

J

Jacobean drama is a term applied to the drama written during the period of James I of England (1603-25). It is derived from his name in Latin 'Jacobus.' The period was remarkable for outstanding English drama including those of Ben Jonson (1572-1637), Webster (1580-1634), Tourneur (1575-1626), Middleton (1570-1627), Dekker (1572-1632), Massinger (1583-1616), Ford (1586-1639) and the later plays of Shakespeare. The King James Version of the Bible (Authorised Version of 1611) was a landmark publication of the period. It is considered the most prominent period of English tragedies and comedies presenting some of the best individualised characters in drama. Sometimes it also includes Caroline theatre as many Jacobean dramatists continued to write under Charles I.

Jester is a person who makes fun of persons or situations. Such entertainers were found in the royal or noble household in the middle ages to amuse the king and the nobility. The jester is presented in motley dress with a cap and bell. Shakespeare introduced such jesters in his plays: Touchstone in *As You Like It*; the Fool in *King Lear*. They have the dramatic function of reflecting other characters of the play.

Jesuit drama developed in the Jesuit schools in the 16th century with the purpose of religious and moral instruction. The first such performance perhaps was at Messina in 1551.

St. Ignatius Loyola founded the Society of Jesus in 1534 catering to education and within a span of 50 years there were about 150 Jesuit schools established. As part of the school curriculum religious drama in Latin used to be performed in these schools based on the Biblical stories as well as the lives of saints. By 1586 the document Ratioatque Institutio Studiorum provided for the staging of tragedies and comedies and in course of time secular plays, ballets and operas were performed. Besides religious themes, stories of national history and classical legends began to be acted on stage. The vernacular language of the region began to replace Latin in writing of these plays as these prospered in Europe in the 17th century. They became spectacular and secular with large casts in magnificent costumes. Prominent dramatists include Calderon De La Barca (1600-1681) the Spanish dramatist known for his *autos sacramentales* (allegorical religious plays); French dramatist Pierre Corneille (1616-1684) wrote *Horace*, *Cinna*, *Polyeucte*. He influenced the Restoration dramatists, especially Dryden and French dramatist Moliere (1622-1673). Moliere was educated at the Jesuit college de Clermont and had a profound understanding of the incongruities of human life as depicted in *L'Ecole des maris, L' Ecole des Femmes, L' Avare, Les Femmes savants, Don Juan, Le Misanthrope*, etc. Others in the Jesuit schools include French novelist and playwright Lesage (1668-1747), popular for his *Gil Blas* and *Don Quixote*; Voltaire (1694-1778) who wrote his popular heroic tragedy *Zaire*; and Italian dramatist Goldoni (1707-1793) who wrote very successful plays like *Il Ventaglio* and *Le Bourru bienfaisant*.

Jig is a brief farce sung and accompanied by dancing which was popular in the Elizabethan and Jacobean theatre. Jigs were performed as separate pieces after a longer play and with political and satiric connotations in some cases. William Kemp and Richard Tarlton (d.1588) were successful performers of jigs. Kemp was a comic actor and dancer who acted in plays of Shakespeare and Jonson. Tarlton is associated with many fictitious anecdotes published in *Tarlton's Jests* in three parts and *Tarltons Newes* out of *Purgatorie*. In Shakespeare's *Hamlet*, Hamlet comments on Polonius : "... he's for a jig, or a tale of bawdry, or he sleeps" (Act II:ii.494). When theatres were closed down in 1642, jigs survived as street theatrical performance. Later, they returned to the stage in the form of trailers announcing the a new play to be performed. In the 18th century jigs took the form of musical farce and afterpieces.

Joculatores are the medieval stage entertainers who sang of heroic deeds and lives of saints.

Jocus in Latin, meaning 'play with words', evolved into 'ludus' in the middle ages which implied play with physical movements.

Juvenile drama refers to 19th century toy theatres consisting of imitative games played by children with paper cutouts of scenery and characters whom they moved on stage on slides. These performances were based on pantomimes, melodrama and operas.

Juvenile lead was the role of young hero or lover played by actors of a Victorian stock company.

Juvenile tragedian was a specialised actor in the Victorian stock company who played a secondary role to the juvenile lead character.

K

Kabuki is a type of Japanese drama involving song, dance and mime popular from the mid-17th century. It comes in contrast with the existing aristocratic and formal No drama with only male actors impersonating female roles. *Kabuki* adopted many conventions from the *nooh* theatre such as the wide shallow stage with actors making their entrances and exits running from the back of the hall to the side of the stage which is usually revolving. It has elaborate scenery and actors wearing rich costumes. Unlike the masked characters in *nooh* theatre, in *kabuki* masks are replaced by maximum make up of characters. These plays depict popular legends and myths with long episodes with intervening dances. There can be three categories of *kabuki* drama: *jidaimono* (histories), *sewamono* (domestic drama) and *shosagoto* (dances). In a dramatic performance a variety of episodes from these categories are presented. The entire performance can be as lengthy as twelve hours and the dramatic framework rather loosely structured. *Kabuki* plays are performed in large theatres, with a *hanamichi*, or raised platform, extending from the back of the theatre to the stage. *Kabuki* has continued to be the most popular traditional dramatic genre. By the mid-1980s *kabuki* became popular in America and troupes made annual appearances in the United States. Some 20th century playwrights have attempted to compromise between traditional Japanese forms and essentially Western idioms. They introduce modern psychology in their treatment of the ancient tales or by making *kabuki*-style plays out of European classics.

Karagoz is a traditional Turkish shadow-puppet play dating back to the 14th century. The name *Karagoz* is derived from the principal character who represents Turkish common man an 'Everyman.' The good Karagoz has his antagonist Hacivatis in these entertainments. The character of Efe is brought in to solve the problems presented in the play which is often a comment on social and political themes. These characters were representative of certain personalities of the 14th century. There are around 30 traditional stories built around these characters. The entertainment consisted of satires, jokes, dances and songs with the puppeteer presenting the dialogue.

King has been often the protagonist in serious drama from classical tragedy, medieval chronicle plays, Elizabethan drama and neoclassical tragedy. He being the monarch has social power in these serious plays. In contrast, in the comedies of the period, ordinary people 'little men' are presented. Sometimes the figure of the fool is associated with the king where his role is one of parodying the monarch.

Kitchen-sink drama is a term that originated with John Osborne's *Look Back in Anger* (1956). It is also associated with Arnold Wesker's *The Kitchen* (1959). It is meant to show in a realistic manner the growth of the working class in drama during the late 1950s. Often such plays centred on the kitchen sink as Wesker's play *Roots* (1959) which opens with washing dishes in the kitchen sink (*see* Angry young men).

Knockabout comedy is a farcical entertainment in which laughter is aroused by presenting physical misfortune. The genre has its appeal with its standard components of provoking laughter with things such as custard pie, banana skins, black eyes, buckets of water, etc. The purpose is to laugh at the childish follies of adults. However, the genre in the hands of dramatists like Samuel Beckett became a medium of expressing profound thoughts.

Kommos is a kind of lyrical dialogue between the chorus and the protagonist in classical Greek drama.

Komos is an ancient Greek form of entertainment prevalent in the city Dionysia, consisting of comic revel and singing wearing animal masks. It is thought to be the origin of Greek comedy.

Komos is a drunken revelry and procession in honour of Dionysus. This is considered the beginning of comedy.

L

Lady Elizabeth's Men is a Jacobean theatre company which began in 1611.

La Mama Experimental Theatre Club is an off Broadway theatre founded in 1961. The theatre experimented with dance and music with a mingling of rock and classical patterns. The club sponsored dramatists like Megan Terry and Sam Shepard. It produced the first rock musical *Hair* in 1967.

Language though a linguistic term has its extended theatrical meaning. Theatrical language can be visual or acoustic. The visual language can be expressed in movements, postures, facial expressions, colour, lighting and set design. The acoustic language consists of dialogue, voice modulation and sound effects. There is also the musical language which emerges from the rhythm of the stage movement with its volume, tone, pitch, etc.

Lazzo is the comic fooling in the *commedia dell'arte*.

Lead is the central role played by an actor or actress in a Victorian stock company.

Leap is a dramatic effect produced by an acrobatic jump in a Victorian melodrama.

Legitimate theatre refers to serious drama that was performed by patent theatres according to the Theatres Act of 1737, namely, Drury Lane and Covent Garden. The term is abbreviated as 'legit', meaning straight drama of serious nature without songs, dances and interludes.

Leicester's Men is the name given to the Elizabethan company of men who acted under the patronage of the Earl of Leicester before he died in 1588.

Leitmotif is a German term (*leitmotiv*) meaning 'leading motif' coined by Hans von Wolzugen in reference to a musical theme that runs through an opera. The device was used in the operas of Richard Wagner (1813-1883). Thomas Mann (1875-1955) used it as a literary device by which an image, symbol or phrase is frequently repeated in a work, associated with a particular character or situation. In drama, a leitmotif gives information on the character who uses it or offers an ironic comment on the action, e.g., in Ibsen's *The Wild Duck* (1884) a wounded wild duck gets into a dark attic and lives there symbolising the relationship between various wounded characters in the play and their painful experiences.

Levels are the different heights from which a character communicates with each other and the audience. To facilitate this various things like a platform, stairs or galleries can be used. This device also indicates the positions of the characters: the gods make their appearance above; angels descend from above.

Libretto in Italian means *libro* (book). It is the text of an opera or other staged musical work. The term sometimes also refers to the text of an oratorio or to a ballet scenario. In the libretto of a musical, the dialogue is called the book; and the song words, the lyrics. A libretto is shorter than a play as it takes more time in singing than speaking with several repetitions as in 18th century operas. Popular English librettists include J.B. Priestley, W.H.Auden and Michael Tippett.

Licensing Act came into effect in 1737 by which Lord Chamberlain had the responsibility and power to give licences to theatrical performances other than those performed by the patent theatres. This made theatre come under strict political control which made dramatists like Henry Fielding turn away from satirical drama to fiction (*see* censorship).

Light is a dramatic language which illuminates the actors, actions and sets. It is used to focus attention on a character or a particular action or expression. Lights of different intensity and colours can depict different moods in a drama, e.g., Expressionist theatre used powerful lights in comparison to the theatre of naturalism that insisted on natural lighting. Artificial lighting is a modern dramatic device as plays up to the Elizabethan times were performed in the open air theatre in daylight. Torches or candles were used for evening performances with the establishment of indoor theatres in the 16th century. Tinted glass and bottled liquids were used for colour effects. Reflectors and candelabra were used in the 17th century. By 18th century the candelabra were replaced by lights from the wings and foot-lighting. From the 19th century gas light and limelight were used for better effects on stage as they could be controlled and focused. With the coming of electricity, lighting has become much more complicated and effective in theatre.

Lighting is meant to illuminate the stage, the performers and to create mood. It also controls the focus of the audience. Drama was performed outdoors until the Renaissance, depending on sunlight. Later lamps, candles, gas lamps with coloured filters, reflectors, and mechanical dimming devices were introduced. With the coming of electric lighting in the 19th century stage could be made very bright with proper focusing on the actors. Stage-lighting is done with floodlights for an entire area and focus light for a specific area. Coloured filters called gels are used to make bright white light more pleasing. White light is better balanced with mixing red, blue, and green light. The lights are controlled by a technician who controls the dimmers and switches. Nowadays the controls are done through a computerised control system as all the lights change automatically as pre-programmed.

Light opera is a comic opera parodying a grand opera with characters of a lower social class than those presented in grand opera.

Limelight is the bright light used in the 19th century for spotlighting to give focus of attention to the main actors.

Lincoln cycle is considered a lost cycle of mystery plays. It is thought to be the coventry cycle.

Lincoln's men is an Elizabethan travelling troupe that performed drama.

Line ending refers to syllable ending in verse. If the final syllable is stressed it is called masculine and if it is unstressed it is feminine. Blank verse used in the Jacobean drama helped in giving it a colloquial speech rhythm.

Little Theatre Movement began in England between the two wars and eventually led to the establishment of the Little Theatre Guild in 1946 consisting of several amateur theatres that trained their members and performed on stage. In USA such theatres are known as Community Theatres.

Liturgical drama developed out of the church liturgy and were performed in the church. In the medieval Catholic church such drama was used for instruction of the faithful. By the 10th century the various church services were presented in dramatic form including the Mass (Eucharist) that re-enacted the Last Supper of Christ. Certain feasts were celebrated with theatrical activities, such as the Palm Sunday precession. The antiphons, responses and songs of the Mass and the canonical hours were like dramatic dialogue. In the ninth century antiphonal embellishments known as tropes were being added to the complex musical elements of the Mass. An anonymous three-line Easter trope: a dialogue between the three Marys and the angels at the tomb of Christ from about 925 is considered the origin of liturgical drama. The dramas centred on the two important festivals of Christmas and Easter. The life of Christ from Birth to Resurrection, and the main events of the Christian year from the Annunciation (announcement of Christ's birth to Virgin Mary) to the Ascension of Christ to heaven, were observed in the church. Appropriate episodes were performed by antiphonal chanting between priest and choir or between characters themselves. By the 12th century the liturgical drama was fully developed, but the language used was Latin. As drama developed secular and comic elements emerged such the story of Balaam's ass; the comical spice seller from whom the three Marys bought spices to anoint the body of Jesus after his death, etc. The church authorities moved these plays out of the church due to secular elements in them.

Living Newspaper is a kind of political propaganda drama in the USA in the 1930s. It treated current social and political issues with journalistic techniques and in short satirical scenes. This genre is said to have evolved during the reign of the Red Army in revolutionary Russia. In 1920, the Department of Agitation and Propaganda (Agitprop) was set up by the Communist party leadership to propagate revolutionary ideals through theatrical performances. In England, the Living Newspaper project was pursued by Unity Theatre founded in 1935-36 which produced Communistic and agitational drama (*see* Federal Theatre Project).

Living Theatre is an experimental theatre company founded in New York in 1954 by Julian Beck and Judith Malina. It is characterised by life, revolution and theatre. It used strong visual effects and improvisation. Known productions are *Mysteries* (1964), *Frankenstein* (1965) and *Paradise Now* (1968).

Locus is a station built on a scaffold representing an ideal place like heaven or hell in the medieval drama. The actors used to perform around the locus in the open space.

Long run refers to the performance of a play at the same theatre for a long period of time. A long run gives a steady employment to the actors until they are replaced. Agatha Christie's *The Mousetrap* has run for nearly half a century since its first performance on November 25, 1952, reaching its 20,000th performance in December 2000. Though it is a funny old-fashioned play it is still a very appealing murder story. Christie who died in 1976 considered it successful since it is neither really frightening nor really horrible. The *Mousetrap's* original cast is survived by the film director Richard Attenborough, his wife Sheila Sim and Jessica Spencer.

Long shot is a term used in film and television with reference to a camera shot in a bigger performance. It presents a whole setting and sees characters in relation to one another within that setting.

Lord Admiral's Men is an Elizabethan acting company of Edward Alleyn (1566-1626). Alleyn acted at the head of the company playing leading roles in Marlowe's *Tamburlaine*, *Jew of Malta* and *Dr.Faustus*.

Lord of Misrule is a 15th and 16th century mock character who was appointed to play the role of a king or a bishop in the Christmas revels at the Inns of Court and in the colleges (*see* Feast of Fools).

Low comedian is the leading comic actor in the Victorian farce and melodrama.

Low comedy is a term referring to farcical and coarse type of plays in contrast to the high comedy with its verbal wit and intellectual amusement. Low comedy is used for comic relief or for pure mirth and laughter with buffoonery, ribald jokes, and clowning. Such comedies were mixed with serious drama in the mystery circles, morality plays, Elizabethan period, Restoration comedies. These comical presentations in the mystery and morality plays consisted of portraying the devil and the vices. In the Elizabethan and Restoration comedies farcical subplots on fools and clowns contributed to this genre. Low comedy occurs in Chaucer's *Canterbury Tales*, Samuel Butler's *Hudibras*, Shakespeare's *Merry Wives of Windsor*, Wycherley's *The Country Wife*, etc.

Ludus is derived from Latin, meaning play. In the Middle Ages it referred to war games, circus entertainment and drama involving physical activity and pretence.

Lunch-time theatres were experimental small theatres that grew up in London since 1968. It provided opportunities for writers, directors and actors who could perform with a minimal cost reaching out to a small audience.

Lysiody is a farcical Greek mime in which actors played female parts in male costumes.

M

Machiavel is a villainous character type found in the Elizabethan and the Jacobean drama. The term is derived from the Florentine political philosopher Niccolo Machiavelli (1469-1527). His book *Il Principe* (*The Prince* 1513) was a treatise on stagecraft and justified dishonest means in politics. In it he observes contemporary political scenes with an idealistic vision of an Italian saviour who should expel all usurpers. Often referred to in Elizabethan drama, it is found in the writings of Marlowe, Webster, Walter Raleigh and Shakespeare. Machiavellian characters occur in Elizabethan drama such as Webster's Bosola in *The Duchess of Malfi*; Shakespeare's Iago in *Othello*; Middleton's De Flores in *The Changeling*. In these the Machiavellian characters were associated with treachery, murder, ruthless schemes, poisoning and different kinds of villainy.

Machinery is derived from Latin 'machina' referring to a mechanical device like a crane used in Greek theatre to facilitate entrances and exits of the gods. As gods appeared through this device it was known as 'deus ex machina.' Alexander Pope explains it in his preface to *The Rape of the Lock* as a term 'to signify that part which the deities, angels or demons are made to act in a poem. In Milton's *Paradise Lost,* the device is used to present supernatural beings (*see* Deus ex machina).

Machine is a term applied to a workshop technique by which actors are directed in a group to interpret a feeling or a word in gestures. It can also be applied to stage equipment or techniques such as Greek *machina*, medieval tableau, and later court masque, opera, ballet, pantomime, etc.

Magody was a rude farcical Greek literary form which is known as different types of mime: *lysiody*, *hilarody* and *simody*. In the opinion of ancient author Aristoxenus of Tarentum, the *magodist* took his plots from comedy. It consisted of low-class comic performance in which male actors played female characters wearing female clothes. In *lisiody* women's roles were played in masculine dress to the accompaniment of flute playing. In *hilarody* the actor wore masculine dress and a golden crown, parodying tragedy. *Hilarody* was later known by the name *simody*.

Main plot refers to the most important sequence of events in a play.

Mainstage production is the main production on the largest stage when there are more than one stage for performance in a theatre complex. The term is also applied to a professional production of a play with greater financial backing and professionalism compared to the amateur workshop performances.

Makeup in theatre consists of the cosmetics used by the actors to enhance or to disguise themselves. Makeup can be used to change facial features so as to emphasise a particular expression of a character. In the Oriental theatre such as Kathakali of Kerala, makeup consists of masking by elaborate paintings of the face with various colours. In Western theatre, makeup helps to stress facial features and to show the difference in age, etc.

Manager in a theatre company is the person who is responsible for arranging performances of the troupe. He raises the income and pays the staff. In Britain, a producer is known as manager.

Mannerist literature is written in an exaggerated and superficial style with idiosyncratic style of the author, e.g., The style of John Lyly and some of the 17th century metaphysical poets. Among the modern writers James Joyce's *Ulysses* belongs to this genre. Mannerist style is ornate with difficult and old syntax, and far-fetched imagery. Mannerism is derived from Italian art of 1520-1600, during the period between the high Renaissance and the baroque style. Artists such as Tintoretto, El Greco, Bronzino and Vasari developed mannerist art. Michaelangelo and Raphael were mannerist in their art towards the end of their career. These artists laid more stress on intellectual preconceptions than visual perception.

Manners is a term used in the Restoration Comedy of Manners (*see* Comedy of Manners).

Mansion is the setting representing the location of a scene in a mystery play or medieval drama. It consists of platforms with settings of heaven, hell, etc. Such mansions were located in the church itself when the religious plays were performed. The clergy acted the various episodes and moved from mansion to mansion and the audience turned towards the scenes accordingly. When plays began to be performed outside the church in the town square, these mansions were set in a line one after the other.

Marionette is a puppet that is operated from above with strings attached to the head and limbs (*see* Puppet).

Marxist theatre refers to drama that propounds the principles and thoughts of Karl Marx (1818-1883). It primarily deals with the working classes and their relation with those in power. Emphasis is laid on communal and social aspects of life with economic needs of man. Sometimes, such plays end with Marxist teachings. In some plays like those of Brecht, it is left to the audience to find a solution to the problem presented, e.g., in Brecht's *The Good Woman of Setzuan*, the heroine is left with the audience with the question to resolve.

Brecht (1898-1956) and Erwin Piscator (1893-1966) made their left wing ideals influence on the social writers in England such as John Arden, Edward Bond and Trevor Griffiths. Arden's *The Waters of Babylon, Live Like Pigs*; Bond's *Restoration, Summer*, etc. belong to this genre.

Mask is a cover to conceal the face. In Greek drama, different masks were used by the same characters, keeping the identity of the particular masks they wore. In *commedia dell'arte* masks covered the upper face. Masks are used in popular and street theatre; oriental theatre such as the Japanese *noh* and *kabuki*.

Masque is a court entertainment popular during the Renaissance with characters performing with masks with occasional dance and song. Masks were used in ancient Greece as part of the classical revival of the Renaissance. Masque is found in the Italian and the French pageants and masquerades from the early 15th century. It used to be performed by the members of the court in disguise. The performance consisted of allegorical and mythical plots and the actors spoke, sang, and danced on in the disguising. It ended with the removal of the masks and a dance in which the audience also joined. The audience participation in the dances is a unique feature of the masque. The performance originated from the practice of mumming and the art of the troubadours.

Court masque was introduced into England in 1512 during the reign of King Henry VIII. It became the most popular form of drama during the reign of James I. Those who wrote masques include S.Daniel, T. Campion, G. Chapman, T. Middleton and J. Fletcher. T. Campion wrote both music and text for his *Masque in Honour of the Marriage of Lord Hayes*. Ben Jonson is considered the most popular writer of court masques in England. He is known for his 30 masques such as *The Masque of Blackness, Love Freed from Ignorance and Folly, Masque of Beauty, The Masque of Queens*, and

Masque of Oberon. Jonson was assisted by Inigo Jones who set music and elaborate stage designs, costumes and machinery. The most important elements of the masque were the dances, the entry, the main dance, and the going off. Jonson also introduced the anti-masque or burlesque dance as a comic foil to the main performance. Shakespeare included short masques in *Cymbeline*, *The Winter's Tale*, and *The Tempest*. Middleton employed it in the final act of *Women Beware Women*. Milton wrote two works in masque form, *Arcades* and *Comus*. Comus is considered a masque only in the wider sense. When the theatre was closed in 1642, masque continued to be present in opera, ballet and pantomime. In the 20th century there was a revival of this genre in the works of the American author Percy Mackaye, known for *Saint Gaudens Masque-Prologue*, and *Sanctuary, a Bird Masque*.

Master of the revels is a term applied to the officer appointed since 1494 under Lord Chamberlain. He was in-charge of the court entertainments. With the Licensing Act coming into effect in 1737, this post was cancelled as Lord Chamberlain directly took over the censorship of plays.

Matinee is a theatrical performance or movies shown in the afternoon.

Mayday, Maying is associated with the spring folk festival celebrated on 1 May. It is celebrated with dance, games and dramatic performances. A queen of May is crowned with flowers and dancing is held around a decorated Maypole. The custom may have originated from the Roman *Floralia*. Various characters of the Robinhood story appear in the dramatic performances.

Mechanical acting is a term coined by Stanislavski which refers to acting by clichés devoid of human feeling.

Mechanism in drama is a device used in heightening the plot with suspense such as peripeteia (reversal of fortune). In general mechanism refers to the construction of a work and the relationship of its parts to the whole.

Medievalism (mediaevalism) is a term in literature referring to the imitation of the arts and manners of Europe in the middle ages (8th to 15th century). Medievalism is characterised by the use of archaism, religious faith and chivalry. In the late 18th and 19th centuries there was a growing interest in the medieval, e.g., Keats' *The Eve of St.Agnes* (1820), Walter Scott's *Ivanhoe* (1819).

Medievalist is a person doing scholarly studies in medieval history, art or culture.

Medieval drama consisted of folk plays, religious and liturgical drama and court revels in the middle ages. The age is known for the development of mystery plays, morality plays, disguising and masques. The religious plays centred on the theme of the conflict between good and evil. Medieval drama began with the religious ceremonies in church. During the Easter Vigil Mass in the Catholic Church, some dialogue was inserted into it for the benefit of the people who did not understand Latin in which service was held. This practice continued in other celebrations of the Mass with stories from the *Bible* being dramatised. These performances were taken event-ually out of the churches and to the town squares as they became a source of distraction to the participation in the Mass (*see* Mystery plays, morality plays, masque.)

Melodrama derived from Greek means 'song drama.' It originated with mime, spoken dialogue or declamation accompanied by music. This form, which began in the ancient Greek theatre, became popular in the 18th century, e.g., *The Beggar's Opera* by the English dramatist John Gay. By early 19th century the term melodrama began to be applied to any play with romantic plot, sensationalism and sentimentality. It followed the structure of tragedy with action, stock characters, and strict morality in which virtue is rewarded and evil punished. The central characters are flat types and the hero and heroine are virtues personified fighting evil in the person of a villain. Nowadays melodrama is applied to any exaggerated acting which is bathetic rather than pathetic in nature, e.g., *Sweeney Todd* (anonymous); *Black-Ey'd Susan* by D. Jerrold; *The Colleen Bawn* by Dion Boucicault; *Rape* by Patrick Hamilton; *The Case of the Frightened Lady* by Edgar Wallace; *Loot* by Joe Orton. Twentieth-century melodrama includes motion picture serials and television soap operas.

Melopoeia is a Greek term used by Aristotle referring to the musical elements in Greek tragedy. The term was used by Ezra Pound to describe music in the poetic lines. It can be applied to poetic drama in a wider sense. T.S. Eliot explains the musicality of drama in his essays 'The Music of Poetry' and 'Poetry and Drama.'

Memory play consists of reminiscent scenes seen through light effects and music. The dramatist uses expressionistic technique in such plays with psychological presentation of characters. The protagonists cling to their happy memories of the past and day dream of happy days to come. *The Glass Menagerie* by Tennessee Williams is an excellent example. In this memory play the narrator Tom regards his unhappy and troubled mother and sister in a mood of guilty sorrow and tender love. In the prologue he says that while the stage magician gives the audience illusion that appears like truth; he for his part gives truth in the guise of illusion. Structurally, the play is a series of seven reminiscent scenes seen dimly as through a film of light and music. And the dingy misery of their lives is made luminous by their bravery, rare in real life. Tom is a would-be poet, but really is a humble clerk in a shoe warehouse as William was at the time of the Great American Depression. The narrator is a character in the play, along with his mother Amanda, the nervous sister Laura, crippled in body and mind. The high point in the play is the visit of the gentleman caller, whose visit Tom has contrived under the pressure of the 'scheming' mother. But it ends up as a tragic-comedy since the only caller they could obtain for Laura was already engaged to marry someone else. The mother Amanda succeed in reviving the glorious past. In the one-evening magic the caller Jim was able to bring into the hopeless life of Laura, a flicker of hope, but the whole episode turns out to be a memorable comic tragedy. The result of it is the lifelong nagging of the son by the unbalanced mother reaching its crescendo when the miserable young man flees his home as his father is believed to have done. This fifth character of the play appears only in a larger-than-life-size photograph dominating the mantle. The father has left the family a long time ago. Tom describes him thus: "He was a telephone man who fell in love with long distance." In his last postcard from Mexico he had written "Hello-Goodbye", and there was no address. This merges into the continuing first scene in which Tom enters parting the portiere and the mother seated at the breakfast table greeting him: "Tom, we can't say grace until you come to the table." Special mention is made of scores of transparent glass animals. This is the glass menagerie fondly collected by the shy inhibited Laura. The fourth wall of the building is transparent and the curtains are gauze to give the effect of a memory play.

Message in drama is a code common to the audience and the actor by which some verbal or visual signals are shared by them. This consists of expressions, postures and gestures and other forms of theatre language.

Messenger is a person who reports offstage events. It is a device used in classical, neoclassical and Elizabethan theatre to avoid violent or unconvincing stage action. The device helps in maintaining suspense and arouses the imagination of the audience. It helps to sum up actions which are lengthy to enact with scene changes. The messenger can help fill the time gaps with information on the main action, e.g., in *Oedipus Rex* Sophocles makes a messenger who tells the king on his birth.

Metaphor is a figure of speech in which similarities of two unlike things are seen as identical. The similarity is only imaginary, e.g., *He is a donkey*. In simile the comparison becomes: *He is like a donkey*. Metaphor is always an implied or compressed comparison. For example, in Shakespeare's "There's daggers in men's smiles"(*Macbeth*) the implication is "Men conceal enmity beneath their apparent good-will, as man might conceal a dagger under cloak". Metaphor can be very effective in presenting strong emotions especially in poetic drama. In Shakespeare's *Macbeth,* when Macduff discovers the murder of the king, he utters:

> Ring the alarm bell: murder, and treason,
> Banquo, and Donabain: Malcolm awake,
> Shake off this downy sleep, Death's counterfeit,
> And look on Death itself: up, up, and see
> The great Doom's image: Malcolm, Banquo,
> As from your graves rise up, and walk like sprites,
> To countenance this horror. Ring the bell.

"To countenance this horror" means to give a suitable accompaniment to this horror you must stalk on like evil spirits.

Metatheatre is a term used by Lionel Abel in 1963 referring to serious plays which are not categorised as tragedies. George Steiner in his *The Death of Tragedy* (1961) argues that the Christian promise of salvation makes tragedy impossible. He considers Arthur Miller's *Death of a Salesman*; Tennessee William's *A Streetcar Named Desire* and Robert Bolt's *A Man for All Seasons* belong to Metatheatre. It is a new name for a subdivision of comedy which calls for resuscitation. This form of melodrama runs through Ibsen, Strindberg, to Beckett.

Method acting is a dramatic term applied to an American school of acting related to the Group Theatre in the 1930s. The school known as 'The Method' under Lee Strasberg, Cheryl Campbell and Harold Clurman developed the concepts of Russian Stanislavski's (1863-1938) naturalism. It called for self-expression in its reaction to the artificial acting styles of the time.

Miasma refers to the kind of pollution due to some kind of impiety which calls for purification or catharsis.

Mickey Mouse is the animated cartoon created by Walt Disney (1901-66) in his cartoon series since 1928 (*see* Disney cartoons)

Middle is the central portion of a plot required by Aristotle in his *Poetics*. A plot or tragic action should be whole and complete in itself. It has a *beginning*, *middle* and *end*. *Beginning* initiates the action that looks forward; *middle* presumes what has gone before and requires something to follow; *end* follows from what has gone before and requires nothing to follow.

Middle comedy is a type of Greek comedy prevalent, between the old comedy of Aristophanes and the new comedy of Menanderc 400 to 338 BC. It consisted of burlesque, parody and literary criticism. It made political and topical references and stressed pleasures of life. Known dramatists of this type were Antiphanes and Elixis. Aristophanes wrote *Ecclesiazusae* and *Plautus* in this genre.

Mime is derived from Greek 'mimos' meaning 'representation.' It is a short dramatic spectacle associated with buffoonery and performed without words. In mime, the meaning is communicated through gestures and movements. Sophron of Syracuse (5th century BC) and Herodas (3rd century BC) wrote mimes. It flourished in the middle ages after the Interludes in the form of *commedia dell'arte*. In it, the actors relied on dumb show with occasional dialogues. With music and dance, mime was popular in the Renaissance and helped to develop ballet, opera and the pantomime. In modern times, mime is derived from *commedia dell'arte* with buffoonery and coarse humour, e.g., Beckett's *Act Without Words I: A Mime for One Player*.

Mimesis is the Greek word for 'imitation.' Aristotle used the word in his *Poetics* while discussing his theory of imitation. Tragedy for him is an imitation of an action. Mimesis refers to the construction of a play and what is put into it. Imitation is not counterfeiting of sensible reality, but the presentation of universals. Imitation is not mere copying of ordinary reality, but an idealised rendering of character in action. By imitation an artist presents imaginative reconstruction of life. An imaginative picture can be more real than the original. Hence an artist is not a false imitator. Mimesis imitates not the created nature, but the creative nature. The aesthetic faculty of imitation produces a higher form of reality. Thus Aristotle seizes the universal and reproduces it.

Minstrel is a musical entertainer in medieval Europe. He sang and told stories with musical accompaniment. He performed acrobatics and other tricks. Some minstrels were employed with the nobility to entertain them with love lyrics, ballads, legends, romances and with acrobatics. But most lived a nomadic life. They organised themselves into guilds after 1300.

Minstrel show is a form of popular entertainment with song and dance in England and America in the mid-19th century. It was begun by T.D. Rice and the Negro groups.

Minimal setting is a stage setting with abstract sets or with simple painted background instead of a box setting. This is done for economic reasons and to suit the play.

Miracle play is a genre that developed from the Mystery Play. It dramatised the divine miracles, lives of saints and the stories of the Virgin Mary. These plays are also called passion, miracle, or saint plays. Mansions were erected around the nave of the church, with heaven usually at the altar end and a hell-mouth at the opposite end of the nave. As the play progressed the performers and spectators moved from one area of the church to the other. Unlike Greek tragedy, the medieval drama did not always display conflict and tension as its purpose was to dramatise the salvation history. Though the liturgical drama was enacted for its didactic qualities, in course of time entertainment and spectacle began to increase. This necessitated drama to be taken to the market squares with the same physical arrangement. Though still religious in subject-matter, the main intention was entertainment. These were called miracle plays and there are records of cycles of miracle plays in many parts of England from the 14th to 16th centuries. Miracle plays survive from Chester, York and Wakefield. The Chester cycle had 25 plays; the York cycle: 44 plays and the Wakefield cycle: 32 plays. The themes begin with the Fall of Lucifer and end with Doomsday. They include stories of Creation, Fall, Cain and Abel, Noah, Abraham and Isaac, and the various stages of Christ's life. By the 14th century the production of plays was associated with the Feast of Corpus Christi and had evolved into cycles of as many as 40 plays. Though these cycles are similar to the liturgical dramas, they can be considered a separate development. They were produced by the community as a whole every four or five years. The production of each play was assigned to a trade guild, with an attempt to correlate the guild with the subject of the play—the boatwrights, for instance, might stage the play of Noah. Since the performers were often illiterate the plays tended to be written in an easily memorised doggerel type of verse. Three major forms of staging were employed. Pageant wagons were most common in England. The former mansion became an elaborate rolling stage, that would move from place to place in the city. Spectators would assemble at each location; the participants would perform on the wagons and on a plateau created on the street or with an adjoining platform.

Mise-en-scene is a French term meaning 'action of putting on the stage.' It refers to the total dramatic production with its sets, costumes, visual effects, scenery, props and techniques.

Mixed media performance is a multimedia montage in which live dramatic performance is mingled with slide projections, film sequences and music. With computer graphics and animation, such performances are very appealing to 21st century audience.

Modernism is a term applied to several tendencies in the arts prominent in the first half of the 20th century. It comes directly after the Victorian age in 1887. The First World War gave a new direction to literature and the real new poetry began by 1914. It ended an era of idealism and filled people with bitterness and despair. The literature of this period was deeply influenced by the psychology of Freud and the anthropology Sir. J. Frazer's *Golden Bough*. Emphasis was given to the irrational and the unconscious in man. The age was one of experimentalism and *avant-garde* trends as it rejected traditional Victorian forms in literature. Delving into the 'stream of consciousness' in human mind was an essential feature of the time. The aesthetic vision of Modernism broke with the immediate past traditions and looked for experiments in form and style. In drama, modernist tendencies are seen in Theatre of the Absurd, Anti-Play, Expressionism, Stream of Consciousness, Theatre of Cruelty, etc.

Momus is the Greek god of ridicule who is the patron of clowns.

Monologue is a single person speaking alone with or without an audience, in the form of a speech, a prayer, a lament or a love song. Monologues can be of different types such as monodrama, soliloquy, solo, and dramatic monologue. An entire work or a part of it can be written in the form of a monologue, e.g., Samuel Beckett presents a single character in his *Krapp's Last Tape*.

Montage is a term coined by Bertolt Brecht. He took the concept from the photographic technique of John Heart-field (1891-1968) and the cinematographic technique of Eisenstein (1898-1948). By montage Brecht means a quick succession of contrasting and unrelated scenes that depict life. This he employed in his epic theatre (*see* Epic theatre).

Mood is the atmosphere and feelings of a character. The mood is communicated through the attitude of the character through speech, voice modulation and actions and postures. It also calls our attention to the various theatre languages. In the hands of a dramatist the mood is made more effective by costumes, entrances and exits, lighting, sound effects and music. For instance, Chekhov uses moods in a very effective manner in his plays (*see* Atmosphere).

Moral interlude is a name by which some morality plays with comic effects are known. It has common elements of morality plays and interludes. The humorous element is stronger than the didactic element in a moral interlude, e.g., *Lusty Juventus* (1550) by Weaver.

Morality play is a dramatised religious allegorical play of the late medieval times. During the period when miracle plays were popular, folk plays, secular farces, and pastoral dramas emerged by anonymous authors. All these influenced the evolution of the morality play in the 15th century. It does not deal with Biblical stories but with personified abstractions of virtues and vices, constantly waging war for man's soul. These were usually performed by professionals such as the minstrels or jongleurs. The themes included the Seven Deadly Sins corrupting man, and Mercy and Peace pleading with God. The allegorical characters include such figures as Death, Gluttony, Good Deeds, and other vices and virtues. The earliest Morality Play was *The Castle of Perseverance* (c. 1425) in which the Good Angels and the Bad Angels with the Deadly Sins fight for the soul of man. The most famous among these plays is *Everyman* which dealt with a person's journey through life. Everyman meets characters named after qualities they represent such as Strength, Discretion, Beauty, and Five Wits. They all desert him one by one except Good Deeds. Thus a typical morality play deals with the individual and his confrontation with death. It consists of long debates between allegorical characters representing virtues and vices. Often a man is on his march towards death and these virtues and vices accompany him on his final journey. Some elements of this genre is employed by Marlowe in *Dr. Faustus* and Shakespeare in *King Lear* and *Macbeth*.

Motif is a character, an incident, a concept or an image which recurs as a theme. It is a synonym for leitmotif (*see* leitmotif), e.g., the passage of time is a recurrent theme in Shakespeare's Sonnet sequence. In folklore common motifs are found, e.g., in Malory's *Le Morte d' Arthur* the theme of the quest for the sword occurs as a motif " 'I command,' said the Archbishop, 'that ye keep yourselves within your church and pray unto God still; that no man touch the sword till the high mass be all done.' When all masses were done all the lords went to behold the stone and the sword...." In drama examples of motif is found such as Shakespeare's disease images in *Hamlet*; food images in *Antony and Cleopatra*; Ibsen's references to photography in *The Wild Duck.* In Western music motif is a short melodic or rhythmic segment of a theme that repeats throughout a composition. Although a motif is often repeated in a slightly varied or elaborated way, it carries a recognisable form throughout the composition.

Motion is a puppet play on Biblical themes, prevalent in the 16th and 17th centuries. Shakespeare makes a reference to a motion in *The Winter's Tale*: 'a motion of the Prodigal Son' (IV, iii).

Motion picture is the continuous sequence of transparent still photographs projected on a screen in succession to give the optical illusion of motion. Modern motion pictures are synchronised with sound effects to make it a realistic illusion. It is also known as 'film' or 'movie' in the USA and 'cinema' in Great Britain. Motion pictures are classified into feature films, documentaries, and animated films or cartoons. Though they are all similar in their production, they employ different techniques. A feature film normally has three stages of pre-production, production, and post-production. The pre-production stage is the developmental stage when the story and the materials are collected. The production stage is the actual time of shooting, etc., depending on the budget. The post-production is the editing stage when all the sequences are put together. A documentary film is a non-fiction film presenting real-life situations. Such films can be shot on location or can be a collection of archival materials. Animated films are made from a series of drawings or three-dimensional objects and puppets. Walt Disney animated cartoon series are very popular with kids. To produce a motion picture, especially a feature film, requires the collaboration of a large team besides the stars and actors. These include: the producer, screenwriter, director, production manager, assistant director, director of photography, casting director, film and sound editors, composer, and production and costume designers.

Movement refers to the physical movement made on stage with rhythm, music or in silence to appeal to the ear and the eye. Movement has its own visual meaning such as the agitated pacing up and down, enthusiastic run and the like. Movement can also mean the development of the action of the play from event to event.

Multiple settings was a practice in the medieval liturgical drama with several mansions on a platform which gives several settings on stage. Each mansion represents a different locale for the drama. In the 19th century, multiple setting was done by building an entire house on stage and the audience could see the action taking place in the different rooms of the house. Erwin Piscator (1893-1966) in his plays simultaneously presents different activities such as cooking, eating, talking, etc., which take place at different parts of the room on different levels. Alan Ayckbourn in his *How the Other Half Loves* presents simultaneously two couples in their living rooms on stage.

Mummers' play is a folk ritual drama based on the fertility rites, funeral rites and the spring festival. It was widespread in Britain for a long period of time, however only in the 18th century it began to be recorded. According to tradition the play began introducing St. George, the Turkish knight and captain Slasher. They argue and enter into several duels in which one is killed. A doctor enters the scene boasting of his skill and saves the slain. The central theme presented is the death of the year that leads to new life in spring.

Mummer is an actor who participates in a mummer's play.

Musical comedy is a kind of light theatrical entertainment in the form of an opera which developed in the 19th century. It fuses the elements of ballad opera, burlesque and minstrel shows. Such musical comedies are very popular at the Broadway and West End Theatre. Such musicals require large casts, chorus with choreographed songs and music. Popular musical comedy writers are George Edwardes, George Gershwin, Richard Rodgers, Oscar Hammerstein, Abe Burrows, Irving Berlin, George Abbott, Andrew Lloyd Webber, etc. Some popular comedies are *Guys and Dolls* by Abe Burrows; *Annie Get Your Gun* by Irving Berlin; *Pajama Game* by George Abbott. Bernard Shaw's *Pygmalion* has been adapted into the musical *My Fair Lady*.

Music hall is a 19th century institution which began after the patent theatre monopoly ended in 1843. Music hall originally began during the reign of Queen Victoria with the 'song and supper rooms' in London where popular entertainments were held with songs and dance, stand-up comedy, acrobatics and juggling. Women were allowed into the screened gallery only. Such performances were popular in taverns which provided entertainment to the working classes. The entertainment consisted of only male actors singing ballads, madrigals and songs from operas with the accompaniment of music. Later, special halls such as Canterbury, Holborn Empire, etc., were built for the purpose. With the coming of cinema, the music hall is reduced to cabaret, TV and community theatre.

Mystery plays are the medieval epic dramas popular in England from the 13th to the 16th centuries. They are based on the Biblical stories of the Fall, the Redemption and the Final Judgement. Sometimes they are confused with the miracle plays since both deal with religious themes. However, it is to be kept in mind that the miracle plays dealt with the miracles by the saints, while the mystery plays centred on the Biblical stories. The term mystery is derived from 'mestier', meaning trade, and refers to the trade guilds that performed it according to their profession. The mystery plays developed out of the Easter liturgy in the church with *quem quaeritis trope* (whom do you see?) presenting the Gospel account of the meeting between the angel and the three Marys at the tomb on Easter morning. These plays were performed in the church by the clergy during important feasts such as Christmas, Easter, Pentecost and Corpus Christi. Originally in Latin, vernaculars began to be used in course of time. Later, these plays moved out of the church to the church premises and to the marketplace due to the profane elements introduced into them. Trade guilds took up the performances in accordance with their profession. For example, the carpenter's guild would perform Noah's Ark. The plays were performed on wagons with a curtained scaffold. The wagon moved from town to town. The main cycles are York (48 episodes); Coventry (42 episodes); Wakefield (Towneley) (32 episodes); and Chester (25 episodes).

Mythology is the study and interpretation of ancient folk beliefs and traditional stories of gods and heroes in a particular culture. These present in symbolic language the origin of a culture often in supernatural terms. Usually they describe the origin of the world, creation of man and the origin of customs and practices of people, and mysteries of life and death. Myths have been associated with religion, gods and supernatural times. It can be a source of information of a particular culture and its mythical past. Myth is to be distinguished from legends as they contain deeper universal religious phenomena and traditions though with no historical basis. Legends on the other hand deal more with human existence. Sometimes myth is considered synonymous with plot, e.g., the myth of Oedipus' murder of his father and the consequent events. Many plays are based on ancient myths. Bernard Shaw bases his *Pygmalion* on the classical legend of King Pygmalion, king of Cyprus, who fell in love with his own sculpture. Aphrodite gave the statue life and made the beautiful Galatea. In the modern context, the play describes the story of the transformation of a Cockney flower girl, Eliza Doolittle, who is trained to speak like a duchess by the phonetician Professor Higgins.

Mythopoeia refers to the making of myths by writers who base themselves on a framework of myths. This myth making is an elaboration of a story by an individual or a community which often leads to a dramatic form. For example, the stories of the Trojan war or Biblical stories were transformed into plays. Such mythopoeia is seen in G.B. Shaw's *Pygmalion*; T.S. Eliot's *The Family Reunion* and *The Elder Statesman*; Eugene O' Neill's *Morning Becomes Electra*, etc.

N

Narrator is a character outside the action of a play. He narrates off-stage action and comments on the events. According to Plato and Aristotle, narrators can be of three categories: (i) The narrator who uses his own voice; (ii) The narrator who assumes the voice of another character and speaks like him; and (iii) The narrator who mixes his own and the voice of others, e.g., in *The Statue* the poet John Berryman speaks in his own voice; Byron speaks for Francois de Bonnivard in *The Prisoner of Chillon*; Milton in *Paradise Lost* mixes his own and that of others in the narration. The narrator is very useful in presenting very complex materials in course of a historical or chronicle play involving timespan. The narrator in such a case is a chorus that comments on the action as in Shakespeare's *Henry V*. The device helps reduce the cast and scenes. The narrator provides necessary information to the audience and creates the scene and atmosphere. He can comment on the action of the play as an ideal spectator or can speak directly to the audience. T.S. Eliot in his essay 'The Three Voices of Poetry' refers to the different narrative voices: "The first voice is the voice of the poet talking to himself—or to nobody. The second is the voice of the poet addressing an audience, whether large or small. The third is the voice of the poet when he attempts to create a dramatic character speaking in verse; when he is saying, not what he would say in his own person, but only what he can say within the limits of one imaginary character addressing another imaginary character."

Nativity play belongs to the cycle of mystery plays and depicts events at the birth of Christ, e.g., *The Second Shepherds' Play* presents the story of the shepherds who receive the angelic message of the birth of Christ and their visit to the manger at Bethlehem.

Naturalism in literature calls for an objective and empirical presentation of human beings. It differs from realism. Naturalistic writers reject free will in man and believe that human behaviour is controlled by instinct, emotion, or social and economic factors. Man is a passive victim of natural forces. It accepts the biological determinism of Charles Darwin and the economic determinism of Karl Marx. Naturalists refused to idealise experience as all human experiences are subject to natural law. Naturalism was first noticed in the 19th century French authors Edmond Louis Antoine de Goncourt, Jules Alfred Huot de Goncourt, and Émile Zola. Zola tried to apply methods of scientific observation to the depiction of pathological human character. In his essay, *The Experimental Novel* (1880) he examines his theory of literary naturalism. American novelist Frank Norris deals with naturalism in his novel *McTeague* (1899). Other American and British naturalistic writers include Sherwood Anderson, John Dos Passos, Theodore Dreiser, James T. Farrell, George Moore and George Gissing. Ibsen's *Ghosts* is a naturalistic drama dealing with hereditary disease.

Naturalistic drama became popular in the late 19th century which sought to depict life as it is. It began from the naturalism of Zola and went beyond the realism of Ibsen. The movement spread from France to Germany, England, Russia and America. Known dramatists who wrote in this genre include Henri Becque, Antoine, Strindberg, Hauptmann, Galsworthy, N.C. Hunter and Terence Rattigan.

Natya is derived from Sanskrit referring to a form of Indian dance drama which performed primarily scenes from the epics *Ramayana* and *Mahabharata*. It consisted of an actor presenting pantomime (*abhinaya*) and the narrator (*bhagavatar*) chanting the lines.

Nautical melodrama is a form of romantic melodrama on shipwrecks, smuggling and piracy, popular in the late 18th and early 19th centuries. Such a melodrama had the usual innocent victim, the villain and the hero. The hero is a sailor who is away at sea and returns on time to save his woman in distress. He is patriotic and ready to die for his country.

Negritude is a black cultural movement begun in 1932 in Paris which influenced many black writers in the French-speaking world. They sought to uphold traditional African values and resisted the attempt of the whites to absorb the blacks into the white man's world. The leaders were Leopold Sedar Senghor and Aime Cesaire.

Nemesis means retributive justice often referred to in the case of tragic heroes. 'Nemesis' is the Greek goddess of retribution who punishes erring humans.

Neoclassicism known by various names, 'Augustan Age', 'Age of Reason' or 'The Enlightenment' is a movement in literature which imitated the great classical authors of the ancient Greece and Rome. Aristotle's *Poetics* (4th century BC) and Horace's *Ars Poetica* (c.20 BC) became the dominant literary influences on the writers of the period with the principles of decorum and instruction. They took up to the Aristotalian Unities of time, place and action. This resurgence began with the French literature in the 17th century and deeply influenced the English literary scene from 1660 to 1780. Neoclassicism stood for reason, judgement, decorum, correctness and argumentation. They used Heroic couplet form in poetry. The Neoclassical beliefs generated a definite vision of man and mankind. Man and his activities were the main subject matter of poetry. They frequently used satire to correct excessive folly, stupidity and corruption which threatened maintenance of good moral order and literary discipline. Alexander Pope wrote, "Order is Heaven's first law". Hence the Neoclassicists were obliged to instruct as well as to please through their works. The period is called classical as it was a revolt against the Romantic exuberance of the Elizabethan period that preceded it. However, they lacked the genius of the Elizabethans and turned to the great classical writers for guidance and inspiration. The period also coincided with the restoration of Charles II in 1660 when the puritan government collapsed. The period, marked by the French influence of Moliere, is evident in the Restoration Comedy of Manners. In tragedy the Neoclassicists imitated the French and the Latin forms and produced the Heroic play. The authors devised many rules and issued the injunction "be correct". Dr. Johnson applied to Dryden the term "Augustan" saying that "Dryden did to English literature what Augustus did to Rome, which he found brick and left marble." The Neoclassical poetry became excessively a town poetry showing no interest in the landscapes and country people. They distrusted emotions and turned to good sense and reason. Important literary figures of this period are Dryden, Pope, Addison, Swift and Johnson.

Neoclassical drama is drama that took classical plays of Greece and Rome. It became popular in France in the 17th and 18th centuries and kept to the classical principles of decorum, didacticism, verisimilitude, unities of time, place and action. Neoclassical dramatists include French Racine; English Ben Jonson, Dryden, Congreve, Goldsmith and Sheridan (*see* Neoclassicism).

Neoplatonism is a philosophical and religious system founded by Plotinus (AD 205-270) which blends Platonic ideas and oriental mysticism. It sets aside the overemphasis of Plato on rationalism and ideas, and stressed more on the intuitive and mystical pursuits of truth. They believed in the hierarchy of the spiritual levels of the individual soul in its communion with the Eternal. Neoplatonism in literature stressed the theory of love based on the concept that earthly beauty is the image of the absolute beauty. It believed in the existence of invisible airy creatures. Art and Nature in their view is the copy of the super-sensuous reality.

New criticism began in the 1940s in the United States after the publication of John Crowe Ransom's *The New Criticism* (1941). The New Critics focused on a piece of literature as an artistic object having certain values in itself. Hence they did not consider that piece in relation to the author's biographical or social backgrounds and his effect on the reader. This called for a close reading of the text and the understanding of the verbal nuances. Many New Critics looked to T.S. Eliot, I.A. Richards and William Empson for inspiration. Richards in his *The Principles of Literary Criticism* (1924) and *Practical Criticism* (1929), encouraged his students to comment freely on unfamiliar poems. He attempted a 'laboratory experiment' by close scrutiny. In America, the prominent New Critics included Cleanth Brooks, Robert Penn Warren, Allen Tate and R.P. Blackmur. Cleanth Brooks and Robert Penn Warren in the preface to the anthology *Understanding Poetry* (1938) wrote, "...conceived on the assumption that if poetry is worth teaching at all, it is worth teaching as poetry". In England, F.R. Leavis took up close reading technique. In his book *Revaluation* (1936) he wrote, "the rule of the critic is, or should (I think) be, to work as much as possible in terms of particular analysis—analysis of poems or passages—and to say nothing that cannot be related immediately to judgements about producible texts." This same principle he followed in the periodical *Scrutiny* (1932-53) which contains some of the sharpest close reading of modern times. His critical method was based on the response of students in the classroom like Richards and the American New Critics Cleanth Brooks and John Crowe Ransom. The basic assumptions of New Criticism are summarised in Rene Welleck's and Austen Warren's *Theory of Literature* (1949).

New comedy is the Greek comedy which emphasised realistic depiction of life without supernatural or poetic elements in it. It was a popular Greek form from 330 BC to 150 BC. Such comedies presented young lovers pining for each other. Their love is thwarted but ends in happiness. The drama has stock characters and is presented in five acts with a chorus in between the acts to entertain. These plays required no interior scenes as the action took place before the exterior representing two houses. Prominent exponents include Philemon of Syracuse, Diphilus of Sinope, Apollodorus of Carystus and Menander (342-291 BC), the most prominent among them. Roman dramatists who imitated this genre were Plautus and Terence.

New wave (Nouvelle vague) is a term referring to a new experimental trend in drama and cinema in the 1950s and early 1960s. The term is applied to the plays of authors such as John Osborne, John Arden, Arnold Wesker, Robert Bolt and especially Harold Pinter. Pinter is superb in depicting characters who remain a mystery. In his *Birthday Party* he depicts his absurd characters and situations (*see* Absurd theatre).

Noh (No) theatre is a form of Japanese classical theatre which began as a religious ceremony in the 14th century It evolved from Shinto worship. It took elements of sacred and folk dance like *Bugaku* and is a traditional ritualistic drama. It was at its peak in the 15th century. Noh is also closely related to Zen Buddhism. It is highly stylised with dance and music, extravagant costumes, mime and masks. The drama attempts to evoke a particular mood through the retelling of an incident or story. It is the psychological elements presented through the characters is the most appealing aspect of the play. The drama is very short with one or two acts in prose and verse with a chorus making comments. The drama is enacted on a simple stage with a small balcony for the chorus and a back stage for the musicians. There are over 200 such plays in five types one of which is presented at a religious festival. Many of them have been written by a priest named Kwanami (1333-84) and his son Zeami (1363-1443). The five types of drama include: a drama of praise to God; a drama about a warrior with a battle scene; a drama about a woman; a drama on ghosts; a drama with warlike dance praising the lords and the reign.

Noise off refers to the sound effects required for a dramatic performance. Michael Frayn wrote a farce *Noise Off* presenting all the off stage sounds.

Non-commercial Theatre evolved since 19th century. In Europe and America, it has been known as art theatre before World War I. Later, it came to be called Experimental theatre and Fringe theatre. In New York City, it is known as Off Broadway and Off-Off-Broadway. The non-commercial theatre aimed at staging serious literary, artistic, and*avant-garde* drama. It experimented with creative productions. Unlike commercial theatre it is low-budget in production and does not aim at profit making. It depends entirely on donations or subsidy from government. Those companies that cannot obtain adequate funding usually face bankruptcy after a short time or else are forced to compromise their ideals to survive (*see* Commercial theatre).

Nursery, The is a school for actors begun by Thomas Killigrew (1612-83) during the Restoration period.

O

Objective is the purpose or intention a character has in a play, e.g., in *Othello* Iago is ruled by the 'green eyed monster' jealousy and is determined to wreck Othello's love for Desdemona.

Objective correlative is a term coined by T.S.Eliot to explain how emotions can best be expressed in poetry and drama. In his essay, 'Hamlet and His Problem', he says that emotion cannot directly be transmitted from the poet to the reader but has to be objectified into something suggestive of it. In this way the object evokes the same emotion in the reader. "The emotion and the object should become indissolubly one within the structure of the poem or the drama, so that the one spontaneously evokes the other." According to him, *Hamlet* has been an artistic failure as Hamlet's complex emotions have not been properly objectified. In his opinion, "The only way of expressing emotion in the form of art is by finding an 'objective correlative'; in other words, a set of objects, a situation, a chain of events which shall be the formula of the particular emotion; such that when the external facts, which must terminate the sensory experience, as given, the emotion is immediately evoked." Eliot gives the example of Lady Macbeth's sleep walk as an example of objective correlative. It communicates her state of mind by "a skilful accumulation of imagined sensory impressions; the words of Macbeth on hearing his wife's death strikes us as if, given the sequence of events, these words were automatically released by the last event in the series. The artistic 'inevitability' lies in this complete adequacy of the external to the emotion." The term describes poetry that is pure image.

Obligatory scene is a scene the audience anticipates in a play as they are led to it through the development of the plot, and the dramatist is obliged to include it. Such scenes are of intense emotional climax.

Obstacle is a character or a situation in a play that prevents the protagonist from achieving his objective.

Off-Broadway is a term referring to the *avant-garde* theatre productions away from the Broadway area of New York City in the 1950s. It is characterised by experimental low budget productions. A few of such theatres are John Houseman Theatre, Sullivan Street Theatre, Circle in the Square, etc. Off-Broadway plays include Brecht's and Weill's *The Threepenny Opera*, Uhry's *Driving Miss Daisy*, Harling's *Steel Magnolias*.

Off-off-Broadway refers to the low budget skits and plays performed in warehouses, churches and cafes, especially in the Greenwich village. These improvised plays had also the audience participating in it. Many of these plays are found in the *Best Short Plays of 1968* edited by S. Richards.

Offstage is when an actor is out of sight of the audience.

Onstage is when an actor is in sight of the audience.

Old comedy originated from the Greek choruses in the fertility rites and processions in honour of Dionysus in Athens around 487 BC. It consisted of much satirical buffoonery, parody, and political propaganda. It was bawdy and at times obscene. Such old comedies had various parts: (i) a prologue in which a 'happy idea' was announced; (ii) parados (entrance of the chorus); (iii) Agon (debate and decision over the 'happy idea'; (iv) Parabasis (chorus addressed the audience with the ideas of the dramatist); (v) Episodes of the 'happy idea'; and (vi) Festive celebration. Old comedy is often referred to the plays of Aristophanes (448-380 BC) such as *The Wasps*, *The Clouds* and *The Frogs*. These plays had loosely constructed plots in which gods and heroes took part.

Old man/old woman are the stereotyped roles in Victorian melodramas and farces. Often the old man is a figure who exercises powers over his dependants. He obstructs love intrigues of young lovers. Such a character of the old man developed from the Pantaloon in the *commedia dell'arte*. We have typical examples of such characters such as Peter Teazle in Sheridan's *School for Scandal*; Lady Wishfort in Congreve's *The Way of the World*.

Olio is a collection of musical selections which are performed during intermissions of a melodrama.

Ombres chinoises is a Far Eastern shadow play using puppets, popular in Paris in the 18th and 19th centuries.

One-act play is a short 20 to 50 minutes play with few characters with no change of scene, which developed from the experimental 'little theatre' movement in Europe and America towards the end of 19th century. It is distinct from the earlier interludes, afterpiece or vaudeville skit performed in course of a lengthy play. Chekhov, Strindberg, W.B. Yeats , J.M. Synge and Beckett are known for their one-act plays.

One-man/one-woman show is a performance by a single actor usually accompanied by musical accompaniment. Such shows can vary in content. It can be autobiographical, impersonation or a collage presenting excerpts from plays or poems.

Open stage is one that has the audience on its three sides like the arena stage. It has no curtain or the proscenium arch. Open theatre was popularised in the 20th century by William Poet and Harley Granville Barker. National Theatre and Royal Shakespeare Company use open theatre today.

Open Theatre is a theatrical group began by Joseph Chaikin in 1963. The group experimented with short pieces with dance, mime, chorus and other improvisation, e.g., *The Serpent* (1967) is based on the Biblical stories of Genesis such as the eating of the forbidden fruit, the killing of Abel, etc., with images of death from the contemporary situations like the assassination of President Kennedy and Martin Luther King. The Open Theatre centred on group activity has been influenced by Stanislavski, Artaudi's theatre of cruelty, and Grotowski's theatre of laboratorium.

Opera is a dramatic performance in which all or part of the dialogue is sung with choruses, recitatives, arias, orchestra, instrumental overtures, interludes and accompaniments. Opera began in Italy in the late 16th and early 17th centuries preceded by Italian madrigals in which dialogue was set to music. Renaissance court spectacles of pageantry, music, and dance had influence on its development. Rinuccini's *Dafne* is the first opera which attempted to revive the classical Greek Tragedy. From Italy baroque operas flooded Europe in the 18th century. It became very popular in the halls of princes and the public theatres. In France, court operas under the influence of Racine's tragedies became popular. By mid-18th century baroque opera dwindled and more realistic *opera buffa* began. Realistic sentimental and comic operas began to develop with French composers like Gretry, Lesueur and Cherubini. Mozart wrote in the *opera buffa* tradition and Beethoven in the realistic tradition of Cherubini. France, Germany, and Italy developed characteristic operatic styles during the 19th century, all reflective of the romantic movement. Giuseppe Verdi is considered the father of Italian opera with his infusion of vigour and rhythmic vitality. Verdi's last two operas, *Otello* (1887) and *Falstaff* (1893), adapted Shakespearean plays to the operatic stage. In Germany, Wagner's influence pervaded virtually all subsequent operas. Modern composers mingle symphonic techniques with folk, popular, or jazz styles into their operas.

Opera never took roots in England as an indigenous form as in the rest of Europe. In the 17th century England. Purcell is an exception to this with his opera *Dido and Aeneas*. In Britain, Benjamin Britten is well known for his operas such as *Peter Grimes* (1945), *Albert Herring* (1947), *The Turn of the Screw* (1954), *A Midsummer Night's Dream* (1960), and *Death in Venice* (1973). The first American grand opera was *Leonora* (1845) by William Henry Fry. Later works like *The Scarlet Letter* (1896) by Walter Damrosch, were European in style. In the 20th century emphasis has been given to the operatic ensemble, with the conductor, the scenic designer, and the stage director assuming roles with the singers. The Italian Franco Zeffirelli is a prominent personality in neo-romantic revival in opera staging and design during the early 1960s. Other known stage directors are British Jonathon Miller, and Americans Frank Corsaro, Sarah Caldwell, and Peter Sellars. Modern composers have taken to multimedia techniques with electronic and synthesizer music. Composers like Leonard Bernstein blends dance, electronic music, and novel stage techniques in operas.

Operetta is a stage play with music, songs and dance interspersed often with satirical dialogue which developed from the French *opera bouffe*. It is distinguished from opera from its spoken comical dialogue. In the 18th century it was a short opera, but in the 19th and 20th centuries it came to be a play with music and of popular appeal. Sheridan's *The Duenna* (1775) is an early examples in England. The English operetta developed from the short ballad opera like that of John Gay's *The Beggar's Opera* (1728). Gay's political and social satire influenced others such as playwright Bertolt Brecht and composer Kurt Weill. Sir Henry Bishop's *Clari, or the Maid of Milan* (1823) is known for the tune "Home, Sweet Home." Other known English operas are of Sir Arthur Sullivan and Sir William S. Gilbert (*see* Opera, Ballad Opera).

Oratorio is a musical composition which is semi-dramatic. It is often written with a religious tone and not meant for acting. Handel's *Messiah* (1742) and *Samson* (1743) are written in this genre.

Orchestra/orkestra refers to the dancing area of the Greek and Roman theatres. It was a circular area with an altar in the centre to Dionyso, the god of dramatic festivals. Originally, this was a large area where the two slopes of the hillocks met. Later it was placed below the skene. The paved orchestra tended to be very small. Later, in the Greco-Roman theatre, the skene began to extend to the orchestra area.

Oratory refers to the art of public speaking which was taught in classical rhetoric.

Organic is a term used in literature in contrast to the mechanical. It refers to 'life and growth'. It is based on Coleridge's conception of imagination and fancy. The term organic is used for literary works that continue to evolve due to their vitality. For example, a 'farce' is mechanical as it is fixed and conventional in form.

Originality is the quality an author possesses by which he introduces spontaneously novelty and innovation in his writing based on some organic principle. However, according to T.S. Eliot, 'that which is absolutely original is absolutely bad'. He held the view that every writer is dependent on the past traditions. Originality consists of reshaping of the materials held in common and bringing these into relation with something new in the writer's own time. In '*Tradition and the Individual Talent*', he writes: " ... the historical sense involves a perception, not only of the pastness of the past, but of its presence; the historical sense compels a man to write not merely with his own generation in his bones... . No poet, no artist of any art, has his complete meaning alone. His significance, his appreciation is the appreciation of the relation to the dead poets and artists. You cannot value him alone; you must set him, for contrast and comparison, among the dead…what happens when a new work of art is created is something that happens simultaneously to all the works of art which preceded it…."

Origins of drama: According to tradition drama originated in the primitive religious rituals. Sir James Frazer from his anthropological studies explains certain rituals, charms and myths. Secular drama developed from ritual ceremonies (*see* Introduction: What is drama?)

Ostension is showing a thing as it is without any allegorical meaning. In a naturalistic drama things are portrayed as they are and the audience know what the author intents, his dreams and wishes. At times ostension can be stretched further in naturalistic plays as for example holding an empty cup and inviting the audience to fill it as presented by the chorus in Shakespeare's *Henry V*. Here the ostension is of a double nature: the real holding of the cup and the desired response of the audience. The traumatic action grows between the actual and the desired.

Outdoor theatre is the theatre in the open air until roofing was done over the theatrical space in course of time. Open space with sunlight was used for dramatic performance in the Greek amphitheatre, Cornish rounds, Elizabethan theatre and the *commedia dell'arte*. From the 17th century there is the development of roofed and well-lit theatres.

Overhearer is a character who overhears a conversation between characters on stage who are unaware of his presence. However, the audience sees him or her. Such an overhearer is used by dramatists as a device to heighten the plot by which a secret is known to someone who would act accordingly. Suspense is aroused with such dramatic irony, e.g., in Othello, Shakespeare lets his hero listen to a conversation between Iago and Cassio about Bianca and misunderstands it to be about his wife Desdesmona. The misunderstanding finally leads to a tragic end.

Overplot is the context in which the play was originally written as part of a celebration or festivity. The term has been suggested by the American critic Harry Levin. For example, Shakespeare wrote his comedy *The Merry Wives of Windsor* (1597) on the occasion of George Carey, Lord Hunsdon's installation as knight of the Garter on 23 April 1597. The passage alluding to the Garter Feast is found only in the Folio text of 1623. In course of time the over-plot is forgotten by later audiences.

Over the top refers to highly exaggerated performance. It occurs in tragedy when a performance goes out of the conventional expectation of the audience. In such a case, the character goes out of his range and tries to give an unexpected and unconvincing interpretation. 'Over the top' cannot be applied in the case of comedy as it has clowns who are expected deliberately to exaggerate in order to arouse laughter.

Overture is the music played before a musical play begins.

Oxford's men is a company of actors sponsored by the Dukes of Oxford in the 16th century.

P

Pace is the tempo, rhythm or the speed of a play. Tragedies are slow-moving while comedies have a faster tempo.

Pace-egging play is a mumming play associated with the Easter Monday practice of the Easter-egg. It used to be a practice in Lancashire and Northern England to decorate with colours hard boiled eggs and rubbing them on each other until they broke. 'Pace' in the North English dialect refers to Hebrew 'Pasch' meaning 'Passover' or Easter.

Pageant is the movable platform or horse-drawn wagon on which episodes of the mystery plays were performed. The wagon had the scenes and sets for the play. It had two storeys of which the bottom portion was covered with curtains and used as dress changing room for the actors and the top portion had the setting for dramatisation. The wagon had a banner of the sponsoring guild in front of it. In course of time, pageant meant a street procession or tableau presentations with songs, dances and dramatic scenes.

Pageant master is the main coordinator of a medieval drama production. He wears ecclesiastical garments and carries a baton along with the prompt book.

Palliata is a Roman form of new comedy presenting contrasting attitudes of the older and the younger generations. Pallium is a Greek cloak worn by actors.

Palsgrave's men is a drama company of the Jacobean times patronised by Prince Henry and known as Prince Henry's men. When he died in 1612 it derived the name Palsgrave's Men.

Palilogy is a rhetorical device by which a word or phrases are repeated for emphasis.

Pan shot is a panorama shot taken by camera with its base fixed, yet can swing from right or left.

Pantaloon is the stereotyped comic character in the *commedia dell'arte* or the old man in the harlequinade who is the object of ridicule by clown and servants. He is a suspicious and greedy old man who wrecks the love of young lovers and is often dressed in a black gown and skull cap. In the Elizabethan times a comical old man was known as a pantaloon. In Shakespeare's *As You Like It* (II,vii) Jaques refers to him as:

> ...the lean and slipper'd pantaloon,
> With spectacles on nose and pouch on side,
> His youthful hose well say'd, a world too wide
> For his shrunk shank; and his big manly voice,
> Turning again toward childish treble, pipes
> And whistles in his sound.

Pantomime is derived from Greek *Pantomimos* (the man who imitates). In the great open-air theatres of ancient Greece and Rome, mime was an important element of acting as the audience could see more easily than it could hear. Pantomimus in Latin referred to a kind of solo performer of ancient Rome who dramatically presented an ancient Greek legend through gestures, movements and masks to the accompaniment of music and a chorus. Pantomime has come to be the art of dramatic representation by means of facial expressions and body movements rather than words. Pantomime was essential to *commedia dell'arte* in the 16th century Italy. Pantomime continued in the 17th and 18th century harlequinade in France and England (an offshoot of the *commedia dell'arte*). It presented the adventures of

Harlequin; his sweetheart, Columbine; and her father, Pantaleone. In England, John Weaver introduced pantomime in 1716 and was further developed by John Rich (1692-1761). John Rich mingled comic episodes from Harlequin stories with serious ones. Harlequinade in London was preceded by a scene in which actors mimed and danced stories from classical mythology. It led to the transformation of the leading character into Harlequin. John Rich made this form of entertainment popular at Christmas. In course of time the pantomime which was the introductory scene became longer and more important than the harlequinade. In the early 19th century Joseph Grimaldi with his acrobatic skills invented tricks and stage machinery. He is known for his creation of the foolish clown Joey. The pantomime eventually became an elaborate stage performance of fairy tales with song, dance, acrobatics and dialogue. In the early 20th century, silent films actors like Charlie Chaplin and Buster Keaton acted and conveyed their stories through mime. Actors like Bill Irwin, David Shiner, and Bill Berky rejuvenated mime performance in the 1980s and early 1990s. Irwin performed his one-man Broadway show *Largely New York* in 1989 which depicted the relationship between a clown and modern technology.

Pantomimus (*see* Pantomime).

Papposilenus is the leader of the satyr chorus in Greek satyr plays popular in the 5th century BC at the city Dionysia (*see* Satyr plays).

Pants part is a technical term referring to a male role being played by a female. In pantomime, the main role of a boy is played by a young girl.

Papering the house is the free ticket distribution to fill a drama house during performance.

Parabasis is derived from Greek meaning 'stepping aside or digression.' It was a device used in old Greek comedy by which a chorus came forward towards the end of the play to address the audience. While doing this it abandons its original costumed dramatic roles. The leader would wear the mask of the author and satirize important personalities or events, e.g., Aristophanes in his *Wasps*, *Clouds*, etc., employs the device. In *Clouds* the parabasis consists of the chorus explaining the author's ideas of comedy and invites the audience to worship clouds.

Parable play is dramatisation of parables which are short narratives with characters that are usually human beings. It is a dramatic allegory which invites the audience to set the story in comparison with another set of events. The parables of Jesus in the New Testament are often set to parable plays such as: the parables of the Good Samaritan, Prodigal Son, Sower and the like. These plays do not always give solutions but arouse suspense in the audience. Such parable plays can present effectively a moral. Ionesco in his *Rhinoceros* (1960) presents a parable play in three acts on the growth of Fascism. It depicts characters as rhinoceros. Brecht in his drama used historical and fictional situations to present contemporary problems and let his audience find their own solution.

Parade is a brief performance done outside fairground booths to attract audience for a dramatic performance.

Paradiso is a stage device used by Brunelleschi (1377-1446) for his play *Annunciation of the Angel to Blessed Virgin Mary*. It used to be performed in the Church of San Felice in Florence. Paradiso referred to a dome in which Angel Gabriel and the cherubim of heaven descend on earth. The dome is lowered from the roof and is raised back to give the effect of heavenly intervention.

Parados is the entrance song or dance by the chorus in Greek tragedy. In the new comedy, parados disappeared and the chorus merely entertained the audience in between the acts, e.g., in *Medea* of Euripides the parados consists of the chorus of Corinthian Ladies (*see* Episode).

Paradox is that which is apparently absurd and self-contradictory but is essentially true. Just as a pun is a form of ambiguity that plays on words, a paradox plays on ideas. Paradoxes have been known since the time of the Greek philosopher Zeno (5th century BC). Many paradoxes are based on false premises. Semantic paradox is based on the structure of language and is used as a rhetorical device. They are unexpected and initially inexplicable. They call for efforts at understanding and if the effort is successful it is delightful to the reader. Paradoxes call for the reader's intellectual participation in the creation of a literary meaning. In general, a paradox involves a contradiction between the physical or material meaning of words and their spiritual, emotional, or supernatural connotation. In drama, paradox can have a serious or comic effect. For example, Brecht in his *Mother Courage* uses paradoxes to give alienation effect. Mother Courage explains her own name paradoxically: "They call me Mother Courage' cause I was afraid I'd be ruined." American critic Cleanth Brooks explores the uses of paradoxes in his *The Well Wrought Urn* (1947). He was inspired by the writings of T.S. Eliot on the metaphysical poets and their use of paradoxes. Eliot's *Murder in the Cathedral* and *The Cocktail Party* are excellent in presenting paradoxical situations. Both these plays present the paradox of Christian suffering and salvation. In *The Murder in the Cathedral,* after the knights stab the archbishop, they address the audience with a pompous, foolish defence of their deed. They move out of stage and the priests appear and thank God for having given them another Saint in Canterbury.

Paradox of acting is considered in the context of two opposite theories of acting that have evolved in modern times, namely, 'actor' and his 'role'. Stanislavski (1863-1938) stressed 'full identification' between the actor and the character played. Brecht (1898-1956) on the other hand emphasised the actor's 'independence' from the character on stage. However, in these two positions there is some sort of an agreement with Henry Irving (1838-1905) who opined that the actor ought to identify himself with the character and yet remain separated to some extent. This brings about a paradox of acting between actor and the role he plays.

Parallelism in drama occurs when there is a correspondence between two characters in similar circumstances. Shakespeare presents such a parallelism in *King Lear*. King Lear and Gloucester are both dispossessed and betrayed in old age.

Paraphrase is elaborating the central ideas of a passage for clarity. It is a rewording of a piece of writing for comprehending the idea. In drama, it helps as a tool in the early rehearsals, helping the actors to understand the sequence of scenes. It helps an actor to improvise and develop more natural movements.

Parapraxis are the accidental mistakes, slips of the tongue, mishearing, etc., which can reveal certain unconscious or suppressed feelings according to Sigmund Freud.

Paraskena/parascenia is the 'side scenes' or the wings of the skene building in the classical Greek theatre.

Parody is a burlesque in comic imitation of a literary work. By it, a composition ridicules another by imitating and exaggerating its content, structure and style. It is a kind of satirical mimicry. A parody has to have close resemblance to the original, yet distorts it creatively. In a parody, a light theme is treated in the style of a serious work, e.g., Cervantes' *Don Quixote* is a parody of the chivalric romances of his time. Chaucer in *The Nun's Priest's Tale* parodies Master Reynard the fox in the widow's barnyard by describing it in a very lofty language and comparing it to the fall of Troy. In English those who have written parody include Alexander Pope, Jonathan Swift, William Thackeray, James Joyce, Max Beerbohm, and Ogden Nash.

In drama parody began with the satyr play and old comedy. Aristophanes's *Frogs* (405 BC) is a parody of the style of Aeschylus and Euripides. Shakespeare parodied some of the writers of his time in his *Love's Labour's Lost*.

Participatory theatre is a modern development in drama by which the audience is made to involve in the performance. The practice began to some extent in the Victorian melodrama which invited the audience to cheer the hero and jeer at the villain.

Passim is a Latin word used to mean 'everywhere or throughout' and is used in footnotes for materials occurring at several places.

Paso is derived from Spanish meaning 'passage'. It refers to the 16th century Spanish procession depicting the passion and suffering of Jesus which led to the marketplace with a short dramatic piece being performed. The term is also applied to a short comic interlude.

Pasquino is the role of a servant in the *commedia dell'arte*.

Passion play is a kind of mystery play presenting the suffering, death, and resurrection of Jesus Christ usually performed on Good Friday. It consists of Jesus's entry into Jerusalem, the trials by Herod and Pilate, the Crucifixion, the burial and the Resurrection. The earliest dramatic representations of the crucifixion in Latin is found in the 13th century based on the liturgical presentation of the *Visita-tio Sepulchri* and the *Victimae Paschali*. These eventually became part of the Corpus Christi festivals and the mystery cycles. At the height of their popularity in the middle of the 15th century, they had developed into elaborate productions requiring three days for performance. During the Renaissance the tradition languished, however after the Reformation these were performed in Germany, Austria and Switzerland. The best known performance of Passion Play is by the residents of Oberammergau in the Bavarian Alps. Dating from 1634, it is performed once in ten years.

Pastiche is a parody with themes and stylistic elements borrowed from artists of a particular school or from works of one particular author. The term is used in a disparaging manner to mock at the lack of originality of the works parodied, e.g., Gerard Alessandrini in his *Forbidden Broadway*, parodies various Broadway performances.

Pastoral is linked to poetry, drama, comedy or fiction that share the conventional pastoral background of shepherds in their rural life.

Pastoral drama is set in the countryside with shepherds and farmers. It has its origin from the pastoral poetic tradition as well as the eclogue and shepherd's play (*see* Pastoral Poetry). During the Italian Renaissance pastoral drama began to emerge such as *Tasso's L'Aminta* (1573); Gnarini's *II Pastor Fido* (1590). John Lyly (1554-1606) and John Fletcher (1579-1623) introduced pastoral drama in England. Fletcher's *The Faithful Shepherdess* is considered the first in this genre. Shakespeare gave pastoral setting to some of his plays such as *As You Like It*, *A Midsummer Night's Dream*, *Love's Labour's Lost*, *Pericles*, *Cymbeline*, *The Winter's Tale* and *The Tempest*.

Pastoral Poetry depicts the innocence of shepherds in their rural world. Following a specific literary convention, pastoral poems can be found as love lyrics, dramatic works and elegies. Classical pastoral poetry originated from the folk songs and ceremonies that honoured the pastoral gods. The first pastoral poems were the *Idylls* written by the Greek poet Theocritus in the third century BC. Later in the second century BC Bion and Moschus wrote pastoral poems. Virgil wrote his *Bucolics* (37 BC) in Latin in imitation of Theocritus. Petrarch (1304-74) and Giovanni Boccaccio (1313-75) wrote eclogues (short pastoral poems) in Latin. These were dialogues between simple shepherds in rustic surroundings expressing moral or philosophical viewpoints. Politian (1454-94) wrote *Orfeo*, one of the earliest dramatic pastorals in Italian. In England, Edmund Spenser wrote *The*

Shepheardes Calendar in 12 pastoral eclogues (1579). This was a model in England and the pastoral spirit influenced other forms of English literature. In drama, pastoral spirit is found in *The Arraignment of Paris* (1581) by George Peele and *Sad Shepherd* (1641) by Ben Jonson. *Arcadia* (1590) of Sir Philip Sidney is a pastoral romance. Lodge, Greene, Thomas Campion, Robert Herrick and Andrew Marvell wrote pastoral lyrics, songs and madrigals. William Shakespeare also used the pastoral convention in *As You Like It* (1600). Moschus (150 BC) wrote his pastoral elegy *Lament for Bion*. This influenced Milton's pastoral elegy *Lycidas* (1637), Shelley's *Adonais* (1821) and Arnold's *Thyrsis* (1866).

Pataphysics is a mock philosophical system of Alfred Jarry (1873-1907) known as the Science of Imaginary Solutions. It was a metaphysics of nonsense devoid of any reason. In his novel *Gestes et Opinions du Docteur Faustroll,* he presented a parody of logic, language and learning. His absurd philosophy is considered as the main source of the Theatre of the Absurd.

Patent theatre were the recognised theatres Drury Lane and Lincoln's Inn Fields by Royal Charters of Charles II on his restoration to the throne. These theatres got the monopoly of staging drama. By the Licensing Act of 1737 Drury Lane and Covent Garden (Lincoln's Inn patent passed on to Covent Garden) got the patent which continued up to 1843.

Pater noster plays were a genre of religious plays used to be performed in York, Lincoln and other places for nearly two hundred years until the suppression of religious drama in 1537. It was John Wycliff (1330-1384) who referred to them as Pater noster plays (*Pater noster* in Latin means 'Our Father': the prayer Jesus taught his disciples) due to its religious nature. These plays focus on the deadly sins and the seven petitions of the Lord's prayer: (1) Hallowed be Thy name; (2) Thy Kingdom come; (3) Thy will be done on earth as it is in Heaven; (4) Give us this day our daily bread; (5) Forgive us our trespasses as we forgive those who trespass against us; (6) Lead us not into temptation; (7) But deliver us from evil. The purpose of such plays was to instruct especially the non-literate faithful in the doctrines of their faith. It is similar to the morality plays which stressed the need for repentance and confession of sins.

Pathos is a Greek term signifying 'feeling' or 'suffering' and is used to signify the suffering of the protagonist in classical tragedy due to certain forces out of his control. This evokes feeling of pity in the reader or the spectator, e.g., in *Prometheus Unbound*, Aeschylus presents the suffering of Prometheus who is punished for defending humans. He is chained on a rock and agonises in pain. This arouses pity and compassion in the audience which is a quality of the drama. Hegel distinguished between 'objective' and 'subjective' pathos. Objective pathos aimed at activity while subjective pathos led to passivity.

Patronage is the financial support given to a literary figure by some wealthy person. In return, he or she is to pay homage to the patron by writing dedications in his praise. It was a practice prevalent in the Royal household until the 18th century England.

Pause is the brief deliberate stop in the course of a dialogue which breaks the dramatic flow. It is used as a device which enables the audience to pay close attention to a character's facial and physical expressions. Such pauses can provide variety and contrast to a scene. Some dramatists specify 'pause' or mark it by three dots or a dash. Modern dramatists such as Jean Jacques Bernard, Samuel Beckett and Harold Pinter used the device effectively in their plays.

Peking opera is the Chinese theatrical performance based on Chinese legends, history and myths with music, song, speech, dance, and acrobatics. The opera has a symbolic setting with characters given symbolic colours according to social rank and position: 'Gold' for immortal persons; 'Red' for high ranking persons; 'Grey' for old men; 'White' for treacherous characters; 'Black' for suspicious persons, etc. Peking opera has been popularised in Europe and America by Mei Lan Feng's tours (1894-1961) and wielded an influence on Brecht's concepts of epic and gestic acting.

Pembroke's men is an Elizabethan drama company. Shakespeare may have written for them before he joined Lord Chamberlain's Men.

Penny gaff is a low theatre performing melodrama in poor urban areas in the 19th century England.

Pepper's ghost is a device with mirrors used in 19th century melodramas to give the effect of transparent ghosts.

Performance art is a kind of fine art involving some degree of improvisation, in which often a single artist draws upon dance, music, drama, sound effects, slides, films, etc., and mixing these forms of expression. This art form is described as 'happenings', 'mixed-means theatre', 'performance art' and 'action art'. In this art form, the various parts of the performance function disharmoniously as in visual-art collage consisting of assembling elements usually found apart. Again, such a performance must be live and spontaneous. It can bring into it social criticism or protest and audience involvement. Performance art originated with the *avant-garde* artists of the late 1950s. American artist Allan Kaprow coined the term *happenings* to describe a one-time event in which people come together to execute new instructions in an open space outdoors. There is sudden discovery and surprise during performance. Happenings later took place within a performance space, e.g., *Moviehouse* (1965) is a piece by American sculptor Claes Oldenburg. He let several artists perform in the seats of a movie theatre while spectators watched from the aisles. Another form of performance art was by the American composer John Cage. He produced a 45 minute untitled piece in which one person read a text, another performed choreography, and a third produced the sounds. By 1970s performance art became more modest usually involving only one person who was writer, director and performer, all in one. The cross-discipline trends with mingling of theatre, music, motion picture images, choreography and language. Lee Bruer produced *Hajj* in 1983. It is an hour long poetry performance during which a woman sits at her dressing table and sees on the mirror her reflection as well as her past projected on screen. In the 1990s, German Pina Bausch incorporated sound and setting with her dance. Elizabeth Streb of USA mixed dance, gymnastics and circus acrobatics. American Laurie Anderson combined music, video, speech, and electronics in her work. Other successful performance artists include Anna Halprin, Meredith Monk, and Yvonne Rainer, Robert Wilson, and David Moss.

Performance group is the environmental theatre troupe of Richard Schechner.

Performer is a person who performs something for an audience. It could range from simple show of skills, dancing, singing, impersonating, depicting historical or fictional characters and the like. Presenting certain complex characters require great physical and psychological expressions. Good performance requires a lot of rehearsals. Some even take years of training such as the Indian dance performances of Kathak, Kathakali and Bharatanatyam; Japanese Bunraku puppet theatre, etc.

Periaktoi is a device by which three-sided prisms with different scenes painted on each side which could be revolved to change scenes. It was used in classical Greek and Roman theatres. During the Italian Renaissance, it was used at the wings. In England, it was introduced by Inigo Jones (1573-1652) for the performance of his masques.

Period is a term used in the history of literature for a convenient and arbitrary division of historical times. We may thus distinguish different periods of English literature such as Ranaissance, Restoration, Augustan, Romantic, Victorian, Modern, Postmodern, etc. Each period is marked by its specific characteristics such as Renaissance is known for creative arts; Augustan for its neoclassical styles; romantic with its stress on emotions and imagination and the like (*see* Periods of English Literature).

Periods of English Literature is classified differently by historians. Given below is a general division for easy reference.

650 to 1066	:	Old English or Anglo Saxon Period
1066 to 1400	:	Middle English Period
1350 to 1450	:	Age of Chaucer
1450 to 1550	:	Chaucer to Spenser
1500 to 1660	:	In general is called the Renaissance comprising different ages according to the reigning monarchs or major literary figures.
		1550 to 1600 Elizabethan Age or Age of Spenser
		1600 to 1625 Jacobean Age or Age of Shakespeare
		1625 to 1649 Caroline age or Age of Milton (1625-60)
		1649 to 1660 Commonwealth Puritan Period
1660 to 1798	:	Neoclassical Period
		1660 to 1700 The Restoration or Age of Dryden
		1700 to 1745 The Augustan Age or Age of Pope
		1745 to 1798 The Age of Transition or Age of Johnson
1798 to 1832	:	Romanticism
1832 to 1901	:	The Victorian Period

1901 to 1914	: The Edwardian Period
1901 to 1936	: Georgian Period
1914 to 1950	: Modern Period
1950-	: Post Modern Period

Period piece is the staging of a play belonging to an earlier period and performed in the costumes and style of that period. At times a modern play can be set in an earlier period like the way Arthur Miller sets *The Crucible* (1953) in the colonial times and is concerned with the Salem witchcraft trials. It was actually aimed at the then widespread congressional investigation of subversive activities in the United States.

Peripeteia/peripety is one of the elements of plot in the Greek drama consisting of the reversal of fortune or the intention of the hero. It implies a change of situation for the hero from prosperity to adversity. For example, in Sophocles' *Oedipus Rex*, Oedipus recognises the truth about his father whom he murdered and married his own mother. Peripety thus leads to a very complex dramatic irony. Aristotle refers to it in his *Poetics*, Ch. VI: "(Peripety) is the change from one state of things within the play to its opposite of the kind described, and that too in the way we are saying, in the probable or necessary sequence of events; as it is for instance in *Oedipus*: here the opposite of things is produced by the messenger, who, coming to gladden Oedipus and to remove his fears as to his mother, reveals the secret of his birth." It is a reversal of the direction of the action in the plot as a whole. Peripety is the change from one state of things in the play to its opposite. In the word peripety is contained the idea of boomerang or recoil effect of one's own action or falling into the pit that one has dug for someone else. Aristotle doesn't say that a peripety can happen only in relation to the hero (*see* Hamartia).

Periphrasis is a round about way of saying or writing something. It is also known as circumlocution. It is a device used in euphemism. In poetry such a circumlocution gives emphasis, e.g., in *Beowulf* 'ancient iron = sword', 'heaven's bliss = sun', 'weaver of peace = woman'.

Periscope ending is a scene at the end of a play which tells the audience what happens to the characters in the future.

Peroration is the concluding section of a speech with an emotional appeal to the audience and summing up the central arguments.

Persona is the character an actor plays in a drama quite different from the actor's own personality. Greatness of an actor is in playing a role that is dissimilar to his own personality and yet making it realistic on stage.

Personification is a figure of speech which ascribes human qualities to abstractions, animals, birds, plants and things of nature. In drama, such personification is done by humanising non-human things. In the medieval morality plays personification was done of virtues and vices, devils and angels. *Everyman*, the popular medieval morality play has personified characters of Fellowship, Kindred, Goods, Good Deeds, etc.

Perspective refers to viewpoint or visual angle. In cinema, film cuts from different cameras can give different perspectives to the audience. In drama, such change of viewpoint cannot be had. But perspectives can be mentally perceived. Modern dramatists like Bertold Brecht in his epic theatre experimented with montage technique in his *Life of Galileo*, placing characters in multiple perspectives to show different sides of Galileo. In some Jacobean plays, 'double perspectives' were employed by which the audience see a character from different angles such as good and evil. For example, Shakespeare's characterisation of Othello in *Othello*; characters in Webster's *The Duchess of Malfi*. In art, perspective means setting an object on a flat surface to give it a three-dimensional effect while seeing it from a particular angle. While constructing the stage, scenic perspective has to be kept in mind to have the appropriate scenic design.

Phallus is the tradition of comic actors in Greece and Rome wearing images of male genitals. It is suggestive of the origin of comedy from fertility rites. Occasionally in *commedia dell'arte* the Pantaloon wore such images.

Phatic communion refers to speech used in social reasons to communicate feelings rather than ideas. For example the casual greetings like 'How are you?'; 'How's weather up there?', etc. Such phrases in the theatre of the absurd with appropriate pause can have great significance. Dramatists like Samuel Beckett, Harold Pinter and Ionesco make use of phatic communion to convey hidden meaning behind with ironic effects.

Phenomenology is a 20th century philosophical movement which investigates *Phenomena* which human consciousness can comprehend. German philosopher Edmund Husserl is the founder of the movement and introduced the term in his book *Ideas: A General Introduction to Pure Phenomenology* (1913; 1931). Phenomenology is the study of the structures of consciousness that enable consciousness to refer to objects outside itself. This study requires reflection on the content of the mind to the exclusion of everything else. Husserl called this type of reflection the phenomenological reduction. Since the mind can be directed toward non-existent as well as real objects, Husserl noted that phenomenological reflection does not presuppose that anything exists, but rather amounts to a "bracketing of existence" that is, setting aside the question of the real existence of the contemplated object. Martin Heidegger claimed that phenomenology should make manifest what is hidden in ordinary everyday experience. French existentialist Jean-Paul Sartre tried to imbibe Heidegger's phenomenology to the philosophy of consciousness. Phenomenology has influenced theology, sociology, psychology, psychiatry, and literary criticism. It is one of the most important schools of contemporary philosophy. This philosophy can be applied to criticism inasmuch as it is devoted to describing the world of the author's consciousness, as manifested in the entire range of his or her works. But more important has been 'reader-response criticism'. For the reader, the work is what is given to consciousness. One can argue that the work is not something objective, existing independently of any experience of it, but is the experience of the reader. Criticism can thus take the form of a description of the reader's progressive movement through a text, analysing how readers produce meaning by making connections, filling in things left unsaid, anticipating and conjecturing and then having their expectations disappointed or confirmed. Another reader-oriented version of phenomenology is called 'Aesthetics of reception'. A work is an answer to questions posed by a 'horizon of expectations'. The interpretation of works should, therefore, focus not on the experience of an individual reader, but on the history of a work's reception and the relation to the changing aesthetic norms and sets of expectations that allow it to be read in different eras.

Phlyax is a type of play in the fourth century BC consisting of mime, burlesque of the classical Greek tragedy and daily comic experiences.

Phobia is irrational and excessive fear of something which is a symbolic substitute for a real threat. Such a phobia being irrational and absurd is treated comically by dramatists. Different types of phobia are agoraphobia (fear of open space), claustrophobia (fear of closed space), acrophobia (fear of heights), pathophobia (fear of disease), nyctophobia (fear of the night), microphobia (fear of insects), zoophobia (fear of animals), hydrophobia (fear of water), etc.

Phoenix society founded in 1919 was meant for the staging of neglected English drama, especially of the Restoration and Jacobean plays.

Physical time is the actual time taken by the audience to watch a play (*see* Dramatic time).

Picaresque is derived from the Spanish *picaro* who is a scheming trickster. Based on such a character a kind of novel appeared in the 16th century known as 'picaresque' such as *Lazarillo de Tormes* (Anonymous) and Aleman's *Guzman de Alfarache*. These are stories of rogues who are depicted as servants of several masters. They continue their wily tricks and finally repent of their misdeed. In English, such picaresque writings appear with Daniel Defoe's *Moll Flanders*, Henry Fielding's *Tom Jones*, Mark Twain's *Huckleberry Finn*, etc. Episodes in the life of such a picaro (rogue) has been turned into episodic plays, e.g., Dale Wasserman's *Man of La Mancha* is based on Cervantes' *Don Quixote*; Roger Miller's musical play *Big River* is an adaptation of Mark Twain's *Huckleberry Finn*.

Picture refers to the overall picture of a set seen from an average seat in the house (*see* Mise-en-scene).

Picture frame is the wooden arch above and on the sides of a performing area in a Proscenium arch stage (*see* Proscenium arch).

Piece bien faite (Well made play) is a term referring to a play with much suspense, well constructed plot, leading up to a crisis and climax, and a final resolution. The term was applied primarily to Victorien Sardou (1831-1908) who got his inspiration from Eugene Scribe (1791-1861). Henrik Ibsen was also influenced to a great extent by Eugene Scribe.

Pierrot is a character from the *commedia dell'arte*. He is a familiar awkward servant in his white face with white loose garments and a sagging hat.

Pin shot is the focusing of a narrow spotlight beam on an actor's head.

Pit is the area below the stage in older playhouses or the ground floor. In the Elizabethan times, it was the standing place for the groundlings. In modern context, it refers to the first rows meant for the orchestra.

Pity and fear is a term derived from Aristotle's *Poetics* where he states that 'tragedy effects through pity and fear the catharsis of the emotions'. Pity and fear are two emotions he describes as specially tragic emotions. Pity is occasioned by undeserved misfortune and fear by that of one like ourselves, i.e., by the misfortune of one like ourselves. 'Like ourselves' means a man of noble nature like ourselves in elemental feelings and emotions. With such a man we identify ourselves and pity his suffering and fear that what has happened to him may happen to us also. Pity and fear are very closely linked. Pity is caused by a sort of pain in the case of somebody who does not deserve it. This pity turns into fear when the suffering seems to be our own and we pity others in circumstances in which we should fear for ourselves. According to Aristotle there can be no pity where there is no fear as well. When the good people prosper we rejoice with them; when they suffer we share their pains and fears—and that is pity. If we ourselves are in terrible suffering and have nothing worse to suffer or fear, we also tend to be incapable of pity because we are absorbed in our own fear and cannot share any more with others. Tragic pity is felt only for the good. Aristotle's pity and fear are sympathy for the good part of mankind in the bad part of their experience. The tragic character in the play has to be far enough removed from ourselves to allow for the possibility of pity—but near enough to ourselves to allow for the possibility of fear. Since tragedy aims at rousing pity and fear it should show undeserved suffering of a good man. There is no tragedy in the situation of a bad man passing from misfortune to happiness, for it makes no appeal to our sense of pity and fear or to that of poetic justice. Shylock is the only case of a bad man rousing our pity as he is 'more sinned against than sinning.' If we pity him, it is because we recognise a certain nobility in his character.

Plagiarism is a literary theft by which a writer copies the ideas of another and presents as his own.

Plant is a clue to a dramatic situation. It is a clue placed in advance to make a scene effective (*see* Pointer).

Plastic scenery means scenery done in three dimensions rather than painted plain on a flat.

Platea is the open space for playing in front of a mansion stage in the medieval drama. It is different from the mansion representing particular locality such as Heaven, Hell, Jerusalem, etc. Platea is a space the actor shares with the audience and had a direct relationship with them. Shakespeare adapted platea as the apron stage.

Platt is an Elizabethan term for noting down the events of a play from entrances to exits with details of all the devices and props used.

Playbill is the 16th century programme with the details of the performance in a theatre. It is given to the audience with some details of the play. Some large playbills were used as posters on walls for publicity.

Play of ideas consists of issues and problems presented through a play. Dramatists like Henrik Ibsen and Bernard Shaw presented social, psychological and moral issues through their plays. Ibsen discusses social problems in his plays: *A Doll's House* (1879) tells of a loveless marriage and an overprotected wife; *Ghosts* (1881) deals with hereditary insanity and the conflict of generations; *Hedda Gabler* (1890) portrays the relationships of a strong-willed woman with those around her. Bernard Shaw examines social complicity of society and its evil in *Major Barbara* (1905) and *The Doctor's Dilemma* (1906). His *Pygmalion* (1914) is a didactic play about phonetics, love, and the exploitation of one human being by another; his five linked parable—plays under the collective title *Back to Methuselah* (1921)—examines human progress from Eden to a science-fiction future.

Play within a play is a brief play performed in course of another play. It was a device prevalent in the Elizabethan and Jacobean theatre, e.g., Shakespeare presents 'Pyramus and Thisbe' in *A Midsummer Night's Dream*; Bernard Shaw's *Man and Superman* (1903), transformed the Don Juan legend into a play. The series of discussions in the third act, "Don Juan in Hell", is a play within a play.

Playwright is the dramatist, the maker of a play.

Playwright's voice refers to certain lines in a play that are typical of the dramatist's feelings on the subject matter. In Classical Greek comedy, the chorus came forward and presented the author's views on various topics. Arnold Wesker, in his *Roots* (1959), makes use of the character of Beatie Bryant to speak out his mind in social criticism.

Pleasant and unpleasant plays is a term derived from Bernard Shaw who divided plays into pleasant and unpleasant instead of tragedy and comedy. He published a collection of plays in 1898 entitled *Plays Pleasant and Unpleasant*. The pleasant plays end happily and are less critical and satirical such as *Candida*, *Arms and the Man*, etc. Shaw's unpleasant plays are very critical and satirical exposing social evils such as *Mrs. Warren's Profession*, *Widower's Houses*, etc.

Pleasure and imitation: Tragedy according to Aristotle gives pleasure: "by raising pity and fear, or terror, to purge the mind of those such like passions, that is, to temper and reduce them to just measure with a kind of delight, stirr'd up by reading or seeing those passions well imitated" (Milton in his Preface to *Samson Agonistes*). The question arises, if people go to a tragedy for catharsis? Nowhere does Aristotle say that in *Poetics*. He mentions Catharsis only once; but refers to 'pleasure' of tragedy several times. "The tragic pleasure is that of pity and fear, and the poet has to produce it by a work of imitation" (Bywater's translation). Butcher translates as "The pleasure which the poet should afford is that which comes from pity and fear through imitation." In tragedy we "rejoice in our grieving". The pleasure is derived from the poet's skill as maker and imitator, from his power to make us follow him. It is "a kind of delight, stirr'd up by reading or seeing those passions well imitated." The pleasure of tragedy is derived from the imitation of emotions and situations which taken in themselves, or taken as they operate in real life, are forms of pain or causes of pain. The tragic poet, by his skill of his art brings the mind into sympathy. Thus he provokes the pure pleasure of exercising thought and emotion and the sense of sight and hearing from painful themes.

Pleasure gardens were popular gardens in London in the mid-17th to late 19th century, that offered people lawns, trees, flowers and refreshments. They could also be entertained with dance, band, circus, puppet shows, mazes, fireworks, theatre with farces and vaudeville.

Plot is the centre of Aristotle's discussion of tragedy in *Poetics*. His word 'mythos' is used for 'legend' or 'story' and is translated 'Plot'. A plot according to him consists of a beginning, middle and end. 'Beginning' initiates action which looks forward to something else. 'Middle' presumes what has gone before. 'End' follows from what has gone before and requires nothing further. In Chapter 5 he speaks of plot as 'unified stories'. In Chapter 6 he calls plot 'the whole structure of the incidents,' and 'the soul of tragedy'. The end of tragedy is plot and it is not a mere arrangement of events. It is the way in which action proceeds. Aristotle gives more importance to plot than character. There is no tragedy without plot, but there can be tragedy without character. (*see* Character). A tragic plot should be whole and complete. It must have certain size (magnitude), neither too short nor too long. It should be aesthetic and utilitarian. Plot should have a certain structure such as: Prologue, Episode, Exode, Parode (Choral song). A plot should have the elements of 'probability' and 'necessity'. The poet's concern is with the possible and not what has happened, but what might happen. A plot should follow unities of 'time', 'place', and 'action' (*see* Unities). In the plot of a play characters come in conflict with rising action, crisis, climax, and falling action with resolution. The plot is something that the poet makes (*Poetics* Ch. 9); but with regard to a story it is immaterial if the poet makes it or not (*Poetics* Ch. 17). When Aristotle says, Tragedy must have "a beginning, a middle and an end" he refers to the poet as a maker. The beginning and end are within the control of the poet. E.M. Forster in *Aspects of the Novel* defines the difference between story and plot. A story begins and ends arbitrarily as they are not governed by reason. The plot is something which the poet makes, e.g., The king died and then the queen died (story); the king died, then the queen died of grief (plot). A plot must have a meaning. The poet who makes the plot with a beginning and end has it within his control as he is the maker. "A beginning is that which is not itself necessarily after anything else" (Ch. 7). The emphasis is on the *necessarily* upon the logic of connection. But the poet may not have to refer to matters supposed to have happened earlier in the story. *King Oedipus* is a fine example. The play begins with the plague in Thebes and the need to release the city from it by discovery and the punishment of the guilty man. The play's process is the process of discovery; its end, the punishment. The initial situation of the plague, etc., is given immediately in dramatic terms. Each step Oedipus takes provides the occasion for revealing some part of the antecedent knowledge which is necessary for the process of discovery. The idea of wholeness of a plot is referred to when he says that it should be "with all the organic unity of a living creature "(Ch.13). Again the concept of order is brought out in Ch. 7: "...to be beautiful a living creature...and every whole made up of parts must present a certain order in its arrangement of parts." The idea of order, harmony, proportion and completeness are all present in the normal Greek idea of what is beautiful.

Plough Monday play is a 16th century English practice of plays performed on the Monday after Epiphany (January 6) or

Monday after Twelfth Night. Such plays were similar to mummer's (St. George's) plays in which characters were farm labourers and dealt with the death of one of them. The play is symbolic of the death and resurrection of the year.

Plug is a line added during laughter of the audience to elicit more laughter.

Poetic drama is verse drama in which dialogue in part or whole is metrical and sometimes rhyming. Usually they are written in blank verse. It may be written in prose as well, but is read like poetry. In the Restoration times heroic dramas were written in heroic couplets (iambic pentameter lines rhyming in pairs). Most of the tragedies and serious plays up to the 19th century were poetic dramas. The term is not to be confused with dramatic poetry. In his essay, 'Poetry and drama', T.S. Eliot claimed that poetry can communicate states which are difficult to communicate through prose in drama. Poetic drama 'without losing that contact with the everyday world with which drama must come to terms... the border of these feelings which only music can express.' Hence, it is the use of musical beat in verse that distinguishes between prose and poetic drama in the opinion of Eliot. Poetic drama deals with life but the characters tend to be more emotional than usual, e.g., Shakesperean plays fall into the category of poetic drama. T.S. Eliot revived this genre in the 20th century with his *Murder in the Cathedral*, *The Family Reunion*, *The Cocktail Party*, *The Confidential Clerk*, and *The Elder Statesman*. Others who attempted the genre include Lascelles Abercrombie, Gordon Bottomely, John Drinkwater, and Lord Dunsaney. W.H. Auden wrote in collaboration with Christopher Isherwood three verse plays, namely, *The Dog Beneath the Skin*, *The Ascent of F6*, and *On the Frontier*. Synge's *Riders to the Sea* is a poetic drama written in prose.

Poetic justice is a term coined by Thomas Rhymer (1641-1713) in his book *The Tragedies of the Last Age Considered* (1678) which critically attacked Elizabethan drama. He was of the view that evil ought to be punished and good rewarded. Hence, literature should reflect some moral purpose giving a sense of poetic justice. In Shakespearean drama, poetic justice is not maintained as along with the guilty person's punishment the innocent too suffer unjustly, e.g., in *Hamlet*, both the evil Claudius as well as Hamlet suffer the same fate.

Pointer is indirect clue to the motivation of a character or a dramatic situation. Such pointers help the audience to get the clues to some secrets and maintain dramatic suspense and irony. 'Pointer' is distinguished from a 'plant' in so far it is likely to be recognised at once as a clue. A 'plant' is a clue which will be recognised only later. Henrik Ibsen uses such pointer in his plays very effectively. In *Ghosts,* Act I, Manders and Mrs. Alving talk about insuring the orphanage against fire which is a clue to the fire that rages by the end of Act II and leads to final climax in Act III.

Point of attack is moment in a play when the action of plot begins. It can happen in the beginning of the first act itself as in *Othello* when Iago decides to wreck Othello. A dramatist can begin the point of attack in later scenes or acts.

Political theatre is drama dealing with political and social events. In it a dramatist analyses social processes and can communicate it directly or indirectly. In direct presentation, the drama depicts its political ideology by attacking sociopolitical attitudes. Indirectly political theatre makes use of allegory and parable to awaken in the audience sociopolitical attitudes. In the 20th century, a political theatre was a medium used by Marxists. Dramatists who wrote in this genre include Weimar Republic (1919-1933), Piscator (1893-1966) and Brecht (1898-1956). Shakespeare's *Henry IV Parts I and II* and *Antony and Cleopatra* belong to political theatre.

Poor theatre is a term applied to theatre that is centred on the actor and his/her involvement with the audience. It calls for a rejection of all artificial elements such as technological devices of light, sound and music, elaborate makeup, costumes and masks. The term has been used by the Polish director Jerzy Grotoswski who experimented with the Polish Laboratory Theatre in the 1950s and 1960s. He aimed on the actor's physical, vocal and emotional resources. His finding revealed that human beings do not act naturally in moments of intense emotional experience such as shock, joy, sorrow; instead they begin to articulate with rhythmic signs, songs or dance. In a moment of intense joy a person can emotionally behave in an extreme manner such as weeping intensely with some vague articulations. In his analysis of extreme situations Grotowski was led to taboo and myths in society. English stage and motion picture director Peter Brook (1925) was influenced by Grotowski and has produced motion pictures that are experimental in nature such as *The Beggar's Opera* (1953), *Lord of the Flies* (1963), *Tell Me Lies* (1968), *King Lear* (1971), *La Tragédie de Carmen* (1984), and *The Mahabharata* (1989). 'Poor theatre' can be understood best in contrast with 'Rich theatre' (*see* Rich theatre).

Popular theatre is a general term for theatre popular among common people such as melodrama, street theatre, political theatre, folk plays, mumming plays, circus, etc. Such theatrical performances are considered crude as they emphasise the body and its physical activity than the use of the head in its intellectual expressions. Recent studies have made popular theatre popular as great dramatists like Shakespeare and Ben Jonson, etc., had recourse to it in the characterisation of fools and clowns.

Portable theatres are the temporary stages built by travelling performers in the marketplaces during country fares and festivals. The usual performances consisted of 19th century melodrama, Biblical and historical stories presented before the modern theatres began. It is also applied to puppet shows and acrobatics performed at the fairground booths.

Portfolio is the folder with the details of a performer such as his resume, photo, reviews of his performance.

Poster is the bill hung to inform the audience about the fares of a show.

Postponement is a device by which a dramatist sustains suspense by adding unexpected materials in course of a serious and tense situation. It breaks the tension of the scene and builds it further to its climax, e.g., Shakespeare adds the farewell scene of Laertes in *Hamlet* (Act I scene iii) in between the information Hamlet gets about his father's ghost and the encounter with it.

Posture is the body position of an actor which communicates several things such as physical makeup, feelings and emotions. An actor can communicate in silence through facial expressions. Postures are basic to tableau presentations which can very powerfully communicate tragic or comic effects.

Practical scenery is scenery that functions on stage such as a fire that cooks food, a real fountain from which water flows, etc.

Pre-acting is a initial performance in mime anticipating a later performance. For example, in *Hamlet,* Prince Hamlet invites a troupe of visiting players to perform a play 'the Mousetrap' about fratricide. This is a play-within-a-play that prepares for fratricidal killings in the play. Such a pre-acting allows the audience to be prepared for what is to come and can focus attention on the various characters.

Premiere is the official first public performance of a play.

Presence is the ability an actor has in drawing the attention of the audience. It can be done by the appeal of his personality, physical features, facial expressions and gait.

Presentational theatre is a variety of performance in which the actors directly address the audience. This device comes in contrast to the representational style in traditional Renaissance and Victorian plays in which the actors speak to the audience indirectly through asides, soliloquies, and through a chorus that make comments. Most African, Oriental, Pre-Renaissance Western, and 20th century *avant-garde* theatre is presentational. The German playwright Bertolt Brecht, in his representational plays, exposed even the lighting instruments and stage machinery to create an awareness in the audience of their witnessing the play (*see* Representational theatre).

Pride is the degree of self-esteem a character has. The higher the self-esteem the better the dramatic action of the play. The Greek concept of 'Hubris' in classical tragedy refers to this overweening pride, confidence or self-complacency that results in arrogance in thoughts, words, and deeds. This attitude arouses the jealousy of the gods who punish the victim of hubris, e.g., in Aeschylus's *Oresteia*, Agamemnon walks on the sacred carpet and is guilty of hubris. Shakespeare in *King Lear* presents Lear a victim of hubris by his imagining himself godlike in power. In comedy, unchecked pride in a character leads to much laughter.

Prince Charles' Men is the theatre company of Edward Alleyn in 1616.

Prince Henry's Men is the name by which 'Lord Admiral's men' began to be called after the death of Queen Elizabeth in 1603.

Principal boy is the main role of the hero in a pantomime played by a beautiful girl wearing blonde wig, high heels, tight clothing and a tunic.

Principals are the leading characters in a play. Some critics consider only the protagonist as the principal in a play.

Prior life refers to the knowledge of the apparent life of a character being presented on stage. The actor playing the role needs to make a detailed study of the character's background such as ancestry, family relationships, talents, taste, etc. Such a pre-knowledge helps the actor to present the character more vividly.

Problem play refers to those plays dealing with a particular social problem in a realistic manner with the didactic purpose of bringing about a change in public opinion, e.g., plays on women's liberation, drug abuse, child labour, etc. It is also known as 'thesis play' or 'propaganda play'. It is a dramatic genre popularised by Henrik Ibsen through his plays such as *A Doll's House* (on exploitation of women); *Ghosts* (on venereal disease and incest). In such plays the protagonist is set in a social problem and the dramatist uses him/her to speak out his ideas. Dramatists who wrote problem plays include Shakespeare (*Measure for Measure; All's Well That Ends Well*, *Troilus and Cressida* etc); Bernard Shaw (*Pygmalion* on English Speech and class system; *Mrs. Warren's Profession* on prostitution, etc).

Producer is the person who sees to the overall administration of a theatrical production. He raises and allocates funds; gets the various persons required such as the cast, the technicians, designers and staff. In cinema the producer is the one who finances the production while the director makes it. Large productions may have several producers such as executive, associate, or co-producers. These will see to a particular aspect of the performance. At times a person who invests money into a production is called a producer. An organisation can be a producer like the Theatre Guild which has been responsible for various Broadway productions from 1920s to 1940s.

Professional players is a medieval term for professional actors who earned a living by it unlike amateurs who acted once in a while during festivals. Such professional actors formed themselves into groups of travelling players who performed tragedies, comedies, masques and acrobatics. Certain of such groups were patronised eventually by the aristocratic families in the Elizabethan times.

Programme is the playbill with the list of the cast with their acting experience as well as relevant information about the play.

Progression is the sequence of events in a plot. However, the chronological sequence and time-flow can be broken with certain effects such as flashbacks.

Prologue is a forward which consists of a speech before the dramatic action begins. It is presented by one of the actors. In Greek tragedy 'prologue' was an early action before the chorus made its entry. Euripides presented a monologue as a prologue to his plays. In the medieval drama a prologue was presented by the master of ceremonies. The practice continued during the Elizabethan and Restoration plays, e.g., the Prologue to Sheridan's *School for Scandal* was written by the great actor David Garrick and refers to scandal mongering:

> A school for Scandal! Tell me, I beseech you,
> Needs there a school this modish art to teach you?
> No need of lessons now, the knowing think;
> We might as well be taught to eat and drink....

In the Naturalist drama the device was dropped. However, in the modern theatre, 'prologue' is reintroduced to give important information about the play and to maintain a warm relationship between the actors and the audience.

Promenade performance is a drama which takes itself to the audience. It is a type of performance based on the medieval mystery plays. Promenade theatre performs the various scenes with flexible staging using 'mansions' of the medieval morality plays. The method of performance establishes direct contact with the audience arousing in them child-like curiosity and wonder. The performance of *The Mystery Plays* at the Cottesloe Theatre in 1985 was a success in this genre.

Prompt book is the copy of the play's script meant for the prompter. On it the stage manager and the director make notes and technical cues during rehearsals.

Prompter is the person who prompts the lines of the script to the actors knowing well the rhythm and pauses of the play. When an actor has skipped portions of the script the prompter has to make on-the-spot adjustments and prompt important lines.

Prompt corner is the place on the left corner of the stage usually just behind the proscenium arch.

Propaganda play is concerned with political and social problems, e.g., Bernard Shaw wrote *Pygmalion* on English Speech and class system; *Mrs. Warren's Profession* on prostitution (*see* Problem play).

Property is shortened as 'prop' referring to stage objects used in the play such as weapons and tools. These props are of different categories: (1) hand props which are handled by actors, e.g., glasses, papers, etc.; (2) Set props are those larger items such as furniture; and (3) Dress props consist of pictures, curtains, etc. Proper handling of props can give realistic touch to acting and was to a great extent used by Stanislavski and Brecht in their plays. Naturalistic film acting encouraged elaborate use of props. Charlie Chaplin was very successful in using various props to induce laughter in his comical acting. In Samuel Beckett's *Waiting for Godot* the dramatist makes use of props symbolically such as Lucky's hat, Pozzo's watch, and Gogo's boots. Chekhov makes use of a dead seagull as a symbol in his play *Seagull* (1896).

Prop manager known as 'prop man' is responsible for arranging all the props for a play. He also sees to the off-stage effects.

Proscenium arch is the structure that separates the main acting area from the auditorium with a picture frame through which the audience watch a drama in a proscenium arch theatre. It was very popular in the 19th and early 20th centuries in most Western theatres. The picture frame gives the illusion of a room through an invisible fourth wall. The term probably originated from Greek 'Proskenion' which was placing of a framed picture behind the scene of action. The Italian theatre used wings and borders. Inigo Jones (1573-1652) adapted the Italian proscenium arch for his court masques. During the Restoration period the performance took place on a front-stage in front of the picture. In course of time the dramatic action began to be performed within the arch. The proscenium arch was used in naturalistic drama in the 19th century fourth-wall plays in which box sets were used. The arch and curtain separated the auditorium from the stage. The arch became a covering for the curtain lines, flies and the stage equipment. The proscenium arch can obstruct the vision of those at the sides and limit stage settings. Modern theatres prefer open stages, however the proscenium arch continues to be present.

Proscenium Theatre has been a Western form of stage variation since the Renaissance. The proscenium is the wall separating the stage from the auditorium. The audience see the play through the proscenium arch (*see* Proscenium arch). There is a curtain that hangs in the space between. The arch hides the curtain line and provides an imaginary space where the actors feel they are not seen by the audience. The proscenium evolved with the purpose of masking scenery and scene changing machinery. It gives an off-stage space for performers to make their exits and entrances. Proscenium being an architectural barrier, it establishes separation between the stage and the audience giving a sense of distance.

Proscenium doors are those opening to the forestage on either side in front of the proscenium arch in the Restoration theatre.

Prose is a kind of written language that has no regular metre and rhyme as in poetry. It is the language of common speech and writing. However, it can have its own rhythmic quality to communicate effectively.

Prose drama is drama written in prose in contrast to poetic drama. From ancient times verse was used in heroic tragedy as well as in the Tudor, Jacobean and Restoration periods. This continued to the 18th and 19th centuries. However, in the 20th century drama began to be written more in prose with the emergence of naturalist dramatists like Ibsen. Dialogue in such prose drama is in prose.

Proskenion is a Greek term referring either to the facade of the skene building with painted set for the play or the acting space in front of it.

Protagonist is derived from 'protos' in Greek. In ancient Greek drama it meant 'first combatant' or 'the principal character' around whom the action revolves. In Greek tragedy, characters were divided into Protagonist (first actor), Deuteragonist (second actor) and Tritagonist (third actor). The concept of the protagonist as first actor began with Thepsis in the 6th century BC. Aeschylus and Sophocles added second and third actors. The conflict in the drama centres around the protagonist. Some plays are named after the protagonist such as Shakespeare's *Macbeth*, *Othello*, *Hamlet*, *King Lear*, *Julius Caesar*, etc.

Protasis in Greek means 'stretching forward' and refers to the opening movement of a play in which characters are introduced. It is followed by epitasis, catastasis and catastrophe.

Protatic character is presented at the beginning of a play to expose the main dramatic situation.

Proverbe dramatique is a French drama to explain a proverb through play-acting done in a game-like manner with proverbial dialogue. It was a practice in the French salons in the 17th and 18th centuries to have such parlour games. Alfred de Musset in the mid-19th century became the master craftsman in the proverbe dramatique.

Psychic distance (*see* Aesthetic distance).

Psychodrama is a therapeutic dramatic presentation meant to help people. It is conducted by a therapist or a director who gives hypothetical situations and problems to the participants and lets them role play and derive solutions. It helps patients assess their own condition and see themselves in a given situation. Psychodrama is not meant for public performance and has no artistic purpose. It can also be performed by a group of players at a crisis management workshop presenting a particular crisis situation in the lives of people. Seeing the performance the audience can be helped in their crisis management.

Psychology is the scientific study of behaviour and experience which has its relevance to drama. Modern psychology collects facts about human behaviour and experience and develops psychological theories. In drama, a character's psychological development as well as his/her relationship with other characters have their impact on its development. To take an example Ibsen employs a great deal of psychology in his character portrayal. In *Ghosts* he puts into the mouth of his protagonist Mrs. Alving a very powerful psychological statement: "I am half inclined to think we are all ghosts, Mr.Manders. It is not only what we have inherited from our fathers and mothers that exist again in us, but all sorts of dead ideas....They are not actually alive in us; but they are dormant...we can never be rid of them ..." Act II). The Pastor and Mrs.Alving debate ways of handling the threatened scandal concerning her dead husband. Ibsen has his eyes upon her shaken psyche. The development of thought in a play can be indicative of the psychology of the author or his social environment. For example Shakespeare's presentation of a character like *Hamlet* is representative of the renaissance man.

Psychotechnique is a term coined by Stanislavski to refer to the inner working of an actor and its impact on himself. The unconscious experiences of the actor has its own influence on his depiction of a character in course of a play, e.g., an actor who is a divorcee may have some unconscious effects on him while acting the role of a husband.

Public theatre is the name by which open-air theatres were known in the Elizabethan times (*see* Open theatre).

Pulitzer Prizes are a series of 21 awards for outstanding contributions in drama, music, letters, and journalism. It was established in 1917 by the will of Joseph Pulitzer, publisher of the *New York World*. His legacy of $ 2,000,000 to found the Columbia University School of Journalism and $ 500,000 of that amount to be given as annual prizes "for the encouragement of public service, public morals, American literature, and the advancement of education." Originally, four categories of American literature, namely, novel, play, US history and American biography, were given the award. The awards are given annually by Columbia University at the recommendation of the Pulitzer Prize Board. The Board appointed annually its juries for each of the categories.

Punch and Judy show is a puppet show performed in fairs and parks. Punch is a hunchback with a long, vicious, hook nose. He is a bullying character in puppet theatre derived from Pulcinella of the *commedia dell'arte*. He is depicted as an aggressive character ill-treating his wife Judy and other characters. Usually he is defeated at the end. The whole show is watched by Toby the dog who sits at the side.

Puncinello is the traditional humpbacked stupid comical servant in *commedia dell'arte* (*see* Punch).

Punch line is the line that is very important in a play which is delivered very carefully at the appropriate time.

Puppets are dolls used in a theatrical performance. They represent human beings, animals, or mythical figures. There are three types of puppets: marionettes, glove puppets (mitten puppets), and rod or stick puppets. The marionettes are operated from above with strings attached to the head, hands, feet, and waist. The glove puppet is operated by hands placed inside glove-dolls and the movements of the head and limbs are manipulated by the finger movements. Punch and Judy shows are performed with glove puppets. Rod or stick puppets are flat or three-dimensional figures operated from below with rods or sticks. Usually the head and neck are supported by a rod. The hands are manipulated by two more rods while the legs hang free (*see* Puppet theatre).

Puppet theatre is an ancient theatrical performance found in ancient India, Egypt, Greece, and China. Often folk-tales are performed in Java with puppets appearing as shadows on a translucent sheet. In the middle ages, European folk artists adapted hand puppets such as the English Punch and Judy, the French Guignol, and the German Kasperle. These puppet shows presented comedy, violent fights, incidents of domestic life. The *Bunraku* or *Joruri* and *Kabuki* theatre of Japan popular in the 16th and 17th centuries used large puppets operated by wires and levers to perform traditional heroic dramas or domestic tragedies. Sometimes black-clad people operate them on stage. (*see* Kabuki). In the 18th and 19th centuries most dramas were also performed by puppets or marionettes in the West. Nowadays puppets are seen in films, television and children's theatre, e.g., noted US puppet TV show "Kukla, Fran, and Ollie"; Jim Henson's puppet shows "Sesame Street" and "The Muppet Show". Puppet shows are performed in modern times with the accompaniment of music with dialogue by the operators. It has a grotesque quality as it can make dead things alive in performance. Puppet shows, being very appealing to children, Walt Disney has brought out several puppet versions of films such as *Bambi*, *Pinocchio*, etc.

Purgation in drama refers to purging of undesirable elements in the audience. A tragedy arouses certain emotions which are quelled by purgation (*see* Catharsis).

Purim plays evolved in the middle ages during the Jewish Purim festival. It is a late Jewish festival commemorating the deliverance of the Persian Jews from the hands of the Persian king Xerxes I. This is recorded in the Book of Esther in the *Bible*. The feast is held on the 14th and 15th days of the Jewish month of Adar in spring, with merriment, almsgiving and chanting verses from the Book of Esther. The celebration is accompanied with masquerades and plays based on the stories in the Book of Esther communicating the message that with Yahweh's help insurmountable battles can be won. Eventually, other Biblical stories were added with folk elements. This became popular with the Yiddish communities of eastern Europe.

Puritanism is a 16th century movement within the Church of England which sought to establish a middle course between Roman Catholicism and the ideas of the Protestant reformers. It had a continuous life within the church until the Stuart Restoration (1660). The term Puritanism is also used in a broader sense to refer to various groups that kept the values of the puritans like the Separatists in the 16th century, the Quakers in the 17th century, and Nonconformists after the Restoration. Often the term Puritanism is applied to rigid moralism, or religious narrowness. Puritan theology is a version of Calvinism and asserts the basic sinfulness of mankind. It also declares that by an eternal decree God has determined that some will be saved through the righteousness of Christ despite their sins. No one can be certain in this life what his or her eternal destiny will be. The experience of conversion was therefore central to Puritan spirituality. Puritanism as a religious movement became a social force under Queen Elizabeth I. In course of time the Puritan influence led to the closure of theatres in 1642 under the Commonwealth (1640-1660). Only during the Restoration of Monarchy in 1660 with the return of Charles II did the theatre reopen with the Comedy of Manners.

Q

Quart d'heure in French means quarter of an hour and refers to a curtain-raiser play or a short one-act play popular in France.

Quarto in Latin means 'in fourth.' It is a size of a book printed on sheets folded into four leaves with eight pages. Many of Shakespeare's plays were printed in quarto. Different editions of the work is called First Quarto, Second Quarto, etc.

Queen's Men is the common name of 'Queen Henrietta's men', a Jacobean theatre company founded by Christopher Beeston in 1625, named after the queen of Charles I.

Queen Ann's Men is a theatre company founded in 1603, named after the queen.

Queen of Bohemia's Men is a Jacobean theatre company founded in 1628.

Queen Elizabeth's Men is an Elizabethan theatre company founded in 1628.

Queen Henrietta's Men is a Jacobean theatre company founded by Christopher Beeston in 1625, popularly known as 'Queen's Men' after the name of Charles I's queen.

Quem quaeritis in Latin means 'Whom do you seek?' It is the question asked by the two angels to the Marys who went to the tomb of Christ and found the stone rolled away and his body missing (Gospel of Luke 24:5). Based on this Easter event medieval liturgical drama used to be performed on the Easter mysteries. *Quem quaeretis* is vital to the development of liturgical drama in Europe.

Qualitative and quantitative elements of drama are discussed by Aristotle in his *Poetics*. The quantitative element of tragedy consists of its development from prologue to exodus. "A tragedy is the imitation of an action that is serious, has magnitude, and is complete in itself... ." A tragedy ought to have six qualitative elements according to Aristotle. " Every tragedy, therefore, must contain six parts which determine its quality. They are Spectacle, Melody, Diction, Character, Thought, and Plot; two of them arise from the means, one from the manner, and three from the objects imitated... . The most important of these six is the Plot... ."

Quid pro quo is a Latin phrase meaning 'something for something' and is applied to a situation of deliberate or accidental misunderstanding or misinterpretation. By this device something is substituted for something else bringing about comic effect. Examples of such device are found in Shakespeare's *The Comedy of Errors*; Jonson's *Alchemist*; Sheridan's *School for Scandal;* Oscar Wilde's *The Importance of Being Earnest*, etc.

Quotation is a 20th century device used in literature by which a text from a literary work is incorporated into another. We find examples in Samuel Beckett's *Waiting for Godot* where he adds lines from Marlowe's *Dr. Faustus* in the dialogue between Didi and Pozzo. Such quotations add dramatic irony to the dialogue.

Quotation titles refer to some titles of books derived from some phrases from the work of an author. For example, Hemingway's *For Whom the Bell Tolls* is from John Donne's *Meditation 17*; Aldous Huxley's *Brave New World* is from Shakespeare's *The Tempest*; Thomas Hardy's *Far From the Madding Crowd* is from Thomas Gray's *Elegy Written in a Country Churchyard*.

R

Radio drama consists of voice and sound effects. It involves no costumes, light effects and other props required in a stage performance. In a radio drama, dialogue is mingled along with the narrative. It is quite difficult to write the script for this dramatic genre as feelings and sense of space have to be communicated through sound effects and change of tone. Examples of radio play include Dylan Thomas' *Under Milk Wood*; Samuel Beckett's *All That Fall*; Louis MacNiece's *Christopher Columbus*; Harold Pinter's *The Go-Between*, etc.

Raisonneur means an ideal spectator or a chorus character who is able to present his view very close to that of an author.

Rake is the inclination of the stage from the front edge which adds to the impression of 'perspective scenery' (*see* Perspective). A steeply raked stage helps in creating an atmosphere of intimacy between the actors and the audience.

Range in drama refers to the different roles an actor is able to play according to his age, sex, voice, physical appearance and personality. A role is offered to an actor keeping in mind his range. However, an actor may have a wider actual range than what is perceived by others. The term can also be applied to an author in reference to his literary sensibility in his social, political, literary background, etc. Hence, when an author writes out of his range, the readers can easily notice it.

Reading is the interpretation of a given script by an actor while performing.

Reader's theatre is a performance of a play to an audience with emphasis on the script which is read aloud. Such a performance does not require the actors to be in their appropriate costumes and perform the required movements on stage.

Rationalism is derived from Latin *ratio* (reason). In philosophy it is a system of thought that emphasizes the role of reason in acquiring knowledge. This comes in contrast to empiricism which gives emphasis to experience. Rationalism is identified with the 17th century French philosopher, René Descartes. Descartes believed that by means of reason alone, certain universal, self-evident truths could be discovered, from which the remaining content of philosophy and the sciences could be deductively derived. He assumed that these self-evident truths were innate, not derived from sense experience. This type of rationalism was developed by Spinoza and Leibniz. It was opposed by the British empiricists like John Locke who believed that all ideas are derived from the senses. In England, Rationalism had its influence on religion and literature of the 18th century.

Realism is a term loosely applied to the observed facts of life and an attempt to describe human behaviour and surroundings as they are. It is generally restricted to a movement that began in the mid-19th century, in reaction to the highly subjective approach of romanticism. The difference between realism and naturalism is harder to define, however, the two terms are often used interchangeably. The distinction lies in the fact that realism is concerned directly with what is observed by the senses while naturalism attempts to apply scientific theories to art. Realism in theatre aims to present people in their daily life situations with their setting and costumes. The language of spoken speech is used in the dialogues on stage. Henrik Ibsen is the dramatist who revolutionised the concept of realistic presentation on stage. He influenced G.B. Shaw, Chekhov and Strindberg. In order to make better realistic presentation on stage Stanislavski began his actor's training method. Social realism in theatre is a Russian concept developed by Anatoli Lunacharsky (1875-1933). Social realism called for adaptation of the classics to people's social life. Psychological realism led to the analysis of human thought and feeling through stream of consciousness method.

Reception is the response of the audience or critics to a literary work. In drama reception depends on Codes and Conventions. Codes can be found in the whispered speech, tone, posture, gestures, facial expressions, type of costumes, etc. When a character speaks besides his personal opinion he may be expressing the attitudes of his social milieu, family or parents. The audience responds to these whispered codes differently. Convention is a code the dramatist shares with the audience. There are codes of behaviour, speech and costumes fit for a particular character in a naturalist drama. A pauper does not behave and dress like a monarch and vice versa. These conventions are at times unnatural devices in a drama as for instance in presenting a drama on conquest the audience suspends its disbelief and regards the stage as a battlefield and the actors as kings and warriors. When the characters speak in soliloquy and asides, the audience understands it as a convention to reveal characters or as comments on actions or persons. 'Reception theory' analyses the social and psychological implications of a text on the audience.

Recognition is defined by Aristotle in his *Poetics* as "a movement from ignorance to awareness". He gives the example of Oedipus recognising the truth that he had killed his father and married his own mother. Such a recognition brings about pain in the character. The audience too feels the pain as the character goes through the process of recognition (*see* Anagnorisis, Discovery).

Reconciliation is a term popularised by Shakespearean critic Andrew Bradley in his *Shakespearean Tragedy* (1904). According to him a tragedy leads to a kind of reconciliation at the end bringing about healing to a stressful situation to the characters as well as the audience. Bradley cites the example of King Lear getting reconciled with Cordelia.

Red Bull is the 17th century theatre in London used by companies like Queen Ann's Men.

Rederijkers are the members of a Flemish rhetoric group in the 16th century that performed in the open air which might have influenced the Elizabethan open air stage.

Reformation was the great 16th century religious revolution in the Christian church meant to reform the practices and doctrines in the Roman Catholic church. It led eventually to the ecclesiastical supremacy of the Pope in the West and the establishment of the Protestant churches. Its leaders were Luther in Germany, Calvin in Geneva, Zwingli in Zurich and Knox in Scotland. They sought to establish the supreme authority of the *Bible* and the doctrine of justification by faith. They rejected the doctrine of the Transubstantiation of the Eucharist, veneration of Mary and Saints and the authority of the Pope. It completely altered the medieval way of life in Western Europe and initiated the era of modern history. The movement dates from the early 16th century, when Martin Luther first defied the authority of the Church. The English revolt from Rome is different from the rest of Europe. The revolt became national as the king and parliament acted together and gave to the king the ecclesiastical jurisdiction previously exercised by the Pope. In England, the political break came with the decision of King Henry VIII to divorce his first wife Catherine of Aragón, being issueless. He married Anne Boleyn in 1533 and made the archbishop of Canterbury approve of his divorce from Catherine. Henry was then excommunicated by the Pope which led the parliament to appoint the king and his successors as supreme head of the Church of England. This led to the establishment of the National Anglican Church. However, Henry VIII remains legendary for his six successive wives.

Regional drama refers to drama with regional characteristics such as dialect, costumes and manners. In the beginning regional elements were strong in the mystery plays belonging to Chester, York and Wakefield cycles. However, with the professional theatre centring in London, regional elements were ignored. Charles II's Royal Charter of 1660 introduced recognised patent theatres, namely, Drury Lane and Lincoln's Inn Fields. These theatres got the monopoly of staging drama. By the Licensing Act of 1737 Drury Lane and Covent Garden (Lincoln's Inn patent passed on to Covent Garden) got the patent which continued up to 1843. This resulted in the disappearance of regional drama. With the rise of Naturalism, dramatists like Ibsen and Chekhov attempted regional drama. However, regionalism became subservient to their psychological and social interests. Fringe theatres and community theatres in recent times have taken to regional presentations. Fringe theatre began as a protest against the established theatre in the 1960s. Effort was made to depict on stage the working classes in the plays of Arnold Wesker and Edward Bond. Thus, community theatre began since 1968 in Britain consisting of fringe groups that presented social problems of racial minorities. *Community theatre* is amateur performances by the residents of a locality. It began since 1968 in Britain. It consisted of fringe groups that presented social problems of racial minorities. In their effort to present situations realistically, they even lived among communities to experience their problems and tensions. In the United States, regional theatres are resident theatres located outside professional theatre centres like the Broadway. Some of the known regional theatres include Guthrie Theatre in Minneapolis, Goodman Theatre in Chicago, Alley Theatre in Houston.

Rehearsal is the practice sessions of a play in preparation for its performance. Rehearsals can take long periods of time depending on the nature of the play. A dress-rehearsal is done before the public performance of a play as it should be with costumes, stage props and techniques.

Relation to characters is establishing the link between one character and the others in a play. The actors who play various roles ought to give the impression that they are connected with one another in actual relationships of blood, friendship, etc., to render a performance as realistic as possible.

Relation to objects is the link established between an actor and the objects and props he /she uses in a performance. For example, an actor wearing the costume of a king ought to feel at ease wearing it as though belonging to him. Such a relationship established makes one act realistically without feelings of embarrassment.

Relaxation is the physical and mental ease an actor experiences in the course of a performance. Muscular and mental tension can divert one's concentration on stage.

Relief is the device used in drama to reduce dramatic tension by giving a new twist to the development of the plot by presenting a new character, changing of the scene, lowering of the emotional intensity by alienation effect, etc. In a tragedy 'comic relief' is brought about by a dramatist by inserting some comical situations as the tragedy progresses, to relieve tension in the audience. This has a psychological effect on the audience, e.g., the episode of the drunken porter in *Macbeth*; the grave diggers in *Hamlet*.

Renaissance meaning *rebirth* is used to describe European history between 1350 to 1600 when there was great revival of learning in humanities, science and exploration. Beginning in the 14th century Italy, it was a time of revival of interest in classical learning, art and creativity. Renaissance began the modern world after the Middle Ages under the influence of the Greek and the Roman models. Humanism is central to the movement and it aimed at preparing the 'universal man' as demanded in the *Courtesy Books*. He had to be a man of strength, character and culture being trained in philosophy, politics, athletics, and various arts. Renaissance literature is imbued with the imaginative spirit of humanism and called for a balanced development of body and mind. It is an era of Reformation and Protestantism led by Martin Luther (1483-1546) who sought liberalism in religion which led to some extreme cases of individualism in religion. In England, the break with the Catholic church was ushered in by King Henry VIII's (1491-1547) revolt due to his divorce of his wife Catherine of Aragon to marry Anne Boleyn. Subsequently, the Anglican church was established of which the monarch became the head. It was an age of scientific discoveries and exploration. Sailors like Christopher Columbus went in search of the new world in 1492. The Copernican theory of astronomy with the sun at the centre of the solar system replaced the Ptolemic concept of a stationary earth. In literature, Renaissance thirst for knowledge led to the revival classical Greek and Roman authors. In literature the exponents of renaissance spirit is found in the Italian Petrarch and Boccaccio; in the English, Johnson, Milton, Sidney, Spenser and Shakespeare. There is a marked growth in vernacular literature, lyric poetry, epic, pastoral poetry, prose and drama.

Renaissance man is the man skilled in all sciences and arts. Renaissance humanism was primarily meant at preparing the 'universal man' as demanded in the *Courtesy Books* which were meant to teach courtiers and others good manners and morals. A Renaissance man had to be a man of strength, character and culture being trained in philosophy, politics, athletics, and various arts.

Renaissance stage is similar to proscenium stage (*see* Proscenium theatre). There is a painted scene on the stage against which an actor is seen. This gives a perspective scenic effect by setting an object on a flat surface to give it a three dimensional effect while seeing it from a particular angle. While constructing the stage, scenic perspective is kept in mind to have the appropriate scenic design. Renaissance stage was used for the Restoration theatre.

Renaissance theatre refers to the form of secular drama of the 15th and 16th century Europe. In England, it comprises the Elizabethan and Jacobean drama. By the middle of the 16th century Protestant Reformation had banned most religious drama and a new kind of secular drama began to develop. There is a movement towards secular themes in drama with the comic and grotesque elements in it. The Renaissance theatre showed great interest in reviving classical drama. It was presented in a new setting in a new form with classical characteristics known as Neoclassicism. The new form of Renaissance theatre began first in Italy in the 15th century with Latin plays. Eventually, they were written in the vernacular modelled on the Roman plays. Since these plays were academic in nature, they lacked vitality. Renaissance art sought the principle of verisimilitude seeking the appearance of truth. This called for a sense of decorum, correctness, ideal, rationality, probability, moral order, etc. There is no mingling of comedy with tragedy. Characters were presented as ideal types. Good was rewarded and evil punished. The Neoclassical dramatists followed the principles of unities of time, place, and action as propounded by Aristotle in his *Poetics*. Accordingly, a play should consist of a single plot, must take place within a 24-hour period, and take place in one place. This helps the audience sitting in a place for a limited time to fulfil the principle of verisimilitude. An attempt was made to recreate the Roman stage architecturally. The most important development was the prospective technique with regard to the stage scenery which consisted of a painting on a flat surface to create the illusion of depth. Such a scenery created the illusion of a real place. The practice of presenting allegorical scenes called intermezzi in between the acts began in the renaissance drama. Eventually mechanical devices began to be used in shifting the scenery. By the end of the 16th century allegorical stories of the *intermezzi* combined with classical productions leading to the evolution of opera and its popularity. *Commedia dell'arte* evolved as a popular form among the general public since the neoclassical theatre catered to the elite. It consisted of performance by troupes of stock characters like the Harlequin and Pantaloon with exaggerated comic characters. In France, the Italian influence in the French court led to the popularity of ballets. Only by the 1630s did Neoclassical drama begin to appeal to the French with the dramas of Pierre Corneille and later that of Jean Baptiste Racine. The greatest French dramatist Molière presented *commedia*-influenced farces and comedies of manners satirising the upper classes and their follies. In England, Renaissance drama developed during the reign of Elizabeth I towards the end of the 16th century. At the universities some academic Neoclassical tragedies and comedies were performed. Breaking from the Neoclassical tradition, English drama tried to satisfy the popular audience with popular forms. Playwrights like Thomas Kyd and Christopher Marlowe began the dynamic drama which led to the dramatic genius William Shakespeare. The plays of this period are classical in structure mingling verse and prose. It adapted the dramatic devices of Seneca, Plautus, and the *commedia dell'arte*. There is a commingling of tragedy, comedy, and pastoral. Strict principles of unities were not maintained. Dramas consisted of a great deal of time and space with multiple plots. Plays were performed in circular open-air theatres. The stage was a platform that thrust into the pit meant for the lower-class audience. There were three galleries around the theatre for the upper class boxes meant for the elite members. These plays used minimal scenery and props and descriptive poetry provided imaginative support.

Later with Jonson court theatre known as the masque developed presenting allegorical stories in dance, music, and spectacle. During the Civil War, the parliament under the influence of the Puritans closed all theatres in 1642 declaring them immoral. Theatre was reopened during the Restoration in 1660 catering only to the coterie circle of the upper class.

Renaissance tragedy refers to the kind of tragedy that developed in England in imitation of the Senecan tragedies. Sackville and Norton in their *Gorboduc* (1562) attempted this form.

Repertoire in drama applies to a theatre company with its collection of plays for a season and a permanent company of actors. These plays can be performed by the company at a short notice. This form of theatre originated for the entertainment of a king's court and the nobility. It was most common in the Elizabethan era (1558-1603) to have such 'Repertory companies' like the Lord Chamberlain's Men. Abbey Theatre is a repertory company in Dublin meant to present Irish plays. Later, its repertory included classical drama as well as Shakespearean and contemporary works. Old Vic Theatre (Old Victorian Theatre) in London is a repertory company famous for staging the productions of William Shakespeare under the management of Lilian Baylis who took charge of it in 1912.

Repetition is a dramatic device by which certain phases, sentences, action or gestures are repeated to impress upon the audience.

Representational theatre is one in which the actors do not directly address the audience as in presentational theatre. Representational style is found in traditional Renaissance and Victorian plays in which the actors speak to the audience indirectly through asides, soliloquies, and through a chorus that make comments. It is illusionistic as it tries to create the illusion of a room, etc., on stage giving the impression of a fourth wall between the actors and the audience. Most

Western theatre since the Renaissance has been representational. There is a tendency in the modern times to mix the elements of both representational as well as presentational theatre. For example, Tennessee Williams in his plays such as *The Glass Menagerie* presents psychological realism with dream sequences. Arthur Miller employs similar technique in his *Death of a Salesman* (*see* Presentational theatre).

Resolution is the denouement by which conflicts and discords are resolved in a play. According to Aristotle in his *Poetics* "Every tragedy is in part complication and in part Denouement. The complication consists of incidents that have taken place before the opening of the play and some of that occur within it; the remainder form the denouement. By complication I mean everything from the beginning of the story up to the point where the hero suffers a change of fortune; by denouement, everything from the latter point to the end" (*see* Denouement).

Restoration theatre refers to drama written and performed during the restoration of monarchy in England in 1660 under Stuart King Charles II. When he and his courtiers returned from exile in France, they brought along the influence of Moliere in drama. The Restoration period of drama continued from 1660 to the end of the century. The prominent dramatists of the period include Etherege, Wycherley, Dryden, Congreve, Farquhar and Vanbrugh. The characteristic theatrical form is the comedy of manners with its witty, cynical, bawdy and amoral tone. Restoration drama concerns the life of the upper classes and their moral laxity and licentiousness. Women characters were introduced into drama instead of young boys playing female roles. The plays were primarily written in verse with a mingling of verse here and there at romantic moments. The comedy of manners had complex and double plots. Scenery was changed in full view of the audience. Music was integrated into the action of the play. Candles and oil lamps provided light effect with coloured and stained glass for colour shades. The Restoration theatre was patronised by royalty and nobility and catered to the aristocracy (*see* Restoration Comedy, Restoration Tragedy).

Restoration comedy denotes that kind of drama which prevailed in England between the restoration of the English King Charles II and the advent of sentimental comedy early in the 18th century. Restoration comedy is also a term that is usually used to refer to the artificial comedy or the comedy of manners that prevailed at that time. Comedy deals eventually with appearance and reality. The comedy of manners is on 'surface of life.' The presence of aristocracy at the centre of action distinguishes comedy of manners from other comedies. Traditionally, comedy deals with the middle or low section. Therefore comedy of manners is styled artificial as they present superficial habits and manners dealing with surface of human existence of a section of society. They do not depict men and women in their emotional sides. There is no study of human psychology as done by Shakespeare. Common characters included fops, country squires, sexually crazy young widows and old women, etc. The comedy of manners had been branded licentious as its common themes were sexual intrigues. Respectable people considered such plays indecent due to their frivolity, corruption and immorality. Dryden is considered the father of the comedy of manners. It is Etherege who established this genre. Later, 'the mannerly and witty' Wycherley had it beautifully brought out in his *Country Wife* which at times sounded very indecent and immoral. Congreve in his *Way of the World* (1700) brought the comedy of manners to perfection. Jeremy Collier in 1698 wrote on *The Immorality and Licentiousness of English Stage* presenting the middle class reaction against it. Soon the sentimental comedy developed in the 18th century. It stood for domestic virtues and the triumph of Christian virtues and preaching to middle class audience. Goldsmith and Sheridan led the anti-sentimental movement.

Restoration tragedy is the Neoclassical form of tragedy that developed after the Restoration of English monarchy in 1660. It followed the Greek and Roman tragedies with strict observance of the rules of unities of action, plot and place (*see* Heroic drama / tragedy).

Retardation is the reduction of the tempo of a particular scene to focus attention on it. Freeze is a kind of retardation by which a sudden break in the flow of the drama is sought with a tableau to make the audience face a dilemma in their understanding of the action of the play.

Revelation is the disclosure of something kept as a secret (*see* Discovery, Recognition, Anagnorisis).

Revels office was meant for the Master of the Revels who was the official organiser of the masques and entertainments at Court or Inns of Court. It had its origin from the early Tudor period during the reign of Henry VII. Sir Thomas Cawarden was appointed in 1545 as the first permanent master of the revels.

Revenge play is a development of the Senecan tragedy with blood feuds and revenge. Blood feuds were common in Anglo-Saxon England, especially during the Middle Ages and the Tudor Period (1485-1603). It was a practice to avenge the death of someone by 'man compensation' which meant killing a kinsman. This practice led even to the extinction of families. At times the feud was resolved by paying blood money or ransom. Revenge tragedies were popular in England from late 16th to mid-17th centuries. During the Elizabethan and Jacobean times, revenge used to be a common theme for plays. The playwrights made use of these plays to exploit the tension in the audience. They would sympathise with the avenger who also succumbed to his fate. The early revenge plays in the Elizabethan period were translations or imitations of the Roman plays of Seneca. *Gorboduc* (1561) is the earliest English revenge play by Norton and Sackville. Thomas Kyd's *The Spanish Tragedy*

(1589) is considered the first great success in the genre and has remained a blueprint for other revenge tragedies. Kyd's skilfully managed, complicated, and sensational plot influenced later psychologically more sophisticated revenge tragedies such as Shakespeare's *Hamlet*. Other known plays in this genre include Christopher Marlowe's *The Jew of Malta*, Tourneur's *The Revenger's Tragedy*, and Webster's *The Duchess of Malfi*. Some of the features of revenge tragedies are: (a) A shocking murder which cries out for revenge. (b) Someone takes it up as a sacred duty to take revenge. (c) The ghosts of those killed ask for revenge. (d) There is a Machiavellian villain who causes widespread bloodshed. (e) Horrors are introduced. (f) Some go mad or feign madness. (g) There is a play within a play which can mirror the core of the main action. (h) The objects of the revenge is often better than the objects of the avengers and (i) The imagery and the language used are proper of violence (*see* Senecan tragedy).

Reversal in drama occurs when an action leads to the opposite effect than what is expected (*see* Peripeteia).

Revesby play is a folk drama that developed from Revesby village of Lincolnshire. The story revolves around a fool who revives from death after being killed by his sons. It is similar to mumming play (*see* Mummer's play).

Review consists of media publicity made for a dramatic performance with some descriptions of the play basing on the plot, dramatis personae and the techniques used. Good reviews can attract large audiences to the performance.

Revival is a new production of a play performed earlier. An ideal revival takes place when a faithful rendering of the original version is made.

Revolving stage is a permanent or temporary stage with several stage settings. By mechanical rotation of the stage different scenes and settings of a play are presented for a performance. The advantage of such a stage is that it can provide different scenes without any delay. The Royal Shakespeare Company used a revolving stage for its production of Victor Hugo's *Les Miserables* in 1985.

Revue consists of an entertainment with songs, dances, comic sketches, skits, readings and commentary. It can present a theme through sequences of events or random scenes with no sequences at all. The programme is preformed with characters entering at different turns and depicting spectacular as well as intimate scenes. It often consists of satires on persons and events. Revue can be very satirical in presenting social and political situations. The revue *Beyond the Fringe* (1961) is a popular Cambridge production. Other known revue series include *George White Scandals*, *Ziegfeld Follies*, etc. *The Ziegfeld Follies* were introduced by Ziegfeld to the American audience and continued the series till his death in 1957.

Rhetoric derived from Greek *rhetor* means 'speaker in the assembly'. In the broad sense, it is the theory and practice of spoken or written eloquence. It refers to the techniques of persuasive public speech in a logical and convincing manner. Spoken rhetoric is oratory. Classical theories of rhetoric were presented by Aristotle's *Rhetoric*, Quintilian's *Institutio Oratoria* and Cicero's *De Inventione*, etc. The classical tradition of rhetoric continued up to the 19th century. It required logical order in invention, arrangement, style, memory and delivery. It is concerned with beauty or forcefulness of style with appropriate figures of speech. In the medieval period rhetoric was one of the seven liberal arts (arithmetic, astronomy, geometry, music, grammar, logic, and rhetoric) taught at the universities. It was applied to three "årtes": letter writing, preaching, and the composition of poetry. In the 18th century rhetoric declined in its importance. However, there is a revival of studies in rhetoric by the first half of the 20th century due to the rising interest in Linguistics and Semiotics. Critics like I. A. Richards, Kenneth Duva Burke and John Crowe Ransom stressed the important role of rhetoric.

Rhythm is the measured flow of aural or visual movement consisting of beat, accent, rise and fall, etc. Rhythm is a basic feature of all the arts, particularly music, poetry, and dance. In prose rhythm gives a balance of sentences by an orderly arrangement of words. In poetry, rhythm is maintained by proper succession of long and short syllables. In drama, it is the regular tempo with which an actor delivers his lines with appropriate movements. Rhythm maintains the dramatic attention of the audience with its rise and fall as required by the dramatic sequence. The director sees to the overall rhythmic movement of the play so as to balance the major climaxes during the sequence. For this purpose, he specifies the tempo of speech with pauses and movements.

Rich theatre refers to theatrical performances with highly modernised and sophisticated technological devices in lights and sound effects, etc., so as to be on a par with television and film industry. The concept of the rich theatre comes in contrast with poor theatre. These terms were used by Jerzy Grotowski when he called for actor-audience relationship as the only essential condition for the success of theatrical performances. He advocated a poor theatre devoid of all technological superfluities (*see* Poor theatre).

Rise and sink is a rapid scene change device used in drama whereby the upper portion of the scene rises above and the lower portion sinks below making way for a new scene.

Rising action is based on the Pyramid principle of Freytag by which a drama develops during the first half with some inciting incident and when the hero makes his plans clear. This leads to intensity, excitement and climax. For example, in Shakespeare's *Macbeth* bewitched by the witches and their prophesies, Macbeth plans the murder of the king after the banquet.

Ritterdrama is a late 18th century Bavarian drama centred on Knight errands, battles and banter.

Ritual is a ceremonial act given importance by repetition and accompanying rites of passage and religious observances. According to tradition, Western theatre began with ritual performances in religious practices. All rituals contain theatrical elements as found in ancient fertility rites, harvest festivals, shamanism, etc. Aristotle's *Poetics* (about 330 BC) Greek tragedy developed from dithyrambs and choral hymns in honour of the god Dionysus. In modern drama, several dramatists attempt to present some kind of rituals, e.g., Jean Genet's *The Blacks* presents a group of blacks perform a ritual killing of a white woman.

Road company refers to a dramatic troupe that goes on performing from town to town. It may have some leading actors belonging to recognised dramatic companies.

Robin Hood is the hero of English legends and ballads of the late 14th or early 15th century. He was an outlaw living in the royal forests of Sherwood and Barnsdale and protected people from robbers and outlaws. He championed the cause of the oppressed and looted the rich and powerful. His friends included Little John, Will Scarlet, and Friar Tuck. The legends give us information on the social conditions of medieval England. In May Day game the King and Queen of May Day give way to Robin Hood and Maid Marian. Robin Hood stories are re-enacted in pantomine. In the modern times, Robin Hood stories have been presented through operettas, dramas, films, and television programmes.

Role refers to the part an actor plays in a drama and the role a person plays in life. Critics speak of 'role distance' and 'role conflict'. Role distance is marked by the way the actor copes up with his role and behaves in a particular situation. Role conflict comes when a character has to play double roles, e.g., the character who plays the role of Othello has to combine the double role of a lover as well as a betrayed husband.

Roleplay is the work of an actor by which he/she plays the role of the character allotted to him/her in a dramatic performance. The success of the roleplay depends on the way the character depicts the role true to its original and to the expectation of the audience (*see* Role).

Role reversal is exchanging roles to arouse laughter and festive mood during celebrations like carnival. In drama, the device is employed to arouse comical laughter in which the servant takes on the role of the master vice versa. Role reversal can be also in the case of mock disguising as done in Shakespeare's *Henry IV* Part I where Falstaff and Prince Hall wear the crown. Role reversal can also take place in tragedy where a monarch becomes subservient to his inferiors as, for example, in *King Lear*, Lear by tragic circumstances loses his powers to his daughters.

Romance is derived from old Latin *Romanice* meaning 'in the Roman Language'. It is a literary form popular in the Middle Ages from fifth century to 15th century concerned with tales of knights, chivalry, and courtly love. These were verse or prose written in the Latin vernaculars, namely, French, Provencal, Italian, Spanish, Portuguese, Romanian, Romansch with their different dialects. A romance had a legendary subject matter with supernatural and amorous elements. The romance is similar to an epic except for the fact that an epic is longer and less concerned with courtly love. Romances are found in Europe since 12th century and continued to be popular till the Renaissance. Originally they were orally transmitted by troubadours and trouvères. Later, they were written by court musicians to entertain and edify the aristocracy. In England, romances have evolved around King Arthur and the knights of the Round Table. Some of the Arthurian romances are *Sir Gawain and the Green Knight, Tristan and Isolt*, *Percival*, or the *Story of the Grail*, etc. In Rome there were romances around the stories of Alexander the Great and in France they were built around the adventures of Charlemagne and his knights. In Renaissance England, Spenser's *Faerie Queene* and Sydney's *Arcadia* are examples of poetic and prose romances.

The term romance is applied to drama based on legendary materials such as Shakespeare's *Pericles*, *The Winter's Tale*, *Cymbeline*, *The Tempest*, etc.

Romance languages are the modern languages of Europe derived from Latin namely French, Provencal, Italian, Spanish, Portuguese, Romanian, Romansch with their different dialects.

Roman drama perhaps began around 350 BC after the Roman Republic began to spread absorbing Greek territories, Greek drama and theatre architecture. In the beginning, Roman dramatic performance consisted of a single player with flute playing. Drama production was originally associated with religious festivals. In course of time the religious performance was replaced by the secular entertainment. Comedy became popular, especially the native Atellan farce. There was much dancing, juggling and acrobatics.

The golden age of Roman play-writing began in the second century BC with the comedies of Plautus and Terence. Seneca reigned supreme in tragedies. Seneca's plays were based on Greek myths with supernatural elements, passion and violent bloodshed. Senecan tragedy followed a five-act structure with soliloquies and poetic speeches. There were only three theatres in Rome as the Romans were afraid of building more theatres and dedicating them to different gods bringing about the wrath of other gods. The structure of the Roman theatre was an adaptation of the Greek form with semi-circular house, a proscenium arch, wings, and orchestra. The orchestra was in small semi-circle as the chorus was minimal. The large stage was about 80 to 100 feet wide with a three-storey facade with three doors. Comedies were performed on the setting of a street in front of three houses. The stock characters wore masks and wigs. Eventually Roman theatre came under attack for its licentious nature and for satirising Christianity. Emperor Justinian banned theatre in the sixth century AD. However, the popular entertainers like the jongleurs and minstrels continued the theatrical tradition.

Romantic comedy is a light drama based on love themes climaxing with the lovers united in a happy ending, e.g., Shakespeare's *As You Like It* , *Twelfth Night*, etc.

Romantic drama refers to drama written during the Romantic period influenced by medieval romances and pastoral traditions. Such drama stresses emotions, exotic and ideal romantic settings as found in Shakespeare's *Comedy of Errors* or *The Merry Wives of Windsor*.

Romanticism or Romantic Movement took place in England and Europe between 1770 and 1848. By the late 18th century in France and Germany there was a shift in literary taste from Classical and Neoclassical conventions. The spirit of Romanticism initially came from French philosopher Jean Jacques Rousseau and German writer Goethe. Rousseau established the cult of the individual and championed the freedom of the human spirit. Goethe and his friends extolled the romantic spirit of the German folk songs, Gothic architecture, and the plays of English playwright William Shakespeare. The term romantic first appeared in 18th century English and originally meant 'romance-like', resembling the fanciful character of medieval romances. According to Lacelles Abercrombie Romanticism is "the opposite not of Classicism but of Realism—a withdrawal from outer experience to concrete upon inner." For Victor Hugo, Romanticism is "liberalism in literature". Theodore Watts Dunton called it "the Renaissance of Wonder." For Walter Pater it was "the addition of strangeness to beauty." Romantics sought to do away with the neo-classical stress on intellect and reason. Hence, it was a revolt against the Neoclassicism of the previous period. It insisted on spontaneity with variety and stress on individualism. The movement took its inspiration from Spenser, Shakespeare and Milton. It was a revival of these great poets with a return to Nature and simple country life. The Romantics were inspired by the ideals of French Revolution: Liberty, Equality and Fraternity. They revolted against everything traditional.

English Romanticism began with the publication of *Lyrical Ballads* in 1798 by Coleridge and Wordsworth. In the preface to the second edition of *Lyrical Ballads* (1800), they present their manifesto of literary romanticism. Wordsworth wrote in the Preface, "...poetry is the spontaneous overflow of powerful feelings: it takes its origin from emotions re-collected in tranquillity." The subject matter of poetry is "to choose incidents and situations from common life... a selection of language really used by men... . Humble and rustic life was generally chosen, because, in that condition, the essential passions of the heart find a better soil in which they can attain their maturity." The watchword of Romanticism was 'Imagination'. The movement was characterised by reliance on the imagination and subjectivity of approach, freedom of thought and expression, and an idealisation of nature. They affirmed the importance of feeling and imagination to poetic creation and disclaimed conventional literary forms and subjects. Imagination was praised over reason, emotion over logic, and intuition over science. This led to a literature of great sensibility and passion. They emphasised a new flexibility of form and freer style. There is an increasing demand for spontaneity and lyricism found in folk poetry and in medieval romance. They rejected regular meters, strict forms, and other conventions of the classical tradition. In English poetry, for example, blank verse largely superseded the rhymed couplet that dominated 18th century poetry. Wordsworth believed in a mystic communion with nature and simplicity of life. It was taking shelter in the lap of nature from the onslaught of industrialism. Since there was a decline in traditional religious beliefs, they made a religion of their own experience. Coleridge emphasised the supernatural and the function of imagination in poetry. Romantic movement believed in the inherent worth of the individual and pantheism. English Romanticism has two phases. The first phase is a reaction against the revolutionary ideals of France. There is the trace of mysticism in the poetry of Wordsworth and Coleridge till 1815. Wordsworth, Coleridge and Southey are known as Lake Poets (since they lived in the lake district) with Burns and Blake form the first generation of English Romantics. The second generation of Romantics (Shelley, Byron and Keats) present a moral revolt and they believed in independence and justice.

The creative energy of the romantic authors went into poetry and dramatic output is very meagre. Wordsworth, Coleridge, Shelley and Byron attempted drama as a literary form. Shelley wrote *The Cenci* and *Prometheus Unbound*. In imitation of Shakespeare, the Romantics tried their hand at poetic drama. Thomas Hardy's *The Dynasts* is a very lengthy epic drama in 19 acts. In theatre, popular entertainment was melodrama and farce. The English theatre revived only towards the end of the 19th century with Bernard Shaw.

Rostrum is a stage platform that is movable, used for stage purposes. They can be of different levels on stage to give emphasis to particular sequences or characters according to their position and power.

Rough theatre is a term defined by Peter Brook in his book *The Empty Space* (1968) in contrast to 'holy theatre'. He discusses the sacred origin of drama and claims that this genre 'makes visible invisible' as it breaks out of the ordinary world. Dramatic art can take an action beyond the ordinary and the spectator can be carried beyond reality. In contrast to the 'holy' element in theatre, there is the 'Rough' element consisting of imperfections and human limitations while presenting the ideal. He refers to the example of the orchestra that performs something pure and beautiful in the form of musical sounds, creates the rough impure sounds of breathing, scraping, etc. However, such roughness is essential to theatre as it is a human activity.

Round character is a character that is life like and grows and changes as in real life in course of the action of a drama or a novel. In contrast a flat character does not grow or change, but is known by certain characteristics. Forster in his *Aspects of the Novel* defines round and flat characters.

Roundhouse is the famous theatre which was taken over by Arnold Wesker in 1964. He took over this 19th century locomotive shed and warehouse to establish the 'Centre 42' (a movement to popularise drama through trade union support). Wesker thus stimulated the kitchen sink drama out of the conventional commercial theatre, (*see* Kitchen sink drama).

Royal court is the theatre in Sloane Square in London. It is known for its contribution to the development of modern drama since 1956. It was founded to perform new English and European drama. Plays such as Osborne's *Look Back in Anger* (1956), and John Arden's *Sergeant Musgrave's Dance* (1959) were performed in the Royal Court. It has encouraged Fringe groups, touring companies and experimental writers.

Royal National Theatre located on London's South Bank is the result of over hundred years of effort and planning. The large complex, designed by Sir Denys Lasdun, was inaugurated by its patron Queen Elizabeth II in 1976. It was built under a special Act of Parliament. The building has three separate theatres with a seating capacity of 2,500 people. The theatre has an open-stage, a proscenium stage and a rectangular room. There is also a studio in the complex meant as an experimental workshop for new writers. The theatre has a rich collection of classical, contemporary, and other world drama. The upkeep of the theatre is through financial assistance from the Arts Council of Great Britain as well as through the income generated through performances.

Royal Shakespeare Company was formally established by Sir Peter Hall in 1961 building on the existing theatre company at the Stratford Memorial Theatre in Stratford-upon-Avon.

The company is known today for the performances of dramas by William Shakespeare and his contemporaries. It also performs classical and contemporary world drama.

Royalty is a term referring to the remuneration made to a playwright for the publication or performance of his/her play.

Royalty and nobility tale is historical or fictional story concerning royalty and nobility. These appear in folktales and children's stories such as the 'Arabian Nights', 'Arthurian Legend', etc.

Rules of drama are the literary conventions, customs and codes associated with drama. These have been defined by Aristotle in his *Poetics*; Horace in his *Ars Poetica*; Longinus in his *On the Sublime*, etc. According to Aristotle a tragedy must include six elements: Spectacle, Melody, Diction, Character, Thought and Plot. He also speaks of strict rules concerning Unities: of Plot, Time and Place. Rules of drama vary according to the different literary movements: Classicists and Neoclassisists insist on order, decorum, reason, thought; while the Romantics insist on feelings, emotions and psychological elements.

Run refers to the continuous performance of a play in a city or town which brings financial gain to the company.

Run through as the term implies is a running through the entire play or its acts while rehearsing so as to make everyone feel the tempo of the whole act or the entire play. The run through is done without any stop in between for corrections. It can happen that in course of rehearsals of individual scenes, the actors might miss out the rhythm and movement of the entire drama to its proper climax. If such a 'run through' is not done actors will find it difficult to maintain the tempo between the different scenes and acts building up to the climax.

S

Sacra rapresentazione meaning 'sacred representation' is the Italian equivalent of the medieval mystery play. The subject matter consisted of the Passion of Christ. It was performed after the Mass to instruct the faithful with appropriate sermons (*see* Mystery play).

Sacrifice is the ritual offering of a victim or animal to a deity. According to tradition, tragedy began with rituals accompanying rites of passage and religious observances. The Greek theatrical tradition began with ritual performances in religious practices at fertility rites and harvest festivals. Tragedy in Greek is derived from 'goat song' meaning a song sung at the sacrifice of a goat. Hence, the tragic hero is like a scapegoat who is sacrificed to appease the gods. However, in the death of the tragic hero there is some kind of victory as well as defeat. It arouses pity and fear leading to Catharsis (*see* Pity and fear; Catharsis).

Safety curtain is a fire-proof curtain that can be lowered in front of the house curtain in the event of a fire. Such a curtain was introduced to the Drury Lane in 1794.

Sainete is the satirical interlude performed between the acts in the 18th century Spanish theatre.

Satire is a literary art of diminishing a subject by making it ridiculous and evoking amusement and scorn. It uses laughter as a weapon against a butt. A butt may be an individual or a society. Dryden wrote: "the true end of satyre is the amendment of vices by correction." Satire evokes laughter using wit in the form of irony or derision to expose human folly and evil. The Roman poet Horace was the first great satirist who commented with a smile on follies especially in sexual matters and ill-mannered behaviour. Juvenal, a contemporary of Horace, exposed the vices of Roman society in his satires. In imitation of Juvenal, Samuel Johnson wrote *London* (1739) and *The Vanity of Human Wishes* (1749). Beast fables and dream allegories like the 13th century Le Roman de la Rose and the 14th century *Piers Plowman* of William Langland are satires. Chaucer uses satire in *The Canterbury Tales*. *Don Quixote* of Cervantes is a great satire on knight-errantry. Satires in English include Ben Jonson's *Volpone*, *Alchemist*; Samuel Butler's *Hudibras*; Dryden's *Absalom and Achitophel*; Pope's *The Rape of the Lock*, and *Dunciad*. Swift, Addison, Steele, Fielding, Shaw, Galsworthy and Bennett are also known satirists. Satire plays are found from ancient times as in the comedies of Aristophanes. In the first century BC Latin poet Horace employed gentle satires known as Horatian satire while Juvenal employed more biting ones. Satire is used for comedy with wit, irony and exaggerations to expose the follies of society and individuals. It becomes a means of social criticism as well as correction. Noted English satirical dramatists include Ben Jonson, Oscar Wilde, Bernard Shaw, the absurdists and others. Shaw's *Arms and the Man* is a satire on war. Brecht's parable plays are some kinds of satire with alienation effects. There was a satire boom in the 1960s with the satirical revue *Beyond the Fringe* (1960) by Allen Bennet and others.

Satyr plays are humorous comic skits with mythological heroes and a chorus of satyrs prevalent in the fifth and fourth centuries BC. These were added to the tragic triologies performed for Athenian drama competition. A satyr play provided comic relief with a burlesque based on mythical stories using obscene language. The chorus in a satyr play used to be played by men with horse tails and ears. Aristotle in his *Poetics* refers to tragedy having its origin in performances by actors dressed as satyrs. Aeschylus' tragedies were presented as trilogies (groups of three) bound together by a common theme. After each trilogy there was a satyr drama. The only complete surviving satyr play is Euripides' *The Cyclopes*.

Scaffolds are the platforms used as stages for mystery plays. These scaffolds used to be constructed in the marketplaces for the procession on Corpus Christi feast-day and for the performance of the mystery plays.

Scapegoat is derived from the Jewish tradition of a goat on which the high-priest laid the sins of the people in a symbolic manner and let it into the wilderness (cfr. Leviticus xvi). The term is applied to someone who is treated harshly to bear the misdeeds of others. It can be a psychological syndrome in people to make someone a scapegoat. In Greek 'tragedy' means 'goat-song' applied to ritual worship of gods. Tragedy occurs in the life of a good man when due to some error of judgement he comes under some tragic circumstances and is like a scapegoat in society. Tragic heroes like Oedipus, Othello, King Lear, etc., are such scapegoats. In absurd theatre like Harold Pinter's *The Birthday Party* the character of Stanley is a victim of psychological oppression by Goldberg and McCann.

Scapino is a clown figure in the *commedia dell'arte*. He is a cunning liar dressed in green and white striped garments.

Scaramucchio is a boastful servant dressed in black and who is very friendly with women in the *commedia dell'arte*.

Scenario is derived from the *commedia dell'arte*. It is applied to the basic outline of a story. In film and television, it refers to the various directions for the scenes.

Scene is a unit of an act or a play representing an action in a place at a time. It is marked by curtain, black out, change of setting or by entrance and exits of characters.

Scene a faire is a scene that the audience expects as a result of other scenes building up to it.

Scene or setting can be applied to a particular era or place of action in a drama.

Scenery is the background for a play with its location. It can be as a room, sky, forest, mountains, garden, etc. In expressionist drama scenery can be symbolically presented so as to give a particular mood.

School refers to a group of writers who share a common vision and attitude.

School drama is a term applied to drama that developed in the 16th century schools in Europe (*see* Jesuit drama).

Scissor cross refers to a bad movement on stage when two actors move in the opposite direction.

Scissor stage consists of two platforms on either side which can be set with different scenes and can be revolved to effect a rapid scene change.

Scrim is a gauze like transparent material that is dark blue in colour hung in front of a scene. With light reflected on it various effects can be produced. The transparent scrim is invisible and the scene behind is visible through it.

Script is the text as well as the stage directions of a play or a film.

Secrets constitute an important element in a play to provide the sense of suspense. It is through secrets that dramatic irony is brought about by which the audience is aware of it while the characters are ignorant. Sometimes both the audience and the characters are kept in the dark which leads to greater suspense until the secrets are unfolded. For example, in *Oedipus Rex* the protagonist Oedipus is unaware of the fact that he has killed his father and married his mother. However, the audience knows this secret which adds dramatic irony to the play.

Second banana is the close friend of the lead comic character in a play. The term is derived from the old practice of passing bananas between these comical characters.

Sedes is a fixed scenic set used in the medieval times like a mansion.

Self-reflexive is a term applied to actors when they act out certain scenes recollecting incidents in their own lives. Their acting becomes more personalised than acting some other character, e.g., American Alternative theatre in 1960s used self-reflection in their presentation of socialism, feminism, and satire. The term can also be applied to a writer who is conscious of his own artifice and devices.

Semiotics is the science of signs meant for human communication. In drama, semiotics plays an important role as words, sounds and gestures can be very important means of communication. It was Ferdinand de Saussure, the Swiss linguist, who suggested semiotics as a science. Charles S. Pierce established the Science of Semiotics in America by the end of the 19th century. Saussure and Pierce have defined some of the signs in semiotics.

Senecan tragedy refers to the tragedies of Roman dramatist, philosopher and statesman Seneca (4? BC-AD 65) who wrote during the Silver Age of Latin literature. He was a Stoic philosopher who wrote his nine plays based on Greek mythology. His writings are known for their exaggerated rhetoric and blood chilling details with ghosts and magic. Being interested in ethical principles, he was more spiritual than the earlier Stoics. His verse tragedies had a great influence on the Renaissance revival of Classical drama in Italy, France, and England. His themes of crime, horror, and revenge presented with Stoic fatalism was an inspiration to later dramatists. His tragedies were closet dramas meant for recitation rather than for stage performance. He followed the five act pattern with choruses and rhetorical speeches. The English writers Thomas Norton and Thomas Sackville with their *Gorboduc* (1561) introduced the first Senecan tragedy. Other Senecan tragedies include Thomas Kyd's *The Spanish Tragedy*, and Shakespeare's *Titus Andronicus*.

Sensation drama refers to drama employing new mechanical devices to effect spectacular and exciting scenes such as earthquake, accidents and the like. The techniques are better employed in disaster movies with sensational effect as portrayed in *Twister*, *Volcanoes*, *Titanic*, etc.

Sensation memory is the recollection by an actor of certain real sense impressions or sensations like sights and sounds, taste, smell, touch, etc., which brings about effective facial expressions on a character.

Sensibility is an 18th century term to refer to a susceptibility to tender feelings, especially involving the feelings and sorrows of others in contrast to the Neoclassical rejection of emotions. It is the capacity to feel and respond. Sensibility is related to Primitivism, Sentimentalism and Naturalism which are offshoots of Romanticism. T.S. Eliot spoke of "dissociation of sensibility" to imply the split between the sensuous and the intellectual faculties.

Sentimental comedy began to develop in the middle of the 18th century as the stereotyped comedy of manners was getting exhausted and Neoclassical tragedy had practically disappeared. This ushered in sentimental comedy, panoramas, and musical comedies. The comedies of this period are of two types, namely, the old-fashioned witty plays provoking laughter and the sentimental comedies. The sentimental comedies grew in the 18th century due to the rise of the middle classes and as a reaction against the licentious comedies of the Restoration. According to Goldsmith it arose since "the virtues of private life are exhibited, rather than the vices exposed, and the distresses rather than the frailty of mankind." These were meant to refine manners and improve morals, hence lacked humour. These plays praised virtue and the cultivation of sentiment. This genre began with the sentimental comedies by Richard Steele such as *The Tender Husband* and *The Conscious Lovers*. The characters in these plays are middle class. The lovers are not frivolous and they consciously deal with serious domestic problems. The treatment of marriage is a proper affair of love rather than of sentiments. The play is replete with sentimental ideas. Men are waiting to destroy women and the extra-ordinary services they render women are only with self-interest. The sentimental comedy revolves around much moralising and sermonising. The characters were mostly caricatures and were very good or very bad. The features of sentimental comedies can be summed up: (i) They are mawkish and sentimental, (ii) the dialogue is full of moralistic cliches, (iii) there is often a sudden transformation in the villain, (iv) there is much praising of virtue rather than ridiculing folly, (v) Virtue always triumphed, and (vi) these plays attempted to improve society with tears.

Sentimentality is a strong emotional response which the dramatist can arouse in the readers and the audience. The 18th century melodrama had much romantic plot, sensationalism and sentimentality.

Set refers to the locale or the environment in which a drama is performed. It can mean the units of scenery and props used to depict a particular era or place. A perfect set can give the illusion of a reality to the actors performing their roles. This can lead to a most appropriate performance.

Set designer is the one who designs and oversees the construction of the stage setting according to the need of the play and the budget available.

Set piece is a scene from a particular play that is performed out of context in another play.

Set speech consists of certain lines in a drama that have special significance and the actor has an opportunity to demonstrate his/her skills, e.g., in Shakespeare's *As You Like It* Jacques utters his set speech on the 'Seven Áges of Man':

All the world's a stage,
And all the men and women merely players:
They have their exits and their entrances;
And one man in his time plays many parts,
His acts being seven ages...

Shadow show is a kind of theatrical performance popular in the 19th century in which puppet shadows are projected on to a lighted screen. This form is found in the 18th century in China, Java and Bali.

Shot refers to all that is recorded in a camera from the time the director calls for 'action' to the time he calls for 'cut.' A usual shot is for about ten to fifteen seconds. Camera shots can be of three kinds: (i) a *long shot*, (ii) a *medium shot*, (iii) a *close-up*. A *long shot* shows an object from a considerable distance from the camera and in relation to its general surrounding. A *medium shot* shows an object in its immediate surrounding. A *close-up* shows the main object or a part of it. The shots taken on a camera can be of different types such as a *pan shot*, a *tilt shot*, a *travelling* or *tracking shot*, a *crane shot*, a *zoom shot*. In a *pan shot,* the camera has its base fixed and the shots are taken from moving from left or right. In a *tilt shot*, up or down shots are taken with the camera fixed on its base. A *travelling* or *tracking shot* is taken by forward or backward movement of the camera fixed on its base. A *crane shot* is an up and down shot taken with a camera mounted on a crane. A *zoom shot* is taken with a zoom lens which is able to focus on a detail with the zoom device. Shots also depend on the angle from which they are taken such as a high angle shot or a low angle shot. With a high angle shot the camera can reduce the size of objects. The low angle shot is taken from a camera close to the ground and the objects against the sky giving them some prominence.

Showcase is a performance by an actor or a group of actors to show their skills. Such performances can consist of a monologue or a scene. It offers opportunity to producers and theatre companies to assess them and select them for their performances.

Show portal is a structure consisting of a framed teaser (a horizontal drape on top of the stage) and tormentors (a vertical drape at the sides) for a programme.

Sight lines are the imaginary lines drawn between the eyes of the audience and the stage. When the action takes place on stage the audience at the different sides of the hall should be able to establish the sight lines. Directors should ensure that the extra areas on the stage out of the sight lines be blocked from the audience.

Sign is something that stands for something else. In theatre, sign is an important element which is a means of communication. Sign can consist of props, gestures and expressions, lights and sounds, movements, etc. All theatrical languages can be included into the category of sign. Some characters can be presented as sign in a play like in Beckett's *Waiting for Godot*.

Silence is used as a dramatic device by certain dramatists such as Samuel Beckett, and Harold Pinter in the theatre of the absurd. Pinter has even written a play *Silence* in which dialogue is interspersed with phrases from other sections with silence in between. Such silences make the audience ponder over the unsaid utterances of the actors (*see* Theatre of Silence).

Site specific applies to a play that is performed for a specific audience in a particular place.

Situation is the circumstances of the characters or the action in the play. The struggle in the play springs from a critical situation and leads it to the climax (*see* Plot, Climax).

Skene is the wooden building or tent behind the *Proskenium* and at the edge of the orchestra in a Classical Greek theatre. It was used as the dressing room for the actors. The skene had a platform on top of it from where the gods could appear or speak during the play.

Sketch is a small dramatic entertainment or skit like the revue, vaudeville, burlesque, etc., performed within a longer play.

As it is a curtain raiser, a sketch does not have a proper plot or characterisation.

Skit is a piece of banter like a parody or burlesque which caricatures a person or a performance.

Sky dome is the device of suspending a silk over the stage like a dome to give dim daylight effect.

Sky drop is a painted back drop depicting the sky.

Slapstick is a wooden device used by the Harlequin in pantomime to strike his foes and to make loud spanking sound. The term is applied to knockabout comedies with pranks (*see* Knockabout comedy).

Slice of life drama is naturalistic drama depicting real life-like situations on stage. People behave and speak giving the illusion of reality. Such dramas present public places with few scene changes. Plays of Ibsen, Chekhov and Strindberg belong to this genre. In recent times, slice of life drama has led some actors live real life like situations on stage for a considerable period of time, e.g., portraying family life on stage and living so for a period of time.

Sloat is the 19th century device of dropping actors from above on to the stage.

Slang is the informal words and phrases used in ordinary colloquial speech. Slang can be contrasted with jargon and argot or cant. A jargon is a technical language used in a profession. An argot is a secret vocabulary of underworld groups. Slang has its origin in subcultures within a society like the police, computer specialists, armed forces, teenagers, racial minorities, etc. Slang used to indicate the attitudes and values of a particular group. The listener can know about the speaker's background from his/ her slang expressions. For example, the Black Harlem district of New York has slang expressions such as cool for stylish, *The Man* for the law, *Uncle Tom* for a gentle black. Some slang expressions can be widely used such as booze for alcoholic drinks; pot and *marijuana* for drugs; loo for toilet; grub or garbage for food.

Small work refers to certain facial expressions and gestures which do not appear in the stage direction. These come spontaneously from an actor's understanding of his/her role.

Soap opera is a long television or radio serial which attempts to present people in real-life situations. It establishes a relationship between the audience and the characters, e.g., *Dallas*, *Santa Barbara*, *The Bold and the Beautiful*, etc.

Social comedy deals with social manners and customs in a satirical and humorous manner (*see* Comedy of manners).

Social drama deals with social issues, e.g., Ibsen deals with contemporary social problems such as the position of women (*A Doll's House*), the taboo subjects like incest and venereal disease (*Ghost*), middle class hypocrisy, etc. These established him as a great social reformer and moral teacher. He raised drama from the level of pure entertainment to that of an effective means of self-discovery and enlightenment. Bernard Shaw found in Ibsen what was lacking in Shakespeare. Shaw said, "Shakespeare had put ourselves on the stage but not our situations. Our uncles seldom murder our fathers, and cannot legally marry our mothers, we do not meet witches.... Ibsen supplied the want left by Shakespeare. He gives us not only ourselves, but ourselves in our situations." However, Ibsen was not the originator of social drama which was made popular by the French dramatists. Ibsen turned the social drama into the drama of ideas. He questioned in these plays the conventional ideas and beliefs. As Shaw states: "The drama arises through a conflict of unsettled ideas ...and no moral question is raised." These plays are not thesis plays. Ibsen does not offer any clearcut solution or remedies for the evils he spots. He himself has said that his purpose was not to teach a lesson or propound a thesis. The conflict is between clear right and wrong. The villain is as conscientious as the hero. Ibsen's ideas are not those of a propagandist but of a seeker, whc is on the lookout for the best artistic expression of truth inherent in life. He is concerned with contemporary issues.

Hence, they are of universal significance. He chooses his subjects from the world around him. In this he departs from the Greek dramatists who drew from familiar myths and legends. His plays represent average humanity and its concerns. Thus, he made his audience part of his plays. His plays are life-like as he uses everyday prose, eliminates soliloquies, stresses on visual concreteness of settings and detailed stage direction. His themes are universal. He becomes a trendsetter and in his hand drama becomes serious art, a means of self-discovery and awakening than mere entertainment.

Social history of dramatic forms is the study of the changes in attitude towards drama from the angle of the audiences belonging to different places, times and ethnic and cultural sensibilities.

Social realism is a theory of art and literature that developed in Russia in the 1920s and 1930s with the purpose of spreading the Marxist doctrines. The artist became a tool in the hands of the socialist system and was tagged 'the engineer of human souls by Stalin. The term was used by Lunacharski and Gorki. Later, Socialist realism turned more propagandist portraying working classes. Writers like Pasternak and Solzhenitsyn revolted against such an artistic credo.

Social tragedy emerged in the late 19th century presenting the fate of protagonists in their class or social environment. In these social tragedies the characters have their personal freedom that is curtailed by public opinion, for example, in the naturalistic plays of Ibsen such as *Ghosts*, *A Doll's House*, etc. In *Ghosts,* Mrs. Alving, widow of captain Alving, decides to inaugurate an orphanage in honour of her late husband to protect his name as a pillar of society though he had fathered an illegitimate child through his housekeeper. The tragedy leads to the death of her son Oswald due to his inherited syphilis from his father and the fire in the orphanage.

Society for theatre research was founded in London in 1948 with the purpose of promoting records of theatre activities through research and study.

Socio-drama is a group study meant to promote social awareness. The method presents different representatives of society such as a Hindu, a Muslim, a Christian, a black man, a white man, etc. These individuals interact and spend time in a group study.

Sociology of theatre studies theatre in the context of social process taking into account its resources, audience and the public attitude towards it. In the process the cultural and socioeconomic life of society has its influence on it.

Sock is the old term for comedy derived from the Latin 'soccus', meaning, the shoe of the comic actors of Rome.

Soliloquy is a device used in theatre by which a monologue is presented by a character while alone on stage. It reveals his/her thoughts spoken either directly or indirectly to the audience. It is an excellent device in the hands of the dramatist to convey important information on the characters or events. The Latin term 'soliloquium' was perhaps coined by St. Augustine by putting together 'solus'(alone) and 'loqui' (to speak). Elizabethan dramatists employed it extensively. Shakespeare used it very skilfully in plays such as *Macbeth*, *Hamlet*, *Othello*, etc. When soliloquies are put into the mouth of villains in the form of asides or direct address to the audience, they become excellent device for dramatic intensity. For example, Iago's soliloquy in *Othello* aims at 'motive-hunting of motiveless malignity.'

Song in drama originated in classical drama with choral songs and dithyramb. Later, in opera and oratorio, song was employed. Song is employed in drama to depict the mood and feelings of a character and to entertain. Elizabethan dramatists like Shakespeare added songs in their plays, e.g., the drinking scenes in *Othello*; grave-diggers song in *Hamlet*; Orphelia's song when she is out of her mind in *Hamlet*, etc. In modern times, naturalistic drama of Brecht adapted songs in his plays to give the alienation effect, for suspension of disbelief, to link the episodes or to sum up the main ideas of a scene.

Sotie / sottie is derived from French meaning fool and refers to a French dramatic entertainment popular in the 15th and 16th centuries. Soties used to be performed as a curtain raiser to mystery and morality plays, consisting of satirical mockery of the church and state officials such as bishops, clergy, doctors, etc. Basing on such stories Shakespeare introduced comical elements in *As You Like it*, *Troilus and Cressida*, etc.

Soubrette is a comic female specialising in the role of a country girl or maidservant who is very frolicsome and coquettish. Such a character is found in the Neoclassical comedy and opera, often dressed in the garb of a peasant with an apron, etc.

Source refers to the primary oral, visual or documentary materials from which a dramatist has taken the contents for a drama. For example, Shakespeare and the Elizabethan dramatists took historical data from Hollinshed's *Chronicles* (1577). Research into finding the original sources can be useful to the understanding of a dramatist's thoughts and intentions.

Source-book (*see* Source).

Space is the illusion of space created on stage calling for imagination from the audience, the actors, the directors, etc. Space in theatre goes beyond the physical stage and is created by the actors, directors, designers, etc. Lighting effects can increase or decrease space on stage by creating optic illusion. Sound effects too can create the impression of a particular illusory scene, e.g., sounds of vehicles and people can create the illusion of a street. A director creates space by the sets and giving exact movements and postures to actors. In mime, space is created by movements such as a fireplace, office, sitting room, etc.

Spear-carrier is a non-speaking actor who fills the role in a crowd. The term is derived from the practice of such an actor who carried a spear with him.

Specialty is a song or dance performed to entertain the cast of a play. It is not performed for the audience.

Spectacle is one of the six elements of a play as defined by Aristotle in *Poetics*. It comprises the scenery, costumes and the various effects employed.

Spectacle theatres refer to the well equipped playhouses especially in the 16th century Italy.

Speeches in drama refers to each uninterrupted individual speech units of an actor.

Spine is the motivation behind a character's actions according to Stanislavsky.

Stage is the platform or the physical space on which a theatrical performance takes place. Stages can be of different types, shapes and sizes such as arena stage, apron stage, thrust stage, picture frame stage, etc.

Stage crew consists of those behind the scene like the technicians responsible for the performance of a play.

Stage directions constitute the notes given in the script of a play for the actors and the stage crew. These comments specify the movements of character, entrances and exits of the actors, props used, light and sound effects and the settings of the scene. Bernard Shaw gives lengthy stage directions, often meant more for the reader's better grasp of the play and its development.

Stage fright is the fear and nervousness an actor experiences before a performance. Such stage fright can affect the voice and cause forgetfulness in the actor.

Stage imagery consists of the various visual imagery such as scenery used on stage which are meant for drawing the attention of the audience. It may include sets, props, gestures, movements as well as the symbolic language used.

Stage society was founded in London in 1899 to perform plays of quality.

Stage struck happens when a person is obsessed with the desire to be an actor.

Stalls are the seats near the stage.

Stand-in is applied to an actor who learns the part of another actor as a stand-by in case of an emergency.

Stand-up comedy is an entertainment by one or two comedians who arouse laughter by their mimicking social types.

Star system is the method of achieving commercial success in theatre by bringing big actors for a performance and focus attention on them. This was common in the 19th century with such stars as Henry Irving, Sarah Bernhardt, etc.

Star trap is a flap cut on the stage floor and opened to bring a character suddenly on to the stage.

Stasimon in Greek means 'stationary song' and refers to a choral ode in a Greek tragedy sung by the chorus after taking its position in the orchestra.

Static characters are those characters that do not change essentially in the course of a play. Either they are evil or good throughout the play. In contrast to static characters there are the dynamic characters that change in the course of a play.

Static theatre is a term coined by the Belgian author Maurice Maeterlinck (1862-1949) who is the exponent of symbolist theatre. Static theatre used immobile forms and quiet words instead of great dramatic action. It was a reaction against naturalism in theatre and was primarily religious in nature. In such performances the audience is made to feel reconciled with the fate of events and find a kind of comfort, e.g., in a play depicting the crucifixion of Christ, the Mother of Christ does not lament and cry aloud; instead there is a silent grief with a certain composure and calm. Maurice Maeterlinck's plays include *The Princess Maleine*, *Pelléas et Mélisande* and *The Blue Bird*. These plays are set in a dream like atmosphere and presented by suggestion than by direct expression of ideas and emotions.

Stereotype is a type of character who appears in plays after plays such as a cunning servant, a foolish, old man, an innocent heroine, or a calculating villain. Such stereotypes are characters from particular social or religious groups. There can be also stereotype situations, gestures and linguistic jargon employed in drama and literature. The use of stereotypes occur in classical farce, morality plays and neoclassical comedy. The audience expect it as part of the genre (*see* Stock characters).

Stichomythia derived from Greek, meaning 'line talk', refers to a dialogue between two characters in which each one concludes the other's thoughts. It is used in Classical drama and in disputes. The device arouses suspense and comical effect. Dramatists like Shakespeare, Samuel Beckett, Harold Pinter, etc., have employed it

Stock characters represent particular personality types as found in the Greek new comedy, Roman comedy, *commedia dell'arte* and melodrama. These include character types such as the Harlequin the baffoon and servant, the braggart soldier, the Pantaloon the cuckold, the nagging wife, etc. Shakespeare's Falstaff in *Henry IV* is a stock character (*see* Stereotype).

Stock company is a term applied to theatre groups that perform several plays together at the same theatre. Such companies were popular in the 19th century London.

Stock response is the expected response from a spectator to a dramatic performance without any critical judgment such as the spontaneous cheering of the hero and the heroine.

Stock situation is the usual recurrent pattern of relationships or events in drama such as an old uncle or aunt blocking young lovers; husband and wife separated by misunderstanding, etc., e.g., in Congreve's *The Way of the World* Lady Wishfort wishes to block the love of her niece Millamant for Mirabell.

Story and plot: E.M. Forster in *Aspects of the Novel* defines the difference between story and plot. A story begins and ends arbitrarily as it is not governed by reason. The plot is something which the poet makes, e.g., the king died and then the queen died (story); the king died, then the queen died of grief (plot). A story is episodic as the events are simply linked to one another by 'and'. But the plot gives the reason why. And it moves back and forth to give emphasis to certain events. A plot must have a meaning. The poet who makes the plot with a beginning and end has it within his control as he is the maker. In the opinion of Forster Brecht's plays are mere stories and they are episodic as the scenes are connected by 'and'. Instead, in the plays of Ibsen, the scenes develop a plot as they are linked by 'because'. However, both the dramatists are concerned with causality which is a relationship of a cause to its effect. It is through the sequence of events arranged in such a way that a cause-and-effect relationship seems probable (*see* Plot).

Story within a story occurs when another story enters into the main story as a digression. It is a pattern found in the long romances such as the *Arabian Nights*, *Decameron*, *The Canterbury Tales*, etc.

Straight man / woman is the ordinary old, foolish man or woman who appears more foolish than the fool who appears with him on stage. He/she is the one who feeds the lines to the comic fool (*see* Second Banana).

Strangeness is an effect in theatre by which a sense of alienation or estrangement is felt by the audience. Certain strange happenings make the audience get insights into different perceptions of people and events.

Street theatre as the term suggests is a form of entertainment that is performed in the street or marketplaces. It consists of juggling, acrobatics, clowning which have been performed by travelling troupes. In the modern times, the Fringe theatre and the Community theatre belong to this genre. Community theatre began since 1968 in Britain consisting of fringe groups that presented social problems of racial minorities at a particular locality (*see* Fringe theatre, Community theatre).

Striptease is a form of entertainment in which the performer tries to excite the audience by stripping off the clothes. The striptease is a kind of American burlesque from the 1930s in which a female performer gradually removes her clothes as she moves about the stage to music. Gypsy Rose Lee is a prominent performer of the genre, e.g., Tom Stoppard's comedy *Travesties* employs striptease.

Strong curtain refers to a powerful line at the end of an act which leads to some suspense and intensity in the next act.

Strophe is the first division of a choral ode. The chorus would sing the strophe and dance to one direction and move to the opposite direction while singing the antistrophe.

Structuralism is a literary theory and criticism that developed from structural linguistics and structural anthropology that analyse language and literature as structures. It began in the 1960s based on the linguistics of Saussure and Russian Formalism. Structuralists view a literary work primarily in relation to other such works. They look for the 'codes' and 'conventions' that are found in all the works of one genre. Structuralism developed first in anthropology (Claude Levi Strauss), then in literary and cultural studies (Roman Jakobson, Ronald Barthes, Gerard Genette), psychoanalysis (Jacques Lacan), intellectual history (Michael Foucault), and Marxist theory (Louis Althusser). Although these thinkers never formed a school as such, they were labelled under 'Structuralism' in the 1960s and 1970s. Structuralism has its impact in dramatic criticism as it calls for structural relationship between different parts of a play; structural relationship between the play and the audience, etc. The Structuralist Workshop of Michael Kirby produced very formalist plays such as *Photoanalysis* (1976), *Double Gothic* (1978), etc., which draw attention to their own structures. In *Double Gothic* he lets two persons from the audience sit opposite side of the centre stage invisible to each other. They complete two narratives simultaneously intermingling with each other. The narratives fade and increase with light effects. Hence, emphasis is given to the form of the play than its content.

Structure of a play refers to its framework. Plays are structured into acts and scenes. The play can be of different forms such as epic, chronicle, melodramatic and the like (*see* Plot).

Sturm und drang is derived from German meaning 'storm and stress'. It was a German literary movement in the 1770s which protested strongly against the spirit of enlightenment. Their anti-enlightenment spirit made them sense feeling, passion, intuition and inspiration rather than reason. They were influenced to a great extent by Shakespeare. Those who belong to this tradition include Goethe, Schiller, Herder and Lenz.

Style in drama consists of the playwright's particular literary style and taste in the background of the period, its customs, language, costumes, sensibilities, etc. Styles have been categorised according to periods such as Classical, Medieval, Elizabethan, Jacobean, Restoration, etc. At times styles are known by individual authors like Chaucerian, Shakespearean, Miltonic, etc.

Stylised theatre is a form of non-realistic and non-naturalistic theatre in which there is exaggerated movements and speech. Such stylised forms do not give importance to realistic setting and costumes. In a stylised theatre, instead of a forest scenery, the dramatist may use triangles and circles to symbolise trees. The term was used by Vsevolod Meyerhold (1874-1940). Meyerhold rebelled against Stanislavski's techniques of imitative emotion on the stage and realistic drama. He wanted theatre to be different from everyday reality and sought abstract scenic art. He promoted Symbolist plays where the actors moved like stylised puppets.

Subconscious is the area of the mind that is hidden. In drama the Russian author Stanislavski (1863-1938) stressed the need for secret desires to be exposed in the truthful emotions and actions of the performers. He called this effect "psychological realism". Stanislavski found that the actors who recalled their own feelings and experienced and substituted them for those of their characters were able to achieve a special link with the audience. This difficult mental technique allowed performers to break down a text according to the motivations of the character and the beliefs of the playwright.

Subplot is a subsidiary plot in a play that coincides with the main one. It is usually involves a group of minor or subordinate characters. The subplot either reinforces the main plot or comes as a contrast to it. It was a practice in the Tudor and Jacobean drama. Shakespeare's *King Lear* has the 'Gloucester' subplot involving Gloucester, Edmund and Edgar. 'Gloucester' subplot becomes a link between King Lear and the audience. The use of subplot became rare after the 17th century.

Sub-text is a term coined by Stanislavski to refer to the hidden thoughts and feelings beneath a dramatic dialogue. According to him sub-texts are found in the plays of Shakespeare, Chekhov and Ibsen. These sub-texts should be elicited from facial expressions, voice inflections, movements, postures and gestures. Stanislavski encouraged his actors to search for such hidden sub-texts while acting and present them in their performance. Some authors insert sub-texts into the text in brackets. Such a sub-text can be given by the actor or the director while interpreting the role of the character. Such sub-texts can be created in course of the rehearsals by the actors and directors. It calls for the audience's attention read into such hidden sub-texts to appreciate fully a play. Arthur Miller encloses subtexts for his plays in brackets.

Summer stock is a company that offers performances only in summer. Often such companies are sponsored by universities as part of their summer programmes. A stock company may also induct some well known theatrical personalities as well into the production such as actors and directors.

Supernatural element is brought in by some dramatists to add seriousness to the play with out-of-the-ordinary situations that bring about fatal consequences. For example, Shakespeare used ghosts and witches. In *Macbeth,* when Macbeth and Banquo while returning from military campaigns encounter the three witches who prophesy that Macbeth shall be Thane of Cawdor and king. As a consequence, Macbeth is led to his ambition and evil designs to murder the king. In *Hamlet*, supernatural element is presented in the form of the ghost of Hamlet's father. Hamlet is commanded by the ghost to avenge his father's death by killing Claudius.

Supernumerary is applied to an actor in a stock company production who plays a walk-on role involving no dialogue. The term is also applied to the several minor characters in Shakespearean plays such as attendants and ladies in waiting.

Superobjective is the long-range objective of the play with its central purpose. It was Stanislavski who used the term in his method of actor training. According to him the actors must be aware of such a central purpose which will bind them together during the performance and its success. All performances are linked to this motif by the individual scenes and dialogues. For example, in Shakespeare's *Macbeth,* the characters playing the role of Macbeth and Lady Macbeth should be aware of the long-range objective of the play. In Macbeth, there is a growing power hunger; while in Lady Macbeth there is a growing unconscious desire to wash her hands of the murder.

Surrealism is a literary and artistic movement which developed out of symbolism and dadaism in the 1920s. It fought against realism and concerned itself with the world of dreams and the unconscious mind. Its impact on theatre is found in movements such as the theatre of cruelty and the absurd theatre. It was founded by the French poet and critic André Breton. Breton published his *Surrealist Manifesto* in Paris in 1924 and held the view that the irrational is the best mode of perceiving and representing reality. Surrealism emphasized the role of the unconscious in creative activity and employed the psychic unconscious in a more orderly and more serious manner. It was a movement in painting, sculpture and literature. Surrealists stressed hallucination, psychotic utterance, automatic writing and free associations. By using automatism they wrote whatever words came into their conscious mind and regarded these words as inviolable. The authors felt that this free flow of thought would establish a rapport with the subconscious mind of their readers. This purely psychic automatism was modified later by the conscious use of symbols derived from Freudian psychology. In its simple form surrealism is present in modern literature as whatever is visionary and dreamlike. French playwright, Alfred Jarry (1873-1907), with his *Ubu Roi,* is the first to attempt surrealism in drama. *Ubu Roi* derides traditional views of authority by presenting the rise to power of a grotesque and pompous king Ubu. He is a personification of greed, ignorance, and the bourgeois attitudes. The farce is considered the first work of the theatre of the absurd. Jean Cocteau (1889-1963), the French author, is a leading member of the surrealist movement, which emphasized the role of the unconscious in artistic creation. His works *Orpheus*, an adaptation of the Greek myth of Orpheus, and *The Infernal Machine* are excellent surrealistic plays. American playwright Sam Shepard is known for his oblique story lines with mysterious characters. He uses surreal elements with images of popular culture. There is a movement from surreal to the realistic in treating people and situations. Some of his known plays include *Operation Sidewinder* (1970), *Curse of the Starving Class* (1977), *Buried Child* (1978, *True West* (1980), *Fool for Love* (1983), *A Lie of the Mind* (1985), and *Simpatico* (1994).

Suspense is the state of uncertainty which keeps the reader or audience wait in curiosity with regard to the outcome of the story or play. Suspense can be one of uncertainty or of anticipation. Suspense can turn sympathetic when the audience identifies itself with the painful situation of a character. Such a suspense turns intense due to dramatic irony when the audience knows what is going to happen to the protagonist who is unaware of it. Suspense is also maintained due to ignorance of what is going to happen. Shakespeare is a master craftsman who sustains suspense in his plays. For example, in *Hamlet,* suspense is maintained throughout the play as we do not know what is in the prince's mind or whether he will do what has been told to him.

Suspension of disbelief is a phrase derived from Coleridge's *Biographia Literaria* Chapter XIV where he writes: "... that my endeavours should be directed to persons and characters supernatural, or at least romantic; yet so as to transfer from our inward nature a human interest and a semblance of truth sufficient to procure for these shadows of imagination that willing suspension of disbelief for the moment, which constitute poetic faith." According to Coleridge, there needs to be a temporary acceptance of the truth of a story presented in drama or fiction in poetic faith. Hence, one part of the mind accepts the story in faith, while the other part of the mind is aware that the story is fictional. For example, while watching the scene of the strangling of Desdemona in *Othello*, the audience is aware that it is in a world of play-acting and yet the audience temporarily accepts it in poetic faith.

Sussex's men is an Elizabethan drama company.

Swan is an Elizabethan theatre built in 1594.

Sword dance is a dramatic ritual prevalent in Europe symbolising death and new life.

Symbol is derived from Greek 'symbolon' meaning 'mark' or 'sign'. Hence, it refers to anything animate or inanimate that represents something beyond what is perceived. In expressionist and surrealist drama, symbols play a very dominant role. In Shakespeare's *Macbeth* when Lady Macbeth in her sleep walk washes her hands it is a symbol of her guilt being washed. Ibsen very powerfully brings the meaning of the symbolic title he gives to his play *Ghosts* when he lets his protagonist Mrs. Alving utter, "Ghostlike. When I heard Regina and Oswald in there, it was as if I saw ghosts. I almost think we are all ghosts .... It isn't just what we have inherited from our father and mother that walks in us. It is all kinds of dead ideas and all sorts of old and obsolete beliefs. They are not alive in us; but they remain in us none the less, and we can never rid ourselves of them." Ghosts become a symbol of incest and syphilis in the play.

Symbolist drama is an outcome of the 19th century symbolist movement. It was a reaction against the dominant realist and naturalist tendencies in literature. Drama began to be written in accordance with the symbolic ideals of seeing reality beyond human experiences. They attempted to evoke private moods of the audience and readers through the material and the spiritual worlds presented. Symbolist writers attempted to explore the musical qualities of language through sound relationships. Wagner's music drama, and the verse drama of T.S. Eliot and Christopher

Fry are excellent examples of this genre. Known dramatists in this genre include Maurice Maeterlinck (1862-1949), W.B. Yeats (1865-1939), Strindberg (1849-1912), and T.S. Eliot (1888-1965) (*see* Symbolist Movement).

Symbolist movement in literature and the visual arts originated in France in the late 19th century. Symbolism in literature is expressing ideas, feelings, and values by means of symbols or suggestions rather than by direct statements. It was a reaction against the dominant realist and naturalist tendencies in literature. For symbolists imagination is the true interpreter of reality. They discarded rigid rules of versification and Parnassian. The Symbolist movement had its beginning in the poetry of Charles Baudelaire. Symbolist writers attempted to explore the musical qualities of language through sound relationships. Others in the movement include Stéphane Mallarmé, Paul Verlaine, Swedenborg, Poe and Arthur Rimbaud. In English literature, symbolism is found in Blake, Coleridge, W.B. Yeats, Ezra Pound, T.S. Eliot, D.H. Lawrence and others.

Sympathy is sharing the feelings and sufferings of a character. It evokes in the audience joy or sorrow in accordance with the experiences of the character (*see* Empathy).

Synaesthesia is an experience in which the stimulation of one sense elicits a perception that ordinarily would be elicited had another sense been stimulated. For example, a loud noise can register as a blinding light. This happens when an imagined and a real perception are simultaneous. The imagined perception may be confused with or even mistaken for the true perception. Drama is considered naturally synaesthetic as it appeals to the sense of sight and hearing.

T

Tableau in French means 'a little picture.' It is a theatrical term referring to grouping of silent and motionless actors presenting a still picture. The actors pose for a particular scene as, for example, the picture of the Last Supper of Jesus. Some 19th century melodrama and farce had tableaus at the end of the acts. Such tableaus suspend the action of the play and the audience can visualise the situation in the following act. It is a good device to make a final comment on the characters.

Taboo is a prohibition in primitive societies which calls for certain type of behaviour socially or religiously. In religious taboos certain items are forbidden and are considered unclean or sacred. Such items have taboo attached to them for protection against their power. Since drama originated from ancient rituals, taboo is often infringed in them. An example of behavioural taboo is the prohibition against incest. In the case of Oedipus he breaks the taboo of incest in marrying his mother after patricide. Infringement of taboo is often presented in Greek, Jacobean and Neoclassical tragedies such as regicide, patricide, matricide, incest, etc.

Take is a cinematic term referring to a section of a film taken at one shot with the same camera. In theatre, the term is applied to a scene or act that is continuous with no disruption.

Technique in drama consists of the techniques employed by the dramatist, director and actors. Strictly speaking, it refers to acting skills with diction, vocal skills, physical expressions and mental skills of concentration and observation. It also calls attention to the effective use of the stage and the reaching out to the audience besides the personal qualities of the actors.

Take direction is the ability of the actor to respond to the direction given by the director as accurately as possible.

Take it down is the instruction given by a director to an actor to reduce the volume of speech while acting.

Task play consists of a drama built around some task being performed during the whole course of the performance on stage such as building a house, e.g., David Storey in *The Contractor* concerns the building of a reception hall for a wedding.

Tautology is derived from Greek meaning 'the same saying' and refers to repetition of words or concepts in different words, e.g., I myself personally shall see and look after your problem and case.

Tech rehearsal is a rehearsal in which the actors run through a play to try out all the techniques employed in it such as the scene changes, costumes, light and sound affects, etc.

Teichoscopy is a term to describe a dramatic device by which a character on stage describes an off-stage action which is seen by him/her alone through a window or door. The term meaning 'looking through the wall' in Greek is derived from Homer's *Iliad* in which Helen describes a scene she alone sees.

Television drama is filmed drama which is often serialised and televised in episodes taking care of minute details. For instance a lengthy novel can be serialised with its details into a television drama. It is cheaper for the audience than a live theatre. Techniques used on television such as long shot, midshot, and close up shots from varying angles from different cameras with zooming devices can render it very effective to the audience. Television programmes can be of fictional, non-fictional, or live performances. Fictional programmes include soap operas; situation comedies; dramatic series; and motion pictures made for television, including the mini-series. In the last forty years, television has evolved as a major dramatic medium and today it has come to be accepted a powerful dramatic form. Well-known television dramatists include Samuel Beckett, Peter Watkins, Peter Nicholas, Micke Leigh and David Mercer.

Tempo is the pace of a dramatic performance by which the attention of the audience is sustained throughout. A slow tempo can render it boring while a very swift pace can lead to a mix up.

Tendency is a term coined by Stanislavski to refer to the digressions from the overall through-line of a play. Such tendencies are added by a director or an actor intentionally or accidentally (*see* Through-line).

Tennis-court theatres is the practice prevalent in the 17th century Paris of turning tennis courts as theatres. This tendency was introduced into England during the Restoration of monarchy in England when Charles II returned from exile in France.

Tension is the element of apprehension created in the audience in the course of a dramatic performance. Tension is also caused in the actors before and during a performance in the form of stage fright (*see* Suspense).

Tentus is a mansion or locus in the medieval theatre referred to by Lucerne (*see* Mansion).

Terence-stage is a Renaissance stage made of woodcuts for the plays of the Roman dramatist Terence (190-159 BC). Usually it consisted of a mansion. Terence-stage had its influence on the late 16th century Italian stage.

Tetralogy is a set of four plays that are related to one another in structural sequence and theme, e.g., Shakespeare's history plays *Richard II*, *Henry IV Parts I and II* and *Henry V*.

Text in a drama consists of the dialogue as well as the directions for its performance. Stanislavski was of the opinion that the actors and directors ought to be aware of the references to other events between the scenes which he calls subtexts. The actors and directors can give their creative interpretation to such subtexts.

Thalia is considered the muse of comedy (*see* Grace).

Theatre is derived from the Greek 'theatron' meaning seeing place. The term is applied to a building where dramatic performance is held as well as to the performance itself. The term theatre is usually applied only to dramatic and musical plays, but it also broadly includes performances such as opera, dance, circus, carnivals, mime, vaudeville, puppet shows, pageants, etc. (*see* Drama).

Theatre des Nations is an annual drama festival held in Paris since 1954. Different drama companies are invited to perform dramas in their own languages.

Theatre Guild is a New York society founded in 1919 giving opportunities for European plays to be staged in America.

Theatre in Education draws attention to theatre as a means of learning. Exposure given to children in schools through staging of professional drama as well as school plays, can impart knowledge in different fields. Role playing by children can be very instructive in improvising new ways of teaching.

Theatre in the Round refers to a theatrical performance done in an area surrounded by the audience. This method of performance has become popular in the 20th century. The device was employed in the performance of the medieval drama such as *The Castle of Perseverance*. In Russia, theatre in the round was popularised by Okhlopov in the 1930s in presenting realistic theatre involving even the audience. Robert Atkins presented the Shakespearean plays through theatre in the round. In America, such theatres became popular in the universities. In France, Andre Villiers founded the *Theatre en rond* in 1954. Stephen Joseph is a known figure in England who is associated with this form of dramatic performance.

Theatre language includes all kinds of dramatic communications either spoken or unspoken. Unspoken language consists of expressions, postures, movements costumes, scenery, colours, lighting, sound effects and the like.

Theatre libre is a free theatre began by Andre Antoine (1858-1943) which helped in the development of naturalism (*see* Naturalism).

Theatre Nationale Populaire is the French National Theatre founded in 1920.

Theatre of cruelty (*see* Cruelty, theatre of).

Theatre of fact refers to drama in the 1950s that dealt with historical events and facts such as Peter Brook's *US* (1866). It concerns primarily with historical details, however speculative elements are also introduced to render them attractive. Such plays dramatise factual political events arousing political involvement of people.

Theatre of illusion occurs in fourth-wall drama in which actors try to present a naturalist illusion of real people in time and space. They imagine to be unaware of the audience during performance. Hence, such theatre does not make direct address to the audience.

Theatre of panic is intended to present a kind of ritualistic drama arousing terror and awe coupled with an element of farce. The term was coined by the Absurd dramatist Fernando Arrabal who wrote in French greatly influenced by Samuel Beckett and Antonin Artaud. Such drama combined tragedy with buffoonery with religious ceremonies under the inspiration of god Pan, e.g., *The Architect and the Emperor of Assyria* and *And They Handcuffed the Flowers*.

Theatre of silence is a term coined in the 1920s by Jean Jacques Bernard (1888-1972) 'theatre de l'Inexprime', meaning theatre of the unexpressed. In his opinion, the silence and unarticulated expressions are as important as the dialogues in a drama. For instance, in his drama *Martine* (1922), he presents the silent sufferings of the peasant girl Martine. Others who employed the device are Chekhov and Harold Pinter.

Theatre of situations is a term used by Jean Paul Sartre (1905-80) to refer to situations in the lives of actors and the audience as the central focus of a dramatist. His existentialist philosophy defines the role of freedom and responsibility in human situations (*see* Existentialism / Existential Drama).

Theatre of the absurd (*see* Absurd).

Theatre of the ridiculous is a theatre movement that developed in America based on the theories of Antonin Artaud (1896-1948). It developed from the pop and psychedelic art.

Theatre of the straight line is a phrase developed by V. Meyerhold (1874-1940) to present his concept of the relationship between the various people involved in the performance of a drama such as the author, director, actors and audience. In this relationship, the director understands the author's ideas and passes on to the actors who in turn give their free expression in communicating to the audience through performance.

Theatre production refers to the various means by which any of the forms of theatre are presented to an audience. It may consist of dramatic and musical plays as well as opera, dance, circus and carnivals, mime, vaudeville, puppet shows, pageants, etc. The common element in them is that they are essentially visual. At times film/video clippings or recorded sound may be included in a performance. A production has its scripts, scenarios, scores, or choreography. A theatre production can be classified as subsidised, commercial and non-commercial. It may be called experimental or art theatre, community, and academic theatre.

Theatre space varied from time to time. In early times theatre performances were held in the streets, open spaces, market squares, churches, rooms or buildings. Some of the contemporary experimental theatres rejected the formal constraints of available theatres. In these the sense of stage and auditorium is created by the actions of the performers. Most theatre stages are either end, thrust, or arena types (*see* Arena stage, Thrust stage).

Theatre triangle is a term to refer to a drama that is produced as per the strict interpretation of the director. In such drama, the actors have no freedom of personal interpretation and communication with the audience. V.Meyerhold disapproved of such dramatic productions.

Theatre workshop is a touring theatre company established by Joan Littlewood in 1953 at the Theatre Royal in Stratford in London.

Theatricalism is a concept that developed in Russia and Germany in the early 20th century. It came in contrast with naturalism and held the view that a drama is only representation of life and not life itself.

Thesis play is a kind of drama which began in France in the 19th century through Dumas ad Brieux with the purpose of presenting social and political problems. Such plays centering around a problem are known also as problem plays or propaganda plays. Discussion plays in which characters interact with each other through debate is a form of problem play. Bernard Shaw in his *Man and Superman* presents his 'Shavio-Socratic' debate in the third act through the dream sequence set in hell in which four characters discuss the nature of progress, evolution, and the Life Force. Ibsen

(1828-1906), Brecht (1898-1956) and Bernard Shaw are masters in the thesis play with the purpose of communicating their social and political ideologies (*see* Problem play).

Through line is a term coined by Stanislavski (1863-1938) to refer to the main thrust of a play which keeps all the scenes and actions united which can be expressed by a character through a statement. Shakespeare presents such a line in *Macbeth* when the protagonist Macbeth says: "If Chance will have me King,/ Why Chance may crown me,/ Without my stir" (I,iii). Such a statement sums up the attitudes that culminates in the main events of the play.

Thrust stage is a platform stage which projects into the auditorium and is surrounded by the audience on all three sides. This form was used for ancient Greek theatre, Elizabethan theatre, Classical Spanish theatre, English Restoration theatre, Japanese and Chinese Classical theatre, and much of Western theatre in the 20th century. A thrust stage facilitates the actors to have direct communication with the audience in the form of direct address, soliloquy, monologue, asides, etc. The entire backstage is utilised for drops, scenery as well as the entrances and exits. Though a thrust stage can bring a large audience very close to the action on stage, it has the disadvantage of acoustic and masking devices since a sizable part of the audience is on the sides and behind the stage.

Thunder sheet is a strip of metal which is shaken to create thunder-like noise.

Tilt (*see* Shot).

Time is an important element in drama which refers to the passage of time depicted in it. How effectively does a dramatist depict actions and events of a day, a month, or an year or more in a matter of a couple of hours on stage? It requires great skill to present effectively the movement of time in a drama. Drama also depicts certain moment in time and history and analyses how individual characters relate to the past, present and the future. The tempo and rhythm of a play define its *theatre time*. The *dramatic time* of a play comprises of its *plot time* and *story time* (*see* Story and plot). The *plot time* will vary in tempo between acts and scenes. Some dramatic actions are by-passed while others are given prominence which adds to the tempo of the scenes and acts. Besides sub-plots and double plots have their effect on the *drama time*. Attitude to time varies according to the various dramatic genre. In tragedy an individual's life in time is presented leading to death. In comedy emphasis is given to the flow of life leading to celebration.

Timing in drama refers to the speed with which the actors render their lines with appropriate pauses, silences, and movements.

Tireman is the Elizabethan wardrobe manager in the dressing room or the tiring house. He sees to the sets of the play.

Tiring-house is the name by which Elizabethan dressing room was known where the tireman kept the wardrobe. It was just behind the stage forming its back wall and the entrances and exits were made from it. The musicians could play from there. On top of the tire-house was the hut from where actors could come down on stage.

Total-theater is a German term that was applied to an ambitious undertaking to build a *total theatre* for the Weimar theatre and its director Erwin Piscator (1893-1966). The plan was conceived by the architect Walter Gropius in 1926 to build a rotating stage comprising of a theatre in the round, a circular thrust stage and an end stage. There was facility for back projections of films. Picastor was very creative in his presentation of plays with texts adapted to mingle film and animated cartoons on stage. His aim was to communicate his message very powerfully through dance, music, acrobatics, amazing sets and costumes, accompanied by mesmerising sound and light effects. The plan however remained a dream as it did not materialise. The concept of a total theatre was developed in France by Jean-Louis Barrault known for his production of *Christophe Colombe* (1953). In England, Joan Littlewood attempted to popularise the total theatre concept through her production of *Oh, What a Lovely War* (1963).

Tractor play is a kind of Socialist realistic play that evolved in the Soviet Union (*see* Socialist realism).

Touring company is a theatrical company that toured around with a repertory of plays. Small groups of travelling players were found from ancient Roman times. In the 19th century many travelling companies with specific interests such as Feminist or Marxist groups, visited smaller towns away from major cities.

Tradition is a term referring to certain beliefs, practices, customs, works and conventions passed on from one generation to the next. In literature too such a tradition exists. T.S. Eliot in his essay "Tradition and the Individual Talent", brings out powerfully his concept of tradition when he says, "It (tradition) cannot be inherited, and if you want it you must obtain it by great labour. It involves, in the first place, the historical sense...; and the historical sense involves a perception, not only of the pastness of the past, but of its presence; the historical sense compels a man to write not merely with his own generation in his bones, but with a feeling that the whole of the literature of Europe from Homer and within it the whole literature of his own country has a simultaneous existence.... This historical sense, which is a sense of the timeless as well as of the temporal and of the timeless and of the temporal together... ." For example, the Orestes story of Aeschylus reappears in Sophocles' *Electra*; T.S. Eliot's *The Family Reunion*; O' Neill's *Mourning Becomes Electra* and Sartre's *Les Mouches*. In English literature, we may speak of native traditions presented in the writings of Chaucer, the Scottish Chaucerians, Wyatt, Shakespeare and his contemporaries, Donne and some of the 17th century poets, Burns, Blake, Browning, Hopkins, Yeats, Pound, Eliot, W.H. Auden, Dylan Thomas, Ted Hughes and others. The Italian tradition is found in the writings of English poets such as Surrey, Sidney, Spenser, Milton, Keats, Shelley, Tennyson, Arnold, Francis Thompson, etc. In between these two traditions, we find the Neoclassical tradition from the Renaissance to the 18th century as represented by Dryden, Pope, Johnson, Crabbe and others.

Traditionalism is a term coined by Meyerhold (1874-1940) to refer to a method of production in which traditional elements of the original staging of ancient plays being integrated into their modern performances.

Tragedy is a term usually applied to dramatic works in which events lead to fatal conclusions. The term is derived from the Greek meaning 'goat song' due to its association with ritual sacrifice with choral song in honour of Dionysus. According to Aristotle Greek tragedy evolved from dithyrambs which are choral hymns in praise of the god Dionysus and which often told a story. Aristotle in his *Poetics* wrote of tragedy as "The imitation of an action that is serious and also, as having magnitude, complete in itself; in language with pleasurable accessories, each kind brought in separately in the parts of the work; in a dramatic, not in a narrative form; with incidents arousing pity and fear, wherewith to accomplish its catharsis of such emotions." Aristotle also spoke of the six elements of tragedy, namely, Plot, Character, Diction, Thought, Spectacle and Song. Greek tragedy flourished in the 5th century BC and over a thousand tragedies were written of which only some thirty by Aeschylus, Sophocles, and Euripides remain. These tragedies are all in verse form consisting of scenes or episodes with not more than three characters speaking. The scenes alternate with choral songs or odes. Often the stories are based on myth or ancient history and examine the consequences of individual actions on humanity. Most of the events were narrated through dialogue and choral songs as very little of the action takes place onstage (*see* What is Drama? in Introduction). Aristotelian concept of tragedy had great influence on the

Neoclassic concept of tragedy in France and England. Shakespeare and the Elizabethan dramatists attempted new forms such as the revenge tragedy based on the Senecan tragedy (*see* Revenge play, Senecan tragedy). Revenge tragedy continued to be popular in the Jacobean period through dramatists such as Webster, Middleton, Beumont and Fletcher. Tragedy had a decline in the periods that followed until it is revived in the 20th century by dramatists like Ibsen, Strindberg, O' Neill, Arthur Miller, Tennessee Williams and Samuel Beckett. Though a tragedy usually ends in the death of the protagonist, in the naturalistic tragedies of the 19th century the protagonist may not die but he is broken spiritually and psychologically.

Tragic carpet is a carpet that used to be spread on stage to protect the costumes of actors when they drop dead on stage at the climax of a tragedy.

Tragicomedy is derived from the plays of Plautus (254-184 BC.) who mingled elements of tragedy and comedy with gods, kings and servants brought together. Tragedy dealt only with noble characters and ended in death. Comedy on the other hand dealt with insignificant and ridiculous characters and ended in a celebration. Tragicomedy was a mixture of the grave and the light and provided happy ending to a tragedy. It is any drama that does not adhere to the strict conventions of tragedy or comedy. In English tradition, Francis Beaumont and John Fletcher imitated the Italian pastoral play of Battista Guarini *Il Pastor Fido*, and produced *Philaster or Love lies a Bleeding*, a romantic tragicomedy. Shakespeare attempted the genre in his *Measure for Measure*, *The Merchant of Venice*, *The Winter's Tale*, *Cymbeline* and *Troilus and Cressida*. The term can also be applied to Heroic drama (*see* Heroic drama), plays of Chekhov, and the theatre of the absurd of Samuel Beckett and Harold Pinter.

Tragic flaw is a single defect of character in a goodman or an error of judgement a reasonable man makes which leads to tragic circumstances. (*see* Hamartia).

Tragic irony is the dramatic irony associated with the tragic fate of the central characters in a tragedy. For instance, the tragic irony in Shakespeare's *Othello* is Othello's suspicion of Desdemona's fidelity leading to her eventual strangling. In reality she is innocent. In *Hamlet*, we have the example of tragic irony when Orphelia really becomes mad though Hamlet in the play feigns madness (*see* Irony).

Transpontine melodrama is a term applied to very crude melodrama of the Victorian period.

Trap is an opening on the stage floor through which props and characters could appear or exit.

Travelling players are a group of professional actors in the 16th century who went from place to place staging their performance for a living.

Travesty is a burlesque in which a dignified subject is trivialised in the form of a parody, e.g., Tom Stoppard's play *Travesties* is a mock imitation of James Joyce and Lenin presented through the failing memory of Henry Carr.

Trilogy is a sequence of three plays complete in themselves, yet linked to each other in theme and characterisation, e.g., Aeschylus' *Orestia* which consists of *Agamemnon*, *Choephoroe*, and *Eumenides*. In drama competitions in ancient Greece, it was a practice to present trilogies with a satyr play. Shakespeare has his *Henry VI* Parts I, II and III. In the 20th century the genre is revived by Eugene O'Neill with his *Mourning Becomes Electra*; Arnold Wesker with his trilogy *Chicken Soup with Barley, Roots* and *Talking about Jerusalem*. The advantage of trilogy is that it can involve the audience for a longer period of time giving more details of the world of drama. However, it may not be appealing to a very time-conscious audience of modern times.

Triumph is a medieval practice of a victory procession or pageant entering a city.

Trope is derived from Latin *tropus* meaning 'added melody'. The concept developed in the Middle Ages in the form of Latin poems like the *Dies Irae*, *Victimae Paschali* which helped in the development of liturgical drama (*see* Quem Quaeritis).

Troupe means a theatrical company. An experienced actor is called an old trouper.

Tudor drama flourished during the Tudor Period (1485-1603) which began with the accession of Henry VII in 1485 and ended with the death of Elizabeth I in 1603. It was a period in which medieval forms began to give way to Renaissance ideals. Tudor drama includes interlude, morality and chronicle plays. The term Elizabethan is applied to the abundant plays produced after the first permanent public theatre was built in 1576.

Turning point in a drama refers to something that brings it to a crisis point such as an event, a recognition, or a choice that leads to a sudden change in the development of the plot. Such a turning point precedes a rising and falling action. In a tragedy it is a fulcrum point from where the reversal of action begins leading to its catastrophe. Sometimes a play may have more than one turning point, however there will be one central to all. In *Othello,* the event of the handkerchief that falls by chance in Act III, iii becomes a turning point in the play that will lead to the strangling of the innocent Desdemona. Aristotle describes it as *peripeteia* or reversal (*see* Peripeteia).

Two-hander is a short play written for two characters, e.g., Ionesco's absurd drama, *The Lesson* (1951).

U

Uberbrettl is a German theatre founded in 1901 by Ernst von Wilzogen with the aim of presenting clear and short plays devoid of bombastic expressions.

Uber-Marionette is a phrase linked with Edward Gordon Craig (1872-1966) who developed his concept of actors being replaced with super puppets. He wrote plays for his collection of Javanese and Burmese marionettes. These were symbolic and impersonal in presentation (*see* Marionette).

Unconscious is a term in psychology referring to the area of the mind hidden from consciousness. It contains wishes, memories, fears, feelings, and ideas which have no expression in conscious awareness. These find expression in dreams and neurotic symptoms. It was Sigmund Freud who first developed the concept of the unconscious from 1895 to 1900. In his opinion people's behaviour is determined by irrational forces, unconscious motivations, biological instinctual drives and certain psychosexual events during the first six years of life. Originally, Freud used the term Libido to refer to sexual energy and later broadened it to include the energy of all life instincts. These instincts serve the purpose of the survival of human race and individuals. Libido is a source of motivation that goes beyond sexual energy. Freud saw the goal of life as gaining pleasure and avoiding pain. He also postulated the concept *Death Instincts* which accounts for the aggressive drive. Some people have an unconscious wish to die or to hurt themselves or others.

In Freud's psychoanalytic view, personality consists of three systems: the *Id* (the biological component), the *Ego* (the psychological component) and the *Superego* (the social component). These are psychological processes and operate as three discrete segments. The dynamics of personality consists of the ways in which psychic energy is distributed to the *id*, *ego* and *superego*. Since the amount of energy is limited, one system gains control over the available energy at the expense of the other two systems. Human behaviour is determined by this psychic energy. At birth a person is all *id* which is the seat of all instincts and ruled by the pleasure principle. *Id* is illogical, amoral and never matures but remains the spoiled brat of personality. It is largely unconscious or out of awareness. The *ego* is the executive that governs, controls and regulates the personality. It mediates between the instincts and the surrounding environment. The *ego* controls consciousness and exercises censorship as it is the seat of intelligence and rationality that checks the blind impulses of *id*. The superego is the person's moral code and the judicial branch of personality. It decides between right and wrong, good and bad actions. It represents the traditional values and ideals of society as they are handed over from parents to children. Its function is to inhibit the *id* impulses, to persuade the *ego* to substitute moralistic goals for realistic ones and strive for perfection. However, Freud's greatest contribution is his concept of the unconscious and of the level of consciousness which is key to the understanding of behaviour and the problems of personality. The unconscious cannot be studied directly; it is inferred from behaviour. Clinical evidence for postulating the unconscious includes: dreams (symbolic representations of unconscious needs, wishes and conflicts), slips of the tongue and forgetting, neurotic expressions, etc. For Freud, consciousness is a thin slice of the total mind like the greatest part of the iceberg that lies below the surface. The larger part of the mind exists below the surface of awareness. The unconscious stores up all the experiences, memories and repressed materials. Most psychological functioning exists in the out-of-awareness realm. The psychoanalytic therapy makes the unconscious motive conscious, for only when one becomes conscious of motivations can one exercise choice. According to the Swiss psychoanalyst, Carl Jung, the unconscious also consists of a racial unconscious that contains certain inherited, universal, archaic fantasies belonging to what Jung termed the collective unconscious. In drama, the unconscious plays its role to a great extent in the form of dreams, utterances made by the characters unknowingly, soliloquies, facial expressions, gestures, movements, etc. Characters like Macbeth, Iago, Hamlet, etc., are presented very powerfully by Shakespeare with the analysis of their unconscious expressions. Expressionism in drama gives great importance to the unconscious.

Underground theatre is a kind of theatre associated with the beat and hippy movement in the 1960s in USA. It was a revolt against the conventional dramatic form. Nudity, obscenity and audience involvement were the hallmarks of the underground theatre.

Units refer to the movements or sections of a drama for the convenience of performance. The term was coined by Stanislavski.

Unities of time, place and action are the three principles governing a dramatic composition according to Aristotle's *Poetics*. He did not invent them but found the principles of unities followed by the tragedians he knew. In Aristotle's opinion a play should have the unity of a living organism and its action should not last longer than a single revolution of the sun. Aristotle gave emphasis to only the unity of action. He does not say anything about unity of place and refers to unity of time just once. About action, Aristotle says: "The fable should be the imitation of one action, and of the whole of this and the parts of the transactions should be so arranged, that any one of them being transposed, or taken away, the whole would become different and changed." The important thing is to remember how little Aristotle said about time and place. In Chapter 5 of *Poetics* he says, "Epic poetry differs from tragedy... in its length which is due to its action having no fixed limit of time, whereas Tragedy endeavours to keep as far as possible with in a single circuit of the sun." Greek tragedy does not in practice normally exceed 24 hours whereas the imaginary time in an epic may be weeks or years. About unity of place, Aristotle nowhere says anything to the effect that the stage should represent only one place. This limitation was imposed by the necessity of the Greek practice. In the 16th and 17th centuries Neoclassical critics developed the rules of the three unities, prominent among them being Castelvetro. It was the French Jean Mairet who followed the three unities in his tragedy *Sophonisbe*. In England, the unities never found acceptance perhaps due to the influence of Shakespeare who disregarded them except in *The Tempest* and *The Two Gentlemen of Verona*. The Romantics revolted against Neoclassical rules including the rules of unities.

Unity in literature is a concept derived from Plato. A work should have logical structure with the parts interrelated and coherent with each other. It is devoid of digressions and all the parts essentially follow each other. Unity is an essential mark of a plot (*see* Plot).

Universality is the quality of literature by which it is appealing to people irrespective of their particular situations in time and place. Longinus in his *On the Sublime* states that "lofty and true greatness in art pleases all men in all ages." A writer who aims at universal appeal ought to write primarily on human nature and behaviour. We have such writers of universal appeal such as Aristophanes, Juvenal, Ben Jonson, Dryden, Moliere, Pope, etc., who wrote on human behaviour.

University wits refer to a group of Elizabethan playwrights and poets of the 16th century, chiefly Christopher Marlowe, Thomas Nash, Robert Greene, John Lyly, Thomas Lodge and George Peele. The name was given by Saintsbury since they were all Oxford or Cambridge men who often met at the Mermaid Tavern in Bread Street off Cheapside.

V

Vamp trap is a stage trap on stage from where an actor could make his sudden appearance.

Vaudeville is a form of comical opera that developed from the urban ballads and musical drama in the Paris fairs in the 17th and 18th centuries. The term dates from the 15th century valley of Vire in France famous for satirical and humorous drinking songs. By the 18th century such songs were absorbed into pantomime dramas. The English light ballad opera is a development of this form. In the 19th century the term *vaudeville* was applied to a stage performance consisting acrobatics, music, comedy, jugglery, magic, etc. In the early 20th century vaudeville became the most popular form of American entertainment.

Verse drama is a play written in poetic form. The prominent English writers in this genre are T.S. Eliot, W.H. Auden, Christopher Fry, W.B. Yeats and J.M. Synge. T.S. Eliot is the leader of the movement to reintroduce verse into modern English drama. He wrote all his dramas in verse. His *Murder in the Cathedral* is considered the most successful verse drama. According to him, "dramatic verse must justify itself dramatically, and not merely by fine poetry shaped into a dramatic form." The verse employed in drama should absorb the attention of the audience. Certain subjects are best suited to be presented in prose than verse. In his opinion, verse and prose should not be mixed in the same play except for the purpose of giving a jolt to the audience. In *Murder in the Cathedral* he introduces prose passages with this purpose in mind when Becket preaches his sermon which sums up his thoughts about martyrdom. Eliot used a flexible verse form with careful control of rhythm which would be acceptable throughout the play. Shakespeare was superb in this with his gift of musical design which reinforced the dramatic movement. This device is able to accelerate our emotions and gives intensity to the play. However, T.S. Eliot added more variety and controlled the rhythms of his verse than the older verse plays (*see* Poetic drama, Heroic drama).

Vice is a stock character in the morality plays who stands for wickedness. He is presented as a buffoon and servant of the devil. He is crowned with ass' ears. He fights good deeds and is finally driven to hell. Vice appears in morality plays such as *The Castle of Perseverance*.

Villain is the evil character who is the antagonist of the hero and the heroine (*see* Antagonist).

W

Wagon stage is a platform which can be rolled on or lifted from the cellar to the stage with a full scene set on it. This aids to quicken the scene change.

Wardrobe mistress is the person responsible for the costumes of a play.

Weeping comedy is related to sentimental comedy. It arouses tears as well as mirth in the audience. The term is derived from French 'comedie larmoyante' of Claude Nivelle de La Chaussee (1692-1754).

Well made play is derived from French 'Piece bien faite', a phrase coined by Eugene Scribe (1791-1861) to refer to his farces and melodramas which were constructed very logically with various elements of a good drama with climax, reversal of fortunes, suspense, battles of wit, logical denouement, etc. Scribe influenced the English dramatists such as Somerset Maugham and Oscar Wilde.

West End is London's commercial theatre around Shaftsbury Avenue such as the Comedy, the Haymarket, the Lyric, the Apollo, the Prince of Wales, etc. These are known for their glamorous commercial productions. West End is equivalent to New York's Broadway.

Wind machine is a mechanical device to produce sound effects such as the whistling of a wind.

Wings are flats with painted scenes which are used to cover the sides of the stage where the actors wait.

Wit is a term derived from Old English *witan* meaning 'to know.' The word has been applied to mean 'sense' or 'five senses', 'judgement', 'common sense', 'verbal ingenuity', etc. In the Renaissance it was applied to 'mental capacity', 'intelligence', 'wisdom', 'aptitude' and 'genius.' Quick wit meant intellectual liveliness. In the 17th century wit meant 'fancy' and 'imagination.' Hobbes was of the opinion that 'judgement without fancy is wit, but fancy without judgement not.' For Dryden and Pope, wit depends on propriety which is part of neoclassical decorum which is distinguished between wit and humour. Pope in his *Essay on Criticism* used the word several times in different sense. Hazlitt considered wit artificial, and imagination valid. In the 19th century wit was associated with levity. Arnold considered Chaucer and Pope 'lacking high seriousness' due to their wit. T.S. Eliot admired poets who combined wit and high seriousness like the metaphysical poets such as Donne and Marvell. Wit for them meant concentration and intellectual utterance calculated to delight and surprise. Donne is called 'monarch of wit' by Carew. In the modern sense, wit means intellectual brilliance and verbal deftness which is often found in epigrams.

Word play consists of verbal puns and bickering which is also known as verbal fencing. In Shakespeare's *Much Ado about Nothing,* Beatrice and Benedick enter into such verbal fencing:

Benedick: God keep your ladyship still in that mind! So some gentleman or other shall scape a predestinate scratched face.

Beatrice: Scratching could not make it worse an twere such a face as yours were.

Benedick: Well, you are a rare parrot-teacher.

Beatrice: A bird of my tongue is better than a beast of yours.

Benedick: I would my horse had the speed of your tongue...

Workshop is a place where one can get training in acting, directing and stagecraft. A workshop method is an experimental way to explore a play and learn by acting out. As the play is in the workshop it gets touched up for performance.

Workshop production refers to a play in progress and modifications made in it by the playwright, director and the actors. Additions and deletions can be made at this stage.

Y

York cycle is one of the four cycles of medieval mystery plays (*see* Mystery plays).

Youth theatre refers to drama meant for young people. Often these are developed by youth.

Z

Zany is the servant clown in *commedia dell' arte* (*see Commedia dell'arte*).

Zoom is a cinematic device by which the camera lens is adjusted to enlarge or reduce an object by 'zoom in' or 'zoom out'.